CRISIS IN LUTHERAN THEOLOGY

The Validity and Relevance of Historic Lutheranism vs. Its Contemporary Rivals

WITHDRAWN

Volume I
Essays by John Warwick Montgomery

New Edition
with a Fresh Look at the Current Crisis

With a Preface by
Dr. J.A.O. Preus
President, The Lutheran Church-Missouri Synod

BETHANY FELLOWSHIP, INC.
Minneapolis, Minnesota

ISBN 0-87123-073-9

2nd Edition, revised, with additional material,
January, 1973

To
WILLIAM HARDT
Litchfield, Illinois
who knows well that "except a corn of wheat fall into the ground and die, it abideth alone: but if it die, it bringeth forth much fruit."

PREFACE

The name of John Warwick Montgomery is rapidly becoming known throughout the religious press of the world. Dr. Montgomery is not only prolific, he is provocative. He is not only concerned, he is convincing.

It gives me great pleasure to write these few words as a preface to a book of essays, most of which I have read with great pleasure and approval. The doctrine of Holy Scripture is on the cutting edge of virtually every theological discussion in every ecclesiastical paper and in every seminary faculty throughout the Western world. We confidently believe that Dr. Montgomery's essays will do much to edify and to strengthen the church and to set forth clearly and cogently the great Reformation principles of *Sola Scriptura*.

J.A.O. PREUS, President
The Lutheran Church-Missouri Synod

6 January 1967:
The Epiphany of Our Lord

INTRODUCTION

The eminent church historian Winthrop S. Hudson concludes his Chicago History of American Civilization volume on *American Protestantism* (1961) with high praise for Lutheranism and bright hope for its future:

> The Lutheran churches . . . exhibited an ability to grow during the post-World War II years, with the Lutheran Church-Missouri Synod making the greatest gains. The Lutheran churches are in the fortunate position of having been, in varying degrees, insulated from American life for a long period of time. As a result they have been less subject to the theological erosion which so largely stripped other denominations of an awareness of their continuity with a historic Christian tradition. Thus the resources of the Christian past have been more readily available to them, and this fact suggests that they may have an increasingly important role in a Protestant recovery. Among the assets immediately at hand among the Lutherans are a confessional tradition, a surviving liturgical structure, and a sense of community which, however much it may be the product of cultural factors, may make it easier for them than for most Protestant denominations to recover the "integrity of church membership" without which Protestants are ill-equipped to participate effectively in the dialogue of a pluralistic society.

Professor Hudson's analysis is sound and his prediction is well grounded; yet there are disquieting indications that the future of American Lutheranism may fall far short of his expectations. Why? His argument is based squarely on the consideration that, unlike other denominations, the Lutheran Church has been "less subject to theological erosion" and has therefore been able to retain "the resources of the Christian past." But the last decade has made painfully clear to all who have not worn the colored glasses of näiveté that the Lutheran churches in America — the Missouri Synod included — are now experiencing the very "theological erosion" which, as Hudson correctly notes, produces ecclesiastical deadness and irrelevance.

The essays in the two volumes of *Crisis in Lutheran Theology* endeavor to point up the extreme peril of the current theological situation. A conscious effort has been made to include not only papers directed to professional theologians but also essays that laymen untrained in theology will readily comprehend. (In general, the essays in Part One of each volume are orientated to the theologically sophisticated, and those in Part Two are suitable for lay study.) All who contribute to these volumes look with wonder and with thanksgiving to the Lutheran heritage that has provided so clear a testimony to Christ and to His inerrant Word; and every contributor prays the Lord of the Church that these volumes, published in the 450th anniversary year of the Reformation, may rouse sleeping churches from their torpor and drive them to "cast off the works of darkness and put on the armour of light."

7

Charles Porterfield Krauth, who fought and won a not dissimilar battle a century ago, speaks directly to us today in his *Conservative Reformation and Its Theology*; may we have the ears to hear him:

> Had a war of three hundred years been necessary to sustain the Reformation, we now know the Reformation would ultimately have repaid all the sacrifices it demanded. Had our fathers surrendered the truth, even under that pressure to which ours is but a feather, how we would have cursed their memory, as we contrasted what we were with what we might have been.
>
> And shall we despond, draw back, and give our names to the reproach of generations to come, because the burden of the hour seems to us heavy? God, in His mercy, forbid! If all others are ready to yield to despondency, and abandon the struggle, we, children of the Reformation, dare not. That struggle has taught two lessons, which must never be forgotten. One is, that the true and the good must be secured at any price. They are beyond all price. We dare not compute their cost. They are the soul of our being, and the whole world is as dust in the balance against them. No matter what is to be paid for them, we must not hesitate to lay down their redemption price. The other grand lesson is, that their price is never paid in vain. What we give can never be lost, *unless we give too little.* . . . If we maintain the pure Word inflexibly at every cost . . . we shall conquer . . . through the Word; but to compromise on a single point, is to lose all, and to be lost.

JOHN WARWICK MONTGOMERY

15 January 1967:
The Transfiguration of Our Lord

o   o   o

Continued high interest in the *Crisis* volumes, as evidenced by their five printings over a six-year period, has dictated a second edition, with the opportunity to correct minor errors and to include additional essays bearing on the latest aspects of the struggle for a faithful Lutheran confessionalism.

Non-Lutherans who chance upon these volumes should not find themselves in alien territory. Since the work was first published, it has been of considerable service to Christians in many communions (such as the Presbyterian, Anglican, Methodist, Baptist, and Roman Catholic) where deterioration of historic Christian doctrine has paralleled the Lutheran problem on which these volumes especially focus. In actuality, the *Crisis* volumes do not deal narrowly with a crisis in *Lutheran* theology but with the general crisis in biblical and doctrinal authority which has become so endemic in the modern church.

This new edition thus goes forth to serve all those Christian believers who can pray the magnificent words of Duke Henry's Saxon Order of 1539: "O Lord God, heavenly Father, pour out, we beseech Thee, Thy Holy Spirit upon Thy faithful people, keep them steadfast in Thy grace and truth, protect and comfort them in all temptation, defend them against all enemies of Thy Word, and bestow upon Christ's church militant Thy saving peace."

JOHN WARWICK MONTGOMERY

6 January 1973:
The Epiphany of Our Lord

ACKNOWLEDGMENTS

Six of the seven essays contained in this book have appeared previously in several theological journals. The present book has afforded opportunity to make minor revisions and corrections, so that the journal texts of these articles ought no longer to be considered the *textus receptus*. However, readers may well appreciate the following bibliographic listing of all authorized appearances of these essays in print.

"Inspiration and Inerrancy: A New Departure": *The Evangelical Theological Society Bulletin,* Spring, 1965 (complete essay); *Lutherans Alert — National,* May, 1966 and June-July, 1966 (abridged).

"Lutheran Hermeneutics and Hermeneutics Today": *Aspects of Biblical Hermeneutics: Concordia Theological Monthly, Occasional Papers No. 1,* 1966; *Lutherischer Rundblick,* 1967 (in German).

"Current Theological Trends in the Lutheran Church-Missouri Synod": *Lutherans Alert — National,* August-September, 1966 and October, 1966.

"The Law's Third Use: Sanctification": *Christianity Today,* April 26, 1963.

"Missouri Compromise & Aftermath": *Christianity Today,* January 17, March 28, June 6, November 7, 1969; April 9, 1971.

"The Unbridgeable Chasm": *Affirm,* December, 1972.

Three of the essays in the present volume were originally delivered by invitation at conferences of professors, pastors, teachers, and laity of the Lutheran Church-Missouri Synod. My thanks to the program committees of and the participants at those conferences for their interest and encouragement. The conference history of these essays is as follows:

"Lutheran Hermeneutics and Hermeneutics Today": Conference of the Council of Presidents and the joint theological faculties of the Lutheran Church-Missouri Synod, St. Louis, November 29-30, 1965; Central Regional Pastoral Conference of the Northern Illinois District, Lutheran Church-Missouri Synod, La Grange, February 2, 1966; Northern Regional Pastoral Conference of the Northern Illinois District, Lutheran Church-Missouri Synod, Park Ridge, February 15-16, 1966; Northwest Pastoral Conference of the Iowa District West, Lutheran Church-Missouri Synod, Newell, April 20, 1966; Quad-circuit Pastoral Conference of the Iowa District West, Lutheran Church-Missouri Synod, Sioux City, April 21-22, 1966; Michigan District Pastoral Conference, Detroit, April 27, 1966.

"Theological Issues and Problems of Biblical Interpretation Now Facing the Lutheran Church-Missouri Synod": North Dakota District State Pastoral Conference, Jamestown, October 5, 1966; Northern Illinois District Teachers Convention, Chicago, October 13, 1966; Western District Lutheran Teachers

Conference, St. Louis, Missouri, November 2, 1966; Eastern Pastor-Teacher Conference (with participation of the Western Conference) of the North Wisconsin District, Lutheran Church-Missouri Synod, Green Bay, November 4, 1966; Zone 4 Northern Illinois District Lutheran Laymens League Banquet, Lake Zurich, November 6, 1966; Concerned Lutheran Laymen, Brookfield, Illinois, December 4, 1966.

"Current Theological Trends in the Lutheran Church-Missouri Synod": Proviso Lutheran Teachers Conference, Hinsdale, Illinois, May 6, 1966; Iowa District West Pastoral Conference, Carroll, May 25, 1966.

CONTENTS

Part One

THE INSPIRATION AND INTERPRETATION OF HOLY SCRIPTURE

Part Two

DOCTRINE, ETHICS AND THE CHURCH

*Readers who wish to pursue further the subjects discussed in this book are encouraged to consult the asterisked items in the notes to Essay III. Books and articles so designated there are suitable for individual and group study by laymen as well as by the theologically trained. The asterisked citations in this essay thus serve in lieu of a general bibliography of further readings.

Part One
The Inspiration and Interpretation of Holy Scripture

I.

INSPIRATION AND INERRANCY: A NEW DEPARTURE

> If I have told you earthly things, and
> ye believe not, how shall ye believe, if I
> tell you of heavenly things?   John 3:12

In his classic work, *The Progress of Dogma*, James Orr contended that the Christian Church, in each great epoch of its' history, has been forced to come to grips with one particular doctrine of crucial significance both for that day and for the subsequent history of the Church.[1] In the Patristic era, the issue was the relation of the persons of the Godhead, and particularly the christological problem of Jesus' character; the Ecumenical Creeds represent the success of Orthodox, Trinitarian theology over against numerous christological heresies, any one of which could have permanently destroyed the Christian faith. Medieval Christianity faced the issue of the meaning of Christ's atonement, and Anselm's "Latin doctrine," in spite of its scholastic inadequacies, gave solid expression to biblical salvation-history as represented by the Epistle to the Hebrews. In the Reformation Era, the overarching doctrinal problem facing the Church was the application of redemption in justification; Luther's stand for *sola gratia, sola fide* arrested an anthropocentric trend which could have turned the Christian faith into little more than pagan religiosity.

And contemporary Christianity? What great doctrinal issue does the modern Church face? Writing just before the turn of the present century, Orr thought that he could see in Eschatology the unique doctrinal challenge for modern Christianity. Subsequent events, however, have proven this judgment wrong: the doctrinal problem which, above all others, demands resolution in the modern Church is that of the authority of Holy Scripture. All other issues of belief today pale before this issue, and indeed root in it; for example, ecumenical discussions, if they are doctrinal in nature, eventually and inevitably reach the question of religious authority — what is the final determinant of doctrinal truth, and how fully can the Bible be relied upon to establish truth in theological dialog? As the Patristic age faced a *christological* watershed, as the Medieval and Reformation churches confronted *soteriological* crises, so the contemporary Church finds itself grappling with the great *epistemological* question in Christian dogmat-

---

1. James Orr, *The Progress of Dogma* (4th ed.; London: Hodder & Stoughton (1901), *passim*. The lectures comprising this book were originally delivered in 1897. Orr was Professor of Apologetics and Systematic Theology in the United Free Church College, Glasgow.

ics.[2] And, let it be noted with care: just as the Church in former times could have permanently crippled its posterity through superficial or misleading answers to the root-questions then at issue, so we today have an equal obligation to deal responsibly with the Scripture issue. If we do not, future generations of theologians may find that no criterion remains by which to solve any subsequent doctrinal problems, and the theologians of the twentieth century will have gained the dubious distinction of having made their discipline (and the Church which looks to it for its doctrinal guidance) totally irrelevant.

The Ostensible Nature of the Issue

To the unsophisticated observer of the twentieth-century theological scene, it might seem that the present epistemological issue in theology is simply whether the Bible is inspired or not. (Later we shall be reminded that the unsophisticated, like children, often have disarming insight.) However, those who are dissatisfied with the traditional formulations of the Scripture doctrine argue in the strongest terms that the real issue is not whether the Bible is inspired or not, but the *character* and *extent* of inspiration. The claim is made that a non-traditional approach to biblical authority in no way denies the existence of inspiration; it merely defines more closely what is meant by inspiration and how far such inspiration extends in Holy Writ.

Thus it is held that Scripture is inspired as a theological norm — as God's authoritative message in matters spiritual — but that in matters historical and scientific we must recognize the human, fallible element in the biblical witness. "So," writes Roy A. Harrisville of Luther Seminary, "we admit to the discrepancies and the broken connections in Scripture, we let them stand just as they are — this is part of what it means that faith has its sphere in this world and not in some cloud cuckoo-land."[3] And the editors of *Dialog*, in a recent issue devoted to "Scripture and Tradition," are willing

---

2. In this connection it is instructive to note that a recurring theme in present-day "broad-church" Lutheran theological writing is that Bultmann should be regarded as a 20th-century Luther; as Luther directed men from ethical works-righteousness to the saving Christ, so it is argued, Bultmann points men from intellectualistic works-righteousness (i.e., relying on an inerrant Bible) to Christ. (See, for a typical statement of this view, Robert Scharlemann, "Shadow on the Tomb," *Dialog*, I [Spring, 1962], 22-29; and cf. Thomas C. Oden, "Bultmann As Lutheran Existentialist," *Dialog*, III [Summer, 1964], 207-214.) This comparison has the single merit of emphasizing that, as justification was the key theological issue Luther faced, the Scripture problem is the theological watershed of our time. Otherwise, the Luther-Bultmann parallel is completely wide of the mark. As I have written elsewhere: "Whereas Luther turned from moral guilt to confidence in the *objective* facts of Christ's death for his sin and resurrection for his justification, Bultmann turns from his intellectual doubts to *subjective* anthropological salvation — a direct about-face from the objective Gospel Luther proclaimed" (J. W. Montgomery, *The Shape of the Past* ["History in Christian Perspective," Vol. I; Ann Arbor, Michigan: Edwards Bros., 1963], p. 160).
3. Roy A. Harrisville, "A Theology of Rediscovery," *Dialog*, II (Summer, 1963), 190.

(albeit grudgingly) to continue the use of the expression "Scripture is inspired" if by it is meant that "Scripture is God's absolutely authoritative and authorized fundamental witness to revelation" — as long as no attempt is made to apply such inspiration to "an inerrancy of the 'parts,' of the historical and scientific opinions of the biblical authors."[4] In a subsequent issue of *Dialog*, the Lutheran Church-Missouri Synod's *Report of the Commission on Theology and Church Relations* ("A Study Document on Revelation, Inspiration, Inerrancy," 1964) is criticized for not labeling as erroneous the *Brief Statement's* inclusion of the historical and scientific data of the Bible in its definition of inspiration.[5] A more esoteric expression of the same general view is that the Bible is totally inspired — indeed, infallibly inspired — but that such inspiration does not necessarily produce inerrant results in matters historical or scientific, since God's word infallibly accomplishes only what He *intends* it to accomplish (i.e., the revelation of *theological* truths, not the imparting of historic or scientific absolutes).

In sum, then, the present controversy over biblical authority ostensibly centers on a split between inspiration and inerrancy. It is claimed that the former can and should be held without the latter. Not only will the Christian no longer have to defend the Bible against scientific and historical criticism, but he will be freed to enter more fully into a purely faith-relationship with Jesus Christ.

> In the last analysis, a rejection of the doctrine of inerrancy involves primarily a mental readjustment. Nothing basic is lost. In fact, when all the evidence is examined, those essential elements which the advocates of the doctrine of inerrancy have cherished and sought to protect are more firmly supported than ever before. Scripture is the product of inspiration and it is the indispensable source for coming to know God's claim upon us and his will for us.[6]

The contention of the present writer, over against these above-expressed views, is that inspiration and inerrancy cannot be separated — that like

---

4. "Controversy on Inspiration," *Dialog*, II (Autumn, 1963), 273. The same editorial asserts that the inspiration controversy "is surely one of the emptiest"; if so, why devote a journal issue to an attempt to demolish the traditional position on inspiration?

5. Of the Commission's *Report*, the *Dialog* editor writes: "The statement on biblical 'inerrancy' does not come off very well. Admittedly this is a sensitive question and an emotionally laden word in the Missouri Synod; and if public opinion is a determinant, one can understand why the only point raised against *A Brief Statement* — the official document of the Synod which describes the Scriptures as the infallible truth even in 'historical, geographical, and other secular matters' — is the question whether it 'does justice to the rich variety present in the content and mode of the utterances of the Scriptures.' But, synodical public opinion aside, the objection to that sentence in *A Brief Statement* surely is not that it is insufficient but that it is wrong; and the Report ought to say so" ("Right Key — Wrong Melody," *Dialog*, III [Summer, 1964], 165).

6. Dewey M. Beegle, *The Inspiration of Scripture* (Philadelphia: Westminster Press, 1963), p. 187. Excellent critical reviews of Beegle's work are available in *The Gordon Review*, VIII (Double Issue, Winter 1964-1965), 93-109, and in *Christianity Today*, VII (April 26, 1963), 26-30, 39-41.

"love" and "marriage" in *Annie, Get Your Gun,* "you can't have one with-out the other." This traditional position may seem on the surface to necessitate a traditional defense of it, along the lines of the vast number of admittedly drab works on the subject produced by "fundamentalists" since the days of the Scopes evolution trial. However, nothing could be farther from the truth. Note carefully that I have not said merely (as others have said) that inspiration and inerrancy *should* not be separated (i.e., that they *can* be sepa-rated but for various biblical and theological reasons *ought* not to be), but rather that scriptural inspiration and inerrancy *cannot* exist apart from each other (i.e., that to separate them results not just in error, but in plain and simple *meaninglessness*). I am convinced that the dullness and the sameness in standard orthodox defenses of biblical inerrancy point to an impasse in previous thinking on the subject — and constitute a demand for ground-break-ing along different lines. By way of certain new techniques derived from the realm of analytical philosophy, I believe that one can see exactly where the central difficulty lies in the present-day attempt to dichotomize inspiration and inerrancy. The result of this investigation will, it is believed, leave the reader with but two meaningful alternatives: a Bible which is both inspired and inerrant (or better, inerrant because it is inspired), or a Bible which is no different qualitatively from other books.[7] The superficially at-tractive half-way house of an inspired, non-inerrant Bible will be seen to evaporate in the mist — as a concept having neither philosophical nor theo-logical, but only emotive, significance.

The Peculiarity of the Issue

The contemporary advocates of an inspired but non-inerrant view of the Bible appeal constantly to the pressure of recent scholarship as justificating and indeed demanding their viewpoint. A recent letter from a well-known Professor of New Testament Interpretation took me to task for my biblical position on the ground that "a new era of biblical theology began to dawn some twenty-five years ago; and, I believe, any biblical matters cannot ignore what has happened in this field." Warren A. Quanbeck of Luther Seminary has recently argued in more explicit terms that inerrancy was unable to sur-ive the onslaughts of modern historical and scientific scholarship:

> Theologians read the Bible as a collection of revealed propositions un-folding the truth about God, the world, and man. Because the Holy Spirit was the real author of Scripture, every proposition in it was guaranteed infallible and inerrant, not only in spiritual, but in secular matters.
>
> Because of this insistence on the Bible's inerrancy in historical and scientific matters, the blows struck by studies in historical and natural science were crushing in their force. When men approached the Bible as a collection of historical books they saw plainly the human character

---

7. Such a Bible could of course have a higher (quantatitive) degree of *literary* inspiration than the average book (cf. Shakespeare as compared with Mickey Spillane), but this is clearly not the type of "inspiration" with which any theologian (except the unreconstructed, pre-World War I liberal) is concerned.

of its writers and their obvious dependence upon the sources of information available in their day. They recognized also that the scientific outlook of the writers was that of their time, and could not be a substitute for present-day scientific investigation and experiment. When theologians insisted that the religious message of the Bible stood or fell with its scientific and historical information they assumed an impossible apologetic task.[8]

The strangeness in this line of argumentation lies in two principal considerations: (1) The alleged factual errors and internal contradictions in Scripture which are currently cited to demonstrate the impossibly archaic nature of the inerrancy view are themselves impossibly archaic in a high proportion of instances; and (2) the most recent scholarly investigations and intellectual trends bearing on the validity of biblical data have never been more hospitable to inerrancy claims. Let us consider, in this connection, the recent series of anti-inerrancy arguments adduced by Robert Scharlemann:

> Unless one makes all sorts of special qualifications for the term "errors," this statement [that "the scientist can accept the entire Bible as God's inspired Word for it is inerrant"] can simply not be supported by an examination of the Bible itself. Let me cite two examples which, since they are not from the area of "science," are likely to be less provocative.

> A reporter could ask the question, "Was the Greek word *houtos* the first or last word in the superscription on the cross at Jesus' crucifixion?" From Luke (23:38) he would receive the reply, "It was the last." From Matthew (27:37) he would receive the reply, "It was the first." By any normal definition of error, either Matthew or Luke is in error concerning this reportorial matter; perhaps both of them are.

> A second example is the classical one. Matthew 27:9 ascribes to Jeremiah a quotation which is actually found in Zechariah.

> These are not isolated cases. Numerous examples can be found if one is interested in hunting for them. When was Jesus crucified? According to Matthew, Mark, and Luke it was on the 15th of Nisan; according to John it was on the 14th of Nisan. At least one of them must be in error. Unless one so defines "error" that it does not really mean an error in the normal sense; or unless one holds to the word "inerrancy" with a sort of blind dogmatism, the assertion that the Bible is inerrant, "that is, contains no error," simply cannot be supported by the biblical evidence itself.[9]

This account of representative "contradictions" derives in no sense from modern scholarship; the alleged discrepancies have been recognized for centuries and have been dealt with in a variety of effective ways. Haley,

---

8. Warren A. Quanbeck, "The Bible," in *Theology in the Life of the Church*, ed. Robert W. Bertram (Philadelphia: Fortress Press, 1963), p. 23. This book is an outgrowth of the Conference of Lutheran Professors of Theology, and thus well reflects the general trends of Lutheran theological thought in America today.

9. Robert Scharlemann, Letter to the Editor, *The Lutheran Scholar*, April, 1963.

in his great work on supposed biblical contradictions, stated in 1874 what had been obvious to readers of the superscriptions since the accounts were originally set down: "It is altogether improbable that three inscriptions, in three different languages, should correspond word for word;"[10] and in reference to the Zechariah quotation in Matthew, he presents two perfectly reasonable ways of dealing with the problem, both of which are derived from earlier scholarship:

> According to the Jewish writers, Jeremiah was reckoned the first of the prophets, and was placed first in the book of the prophets; thus, Jeremiah, Ezekiel, Isaiah, etc. Matthew, in quoting this book, may have quoted it under the name which stood *first* in it; that is, instead of saying, "by the Prophets," he may have said, "by Jeremy the prophet," since *he* headed the list.
>
> Or, the difficulty may have arisen from abridgment of the names. In the Greek, Jeremiah, instead of being written in full, might stand thus, "Iriou"; Zechariah thus, "Zriou." By the mere change of Z into I [i.e., by later scribal copyists], the mistake would be made. The Syriac Peshito and several MMS. have simply, "by the prophet."[11]

Alleged contradictions of this kind were, in fact, more than adequately handled by such orthodox fathers of the Reformation era as Andreas Althamer.[12] As for the 14th Nisan-15th Nisan crucifixion difficulty, which has also had much attention through Christian history, the most recent biblical scholarship has provided what may well be the final answer to the problem: A. Jaubert, a French specialist on the Dead Sea Scrolls, has shown that two calendars were employed in first-century Palestine (the official lunar calendar and a Jubilees-Qumran calendar) and that there is every reason to believe that the double dating in the Gospel accounts of the crucifixion, far from being a contradiction, simply reflects these two calendar systems.[13]

In point of fact, as Jaubert's investigations illustrate, the present climate of research is more hospitable to an inerrancy approach than was the nineteenth century or the early decades of the twentieth. Archeological work daily confirms biblical history in ways which liberal criticism would have regarded as patently impossible a few decades ago.[14] The Einsteinian-rela-

10. John W. Haley, *An Examination of the Alleged Discrepancies of the Bible* (reprint ed.; Grand Rapids, Michigan: Baker Book House, 1958), p. 154.
11. *Ibid.*, p. 153. Cf. also William F. Arndt, *Does the Bible Contradict Itself?* (5th ed.; St. Louis, Missouri: Concordia, 1955), pp. 51-53, 73-74; and Edward J. Young, *Thy Word Is Truth* (Grand Rapids, Michigan: Eerdmans, 1957), pp. 172-75.
12. Andreas Althamer, *Conciliationes Locorum Scripturae, qui specie tenus inter se pugnare videntur, Centuriae duae* (*Vitebergae*: Zacharias Lehman, 1582). This excellent work, of which I possess a personal copy, treats 160 "discrepancies" and went through at least sixteen editions (1st ed., 1527).
13. A Jaubert, *La Date de la Cène. Calendrier biblique et liturgie chrétienne* (Paris: Gabalda, 1957). I have treated this matter in some detail in my article, "The Fourth Gospel Yesterday and Today," *Concordia Theological Monthly*, XXXIV (April, 1963), 206, 213.
14. For a semi-popular overview of this trend, see Werner Keller, *The Bible As History*, trans. William Neil (New York: William Morrow, 1956).

tivistic reinterpretation of "natural law" has dealt a death-blow to Hume's arguments against the miraculous and has removed the rational possibility of using antimiraculous presuppositions for dehistoricizing such biblical accounts as Jonah-and-the-Leviathan.[15] The collapse of form-critical techniques in Homeric and other classical literary criticism, and the presently recognized debility of that approach even in the literary study of English ballads, has raised overwhelming doubts as to the whole presuppositional substructure of the Dibelius-Bultmann approach to the New Testament documents.[16] All in all, the traditional position on inspiration is able to command more respect today than it has during any generation since the advent of rationalistic higher criticism.

However, there is obviously something to the claim that "a new era of biblical theology began to dawn some twenty-five years ago" — an era which, in spite of developments such as those just described, could not tolerate plenary inspirationism. What has constituted the enormous pressure against the inerrancy view? Why have contemporary theologians found it necessary to ridicule the position and to treat it as a hopelessly outmoded one, in spite of such formidable proponents of it as the philosopher Gordon Clark, the theologian Edward John Carnell, and the New Testament lexicographer W. F. Arndt? Why have such considerations as archeological findings and classical scholarship not moved the mainstream theologians in the direction of plenary inspiration? The answer is most definitely *not* (in spite of loud protests continually voiced) the weight of new factual evidence against an inerrant Bible. Such "evidence" simply does not exist; as we have noted and illustrated, the contemporary critic of an inerrant Scripture is still citing alleged discrepancies and supposed scientific objections which have been adequately dealt with over and over again.[17] *The issue is not empirical; it is philosophical.* That is to say, there has been an alteration in the philosophical Zeitgeist which, apart from the question of particular factural evidence, makes scriptural inerrancy offensive to much of contemporary theological thought. What precisely is this new element in the current climate of theological opinion?

---

15. On the invalidity of Hume's argument in light of the replacement of Newtonian by Einsteinian conceptions of scientific law, see Montgomery, *The Shape of the Past*, pp. 288-93; and C. S. Lewis, *Miracles* (New York: Macmillan, 1947), especially chap. xiii.

16. I have discussed this matter in considerable detail in my lecture series, "Jesus Christ and History," delivered on January 29 and 30, 1963, at the University of British Columbia. These lectures have been published in *His* (Inter-Varsity Christian Fellowship), December, 1964 — March, 1965, and are available as a *His* Reprint (address: 4605 Sherwood, Downers Grove, Illinois). See also in this connection, H. J. Rose, *Handbook of Greek Literature from Homer to the Age of Lucian* (London: Methuen, 1934), pp. 42-43; and A. H. McNeile and C. S. C. Williams, *Introduction to the Study of the New Testament* (2nd ed.; Oxford: Clarendon Press, 1955), pp. 52-58.

17. If the Genesis 1-3 problem here comes to mind, the reader should consult such classic refutations of supposed "scientific error" in the biblical account as are found in two monographs of the American Scientific Affiliation: *Modern Science and Christian Faith* (2nd ed., 1950) and *Evolution and Christian Thought Today* (2nd ed., 1960).

A hint of an answer is provided by Rupert E. Davies in his attempt to refute John Wenham's inerrancy position. Writes Davies:

> I cannot believe that truths which go away into mystery can be expressed once for all in propositional form; and the Bible never claims that they can. Its purpose is to draw attention in many different ways to the saving Acts of God.[18]

Here a suggestion is made that the Bible deals with a different kind of subject-matter than is capable of being expressed propositionally. Biblical truth is not propositional and static, but dynamic and active; its focus is on acts, not assertions.

For the late A. G. Hebert, one of the prime modern opponents of plenary inspiration, the "propositional" view of biblical truth is a relatively recent and unfortunate result of applying scientific categories in the religious sphere.

> The doctrine of Inerrancy was not very harmful in an age which thought of "truth" primarily as belonging to the revelation of God and of the eternal meaning of man's life. The Bible was regarded as teaching chiefly spiritual truths about God and man. It was otherwise when the "scientific age" had begun; truth was now commonly understood as the matter-of-fact truth of observable phenomena, and so great a man as Locke could make the outrageous statement that the existence of God was as certain as the propositions of geometry. The Inerrancy of the Bible was understood as guaranteeing the literal exactness of its every statement. This is the Fundamentalism which has been a potent cause of modern unbelief. This materialistic Inerrancy needs to be carefully distinguished from the theological and religious Inerrancy in which earlier ages believed.[19]

Even if one leaves aside the minor fallacies in this statement (e.g., the confusion of geometry with observable phenomena),[20] one cannot accept the historical explanation of the inerrancy position here presented. Throughout the history of the Church there has been continual concern to maintain and defend the total factual reliability of the Bible. To take only one

---

18. *Is the Bible Infallible? A Debate between John Wenham, Vice-Principal of Tyndale Hall, Bristol, and Rupert E. Davies, Tutor at Didsbury College,* Bristol (London: Epworth Press, 1959), p. 27).

19. A. G. Hebert, *The Authority of the Old Testament* (London: Faber & Faber, 1947), pp. 306-307. Hebert's misrepresentations of biblical orthodoxy as "fundamentalism" have been decisively answered in J. I. Packer's *"Fundamentalism" and the Word of God* (Grand Rapids, Michigan: Eerdmans, [1958]).

20. Locke's statement is grounded in rationalism, not in empiricism, and as such offers no proper analogy to the biblical inerrancy position. Russell and Whitehead, in the *Principia Mathematica,* and Wittgenstein in the *Tractatus Logico-Philosophicus,* have shown that geometrical propositions are tautologous, i.e., that they have no necessary connection with "observable phenomena." Neither the biblical writers nor the plenary inspirationists have argued that biblical truth is mathematical/tautologous; rather, they have asserted that it is observationally reliable (as in the case of the historic revelation of Christ himself).

prominent example, St. Augustine, by all odds the most important theologian of the Patristic age, argued with vehemence for an inerrant Bible. As the definitive study of his biblical position asserts:

> There is no point of doctrine more plainly asserted or more vigorously defended by St. Augustine, than the absence of falsehood and error from the divine Scriptures. . . . Indeed inerrancy is so intimately bound up with inspiration that an inspired book cannot assert what is not true. . . . It is impossible for Scripture to contain contradictory statements. One book of Scripture cannot contradict another, nor can the same author contradict himself.[21]

From earliest times the Church was concerned with the propositional accuracy of the biblical text, for such a concern followed directly from the Church's commitment to the inspiration of Scripture. Actually, the so-called "dynamic," non-propositional view of truth has its origin not in pre-scientific times, but in very recent thinking.

The source of this essentially new approach to the nature of biblical truth, over against traditional plenary inspiration, will become more evident if we look closely at a typical recent expression of it. Let us hear Warren Quanbeck's "re-examination of theological presuppositions":

> Since human language is always relative, being conditioned by its historical development and usage, there can be no absolute expression of the truth even in the language of theology. Truth is made known in Jesus Christ, who is God's Word, his address to mankind. Christ is the only absolute. Theological statements, which have an instrumental function, find their meaning in relation to him; they do not contain the truth nor give adequate expression to it. At best they point to Jesus Christ as the one in whom one may know the truth. Truth is not a matter of intellection only, but of obedient discipleship. Only by "abiding in Christ" can one know the truth.[22]

To any historian of philosophy, the antecedents of this view are patently obvious — and they lie not in the realm of biblical/theological presuppositions, as Quanbeck and other adherents of this position believe, but in the realm of philosophical apriori. The idea that "there can be no absolute expression of the truth" in propositional form has clear alignment with the venerable philosophical position known as *metaphysical dualism,* which in one form or other has always claimed that the Absolute cannot be fully manifested in the phenomenal world. From Plato's separation of the world of ideas from the world of things and the soul from the body, to the

---

21. Charles Joseph Costello, *St. Augustine's Doctrine on the Inspiration and Canonicity of Scripture* (Washington, D.C.: Catholic University of America, 1930), pp. 30-31. Costello's work constituted his thesis for the doctorate in theology, and is fully grounded in the primary works of Augustine. It is noteworthy that Augustine, in the 5th century, effectively treated the Zacharias-Jeremiah "contradiction" which R. Scharlemann presented in 1963 as a decisive counter to biblical inerrancy! (see Costello, pp. 34-37, and cf. our text above at nn. 9-11).
22. Quanbeck, *op. cit.,* p. 25.

medieval "realists" with their split between universals and particulars, through the Reformation Calvinists' conviction that *finitum non est capax infiniti,* to the modern idealism of Kant and Hegel, we see this same conviction in various semantic garbs. It is this absolute separation of eternity and time that lies at the basis of the contemporary theological split between *Geschichte* and *Historie,* as I have indicated elsewhere;[23] and it is most definitely the same aprioristic dualism that motivates much of contemporary theology in its refusal to allow the Eternal to express Himself in absolutely veracious biblical propositions.

But metaphysical dualism is only the minor element in the anti-inerrancy position taken by Quanbeck and others. "Truth," he writes, "is not a matter of intellection only, but of obedient discipleship" and "Christ is the only absolute." Here we see the redefinition of truth in *personal,* as opposed to propositional, terms. Truth is arrived at not through words or through investigation, but "only by 'abiding in Christ.' " Martin Scharlemann, in an unpublished paper presenting this same general approach to biblical inspiration, concludes: "In a very real sense, therefore, it is impossible to speak of revelation as an objective reality, independent of personal reaction on the part of him to whom a disclosure is made. . . . Knowledge is not a matter of acquiring information but of being confronted with God Himself as He is revealed in His Son."[24] Such terminology and conceptual content point unmistakably to the *existentialist movement* in modern philosophy, which, stemming from Kierkegaard, has affirmed that "truth is subjectivity" and that "existence," as manifested in personal relationships, precedes and surpasses in quality "essence," i.e., formal, propositional assertions or descriptions concerning reality.[25] In the hands of its most influential contemporary Protestant advocate, Rudolf Bultmann, existentialist theology claims to "cut under the subject-object distinction"[26] so as to arrive at a "dynamic" view of biblical truth untrammeled by questions of propositional facticity or objective validity.

No philosophy has so captured the minds and hearts of the contemporary world as existentialism; for how can one listen to "propositional" assertions of "objective" ideals when the West has barely survived two terrible self-created holocausts and seems bent on nuclear self-destruction? Only in personal existential relationships does any hope seem to lie. So speaks the average

23. J. W. Montgomery, "Karl Barth and Contemporary Theology of History," published both in *The Cresset,* XXVII (November, 1963), 8-14, and in the *Evangelical Theological Society Bulletin,* VI (May, 1963), 39-49. In this article I deal primarily with the baleful implications of the *Geschichte-Historie* dualism in christology and in theology of history.

24. Martin H. Scharlemann, "The Bible As Record, Witness and Medium" (mimeographed essay), p. 11. The same approach is found in William Hordern's *Case for a New Reformation Theology* (Philadelphia: Westminster Press, 1959), where the amazingly circular statement appears: "Objectivity is possible only when there is a faith-commitment made to objectivity" (p. 44; cf. pp. 62-69).

25. Cf. Jean Wahl, *A Short History of Existentialism,* trans. Forrest Williams and Stanley Maron (New York: Philosophical Library, 1949).

26. Paul Tillich, "Existential Philosophy: Its Historical Meaning," in his *Theology of Culture,* ed. Robert C. Kimball (New York: Oxford University Press, 1959), p. 92.

member of the Western intelligentsia; and, as has happened not a few times in the history of theology, the professional theologian does him one better: in religious life as well, truth can be found only in personality (Christ), and one should discard as irrelevant and harmful excess baggage the traditional view that Scripture offers propositionally objective truth to man. Thus the cultural pressure to existentialism, combined with a powerful tradition of metaphysical dualism,[27] impels much of modern theology to reject inerrancy. Modernity is indeed the source of the new approach to Scripture; but it is not a modernity characterized by new discoveries of empirical fact which have forced modifications of traditional thinking. Rather, it is a modernity of philosophical Zeitgeist.

Bultmann has argued, in defense of his use of existentialistic categories in interpreting biblical data, that existentialism is really not an alien philosophy, but a heuristic methodology that does not commit one to extra-biblical positions. It is almost universally agreed, however, both by professional philosophers and by lay interpreters of existentialism, that this viewpoint does indeed constitute a philosophy, and that its presuppositions (e.g., "existence precedes essence," "the objective-subjective distinction must be transcended," "truth is found only in personal encounter," etc.) can and must be subjected to philosophical analysis and criticism. Such a process of critical analysis has been going on now for some years, and the results have been devastatingly negative for the existentialist position. Indeed, faced with the blistering criticism directed against existentialism by analytical philosophy in particular, contemporary thought is now beginning to move away from Albert Camus' dread city of Oran into more congenial philosophical habitats.

It is now our task to apply the techniques of analytic philosophy to the anti-inerrancy position on Scripture that derives from an existentialistic-dualistic *Weltanschauung*. In doing so, we shall discover, possibly to our amazement, that contemporary theological denials of inerrancy necessarily tie themselves to philosophical stars which are rapidly burning out.

The Meaninglessness of Existentialistic and Dualistic Affirmations

We shall commence our critical task with an examination of analytical technique in general and its application to existentialism and dualism in particular. The relevance of the following discussion to the inerrancy issue will become evident in the subsequent sections of the paper.

While theologians of the last two decades have been especially concerned with the epistemological problem of biblical authority, contemporary philosophy (particularly in England) has likewise focused attention on central epistemological issues. Faced with the welter of conflicting philosophical and theological world-views propounded through the centuries, twentieth-century analytical philosophers have attempted to cut back to the basic question: How can truth-claims be verified? In a brief paper such as this, it would be impossible to discuss the history of this analytical movement, arising from the

---

27. Ironically, to be sure, Existentialism has sought to destroy all metaphysical speculation, including Dualism. But since ‧ Existentialism itself has a metaphysic, it cannot successfully destroy metaphysics; and it often (as here) finds itself a strange bedfellow to other (uncongenial) metaphysical tendencies.

pioneering *Principia Mathematica* of Russell and Whitehead, extending through the "logical atomism" of Wittgenstein's amazing *Tractatus Logico-Philosophicus*, and culminating in the (misnamed) "logical positivism" of Von Mises and the "linguistic analysis" or "ordinary language philosophy" of the later Wittgenstein and Ryle.[28] But, in very general terms, the conclusions of these analytical thinkers can be summarized in regard to the problem of verifiability.

> The criterion which we use to test the genuineness of apparent statements of fact is the criterion of verifiability. We say that a sentence is factually significant to any given person, if, and only if, he knows how to verify the proposition which it purports to express — that is, if he knows what observations would lead him, under certain conditions, to accept the proposition as being true, or reject it as being false.[29]

This "Verifiability Criterion of Meaning" arose from the discovery (set forth by Whitehead and Russell in the *Principia*) that assertions in mathematics and deductive logic are tautologous, i.e., they state nothing factual about the world, but follow from the apriori assumptions of the deductive system. Such "analytic" sentences can be verified without recourse to the world of fact, since they say nothing about the world; but other assertions (non-tautological, or "synthetic" affirmations) must be tested by the data of the real world if we are to discover their truth or falsity.

Thus any proposition, upon inspection, will fall into one of the following categories: (1) Analytic sentences, which are true or false solely by virtue of their logical form, *ex hypothesi*. Such assertions, though essential to thought and potentially meaningful, are often termed "trivial," since they never provide information about the world of experience. Example: "All husbands are married," whose truth follows entirely from the definition of the word "husband." (2) Synthetic sentences, which are true or false according to the application of the Verifiability Criterion set forth above. Such sentences are sometimes termed "informative," because they do potentially give information about the world. Example: "Jesus died at Jerusalem," which can be tested through an examination of historical evidence. (3) Meaningless sentences, embracing all affirmations which are neither analytic nor synthetic. Such sentences are incapable of testing, for they neither express tautological judgments (they are not statements whose truth depends on their logical form) nor do they affirm anything about the real world which is testable by investigating the world. Example: the philosopher F. H. Bradley's claim that "the Absolute enters into, but is itself incapable of, evolution and progress." Such a statement is clearly not tautologous, for it is not deduced from the aprioris of logic, nor is it capable of any test which could conceivably determine its truth or

---

28. For a short introduction to these movements, see Victor Kraft, *The Vienna Circle*, trans. Arthur Pap (New York: Philosophical Library, 1953).
29. A. J. Ayer, *Language, Truth and Logic* (New York: Dover Publications, [1946]), p. 35. Since the publication of the first edition of his work (1936), Ayer has somewhat refined his statement of the "Verifiability Principle" (see his Introduction to the new edition, pp. 5-16); however, in substance, his original statement remains unaltered and its classic simplicity warrants its continued use.

falsity. Thus it is meaningless, or nonsensical (in the technical meaning of "nonsense," i.e., without verifiable sense).

The importance of the analytic approach to questions of truth and falsity cannot be overestimated. As a result of its application, vast areas of philosophical speculation and argument have been shown to lie in a never-never land of meaninglessness — a land where discussion could continue forever without any possibility of arriving at truth or falsity. The analysts have successfully cleared the philosophical air of numerous positions about which discussion of truth-value is a waste of time, because their verifiability is impossible in any case.[30]

It should be emphasized, however, that "category three" statements are meaningless only in the special sense of non-verifiability. When Ayer speaks of the analytical "elimination of metaphysics," one should not conclude that non-testable philosophical or religious assertions do not deserve study. They do: but only from a historical or psychological viewpoint. Such statements as "The Absolute enters into evolution and progress," while not telling us anything about logic or about the constitution of the world, does tell us something (a great deal, in fact) about its formulator, Bradley, and about the history of philosophical ideology. Wittgenstein illustrates the matter well by one of his typically striking parables:

> Imagine that there is a town in which the policemen are required to obtain information from each inhabitant, e.g. his age, where he came from, and what work he does. A record is kept of this information and some use is made of it. Occasionally when a policeman questions an inhabitant he discovers that the latter does not do *any* work. The policeman enters this fact on the record, because *this too* is a useful piece of information about the man![31]

Malcolm, who relates the parable, comments: "The application of the parable is, I think, that if you do not understand a statement, then to discover that it has no verification is an important piece of information about it and makes you understand it better. That is to say, you understand it *better;* you do not find out that there is nothing to understand." Thus analytical philosophy does

---

30. Attempts have been made, of course, to destroy the Verifiability Criterion. Few traditional, speculative philosophers have been happy with Feigl's remark that "Philosophy is the disease of which analysis should be the cure!" But the Verifiability Principle still stands as the best available road map through the forest of truth-claims. One of the most persistent attempts to refute the Criterion has been the effort to show that it is itself a meaningless assertion, being evidently neither an analytic nor a synthetic statement. However, this objection has been effectively met both by Ayer, who argues that the Criterion is actually a definition (*op. cit.*, pp. 15-16) and by Hempel, who shows that it, "like the result of any other explication, represents a linguistic proposal which itself is neither true nor false" ("The Empiricist Criterion of Meaning," published originally in the *Revue Internationale de Philosophie*, IV [1950], and reprinted, with newly appended remarks by the author, in *Logical Positivism*, ed. A. J. Ayer [Glencoe, Illinois: Free Press, 1959], pp. 108-129).
31. The parable was told by Wittgenstein to Stout and is related by Norman Malcolm in his *Ludwig Wittgenstein: A Memoir* (London: Oxford University Press, 1962), p. 66.

not, *pace* its detractors, attempt to silence all discussion of non-verifiable matters; rather, it attempts to limit discussions only to the "understandable" aspects of these matters: namely, to the emotive considerations represented by metaphysical assertions. It is in light of this qualification that we must interpret Wittgenstein's two great assertions, which have so powerfully influenced all subsequent analytical work:

Alles was überhaupt gedacht werden kann, kann klar gedacht werden.
Alles was sich aussprechen laesst, laesst sich klar aussprechen.
Wovon man nicht sprechen kann, darüber muss man schweigen.[32]

Now in practice how does the Verifiability Principle achieve this desirable limitation of speech to what can be said meaningfully and clearly? Let us consider several examples, which will progressively move us into the philosophical-theological application of analytical technique.

(A) "There are angels living on the planet Uranus."[33] This might seem, on the surface, to be a meaningless proposition, for no present test of verifiability exists by which the truth or falsity of the claim can be determined. However (on the assumption that angels are visible creatures), a test can be conceived; it would involve the use of space craft to make the journey to Uranus, whereby, through direct observation, the proposition could be tested as to its truth-value. Thus the proposition, being hypothetically testable, is meaningful. However, let it be noted well, if "angels" are defined in such a way that there is no conceivable way of determining their presence even if one succeeds in arriving at their habitat, then proposition (A) would indeed be meaningless (except as an emotive assertion, such as "I like angels"). Consider Antony Flew's parable, developed from a tale told by John Wisdom:

Once upon a time two explorers came upon a clearing in the jungle. In the clearing were growing many flowers and many weeds. One explorer says, "Some gardener must tend this plot." The other disagrees, "There is no gardener." So they pitch their tents and set a watch. No gardener is ever seen. "But perhaps he is an invisible gardener." So they set up a barbed-wire fence. They electrify it. They patrol with bloodhounds. (For they remember how H. G. Wells' *The Invisible Man* could be both smelt and touched though he could not be seen.) But no shrieks ever suggest that some intruder has received a shock. No movements of the wire ever betray an invisible climber. The bloodhounds never give cry. Yet still the Believer is not convinced. "But there is a gardener, invisible, intangible, insensible to electric shocks, a gardener who has no scent and makes no sound, a gardener who comes secretly to look after the garden which he loves." At last the Sceptic despairs, "But what remains of your original assertion? Just how does what you call an invisible,

---

32. *Tractatus Logico-Philosophicus*, propositions 4.116 and 7.0 (cf. Wittgenstein's "Vorwort"). For a discussion of these propositions in light of the *Tractatus* as a whole, see Max Black's long awaited and just published commentary, *A Companion to Wittgenstein's 'Tractatus'* (Ithaca, New York: Cornell University Press, 1964), *passim*.
33. This is a variation on Moritz Schlick's (now outdated!) propositional example: "There are mountains on the other side of the moon."

intangible, eternally elusive gardener differ from an imaginary gardener or even from no gardener at all?"[34]

This parable shows with utmost clarity how meaningless are religious assertions which are removed entirely from the realm of testability. Is not one of the most fundamental reasons for the strength of the Christian proclamation that "God was *in Christ*" — since apart from God's revelation of Himself in our midst, we could never know with certainty whether the garden of this world had a loving Gardener at all? But more of this later.

(B) "The world was created in 4004 B.C., but with built-in evidence of radiocarbon dating, fossil evidence, etc., indicating millions of years of prior developmental growth." This assertion, made by some well-meaning Christian believers, is a nonsensical proposition.[35] Why? Because it excludes all possible testability. *Any* alleged scientific fact marshalled against 4004 B.C. creation is, by the nature of the original proposition, discounted as having been built into the universe at its creation. Moreover, the statement is reconcilable with an infinite number of parallel assertions, such as "The world was created ten years ago (or ten minutes ago) with a built-in history." Such assertions as (B) are really no different from meaningless cosmological affirmations of the type: "The universe is continually increasing in size at a uniform rate" (obviously, in such a case, our instruments of measurement would *also* be increasing in size uniformly, and would not therefore be capable of yielding any evidence of the increase!). The Christian can take comfort that *his* God is not like Descartes' "Evil Genius" — that He does not introduce deceptive elements into His universe, thereby driving His creatures to meaningless affirmations about the world.

(C) "The resurrection of Christ, though an historical event in the full sense of the term (*Geschichte* and *Historie*), nonetheless cannot be verified by the methods of objective historical scholarship; it is evident only to the eyes of faith." This position, developed by Karl Barth and emphasized in his 1952 debate with Bultmann, is revealed as meaningless when placed under the searchlight of the Verifiability Principle. For how could one possibly know if Christ's resurrection (or any other event) was in fact historical if it could not be tested by the ordinary methods of historical investigation? As a parallel, consider the following argument: "In my backyard is an orange hippopotamus. He is really there, but his presence cannot be tested by any techniques employed to show the existence of the other things in my backyard." Such a claim is nonsense. Either the hippopotamus is there, or he isn't; and if no empirical test will show that he is, then one must conclude that assertions concerning his existence are meaningless. Likewise, if Christ's resur-

---

34. Antony Flew, "Theology and Falsification," in *New Essays in Philosophical Theology*, ed. Flew and Macintyre (London, SCM Press, 1955), p. 96.
35. This was shown in detail by Thomas H. Leith of York University, Toronto, Canada, in a paper titled, "Some Logical Problems with the Thesis of Apparent Age," delivered at the 19th Annual Convention of the American Scientific Affiliation, August 27, 1964, and subsequently published in the December, 1965, issue of the *American Scientific Affiliation Journal* (cf. also the Letters to the Editor in the *A.S.A. Journal* issue for June, 1966).

rection really occurred in history (*Historie*), then historical investigation will indicate it; if not, then one must give up any meaningful claim to the resurrection as a *historisch* event. Either the Orthodox theologians are right, or Bultmann is right; no meaningful middleground exists.

But, it is argued, can we not speak of Christ's resurrection, virgin birth, and other such religious events on the level of *Geschichte*, "metahistory," or "suprahistory"? It is exactly here that we encounter the *dualistic* tradition which, as already noted, constitutes one of the two essential elements in the contemporary anti-inerrancy view of the Bible. What about this eminent tradition of metaphysical Dualism that serves as the most extensive "footnote to Plato" in Western thought? Should we not think of the Absolute apart from earthly flux — God as Otto's "Wholly Other" or as Tillich's "Ultimate Concern," never fully identified with institutions, persons, books, or events in this world? Is it not of tremendous value to hold, with Plato and the medieval realists, that the phenomenal world can never dim the beauties of the eternal world of ideas, and to affirm with Tillich that the "truth of faith" cannot be "judged by any other kind of truth, whether scientific, historical or philosophical"?[36] The answer is simply that, whatever the supposed advantages of metaphysical or theological dualism, and however praiseworthy the motives leading to such dualism, their result is analytical meaninglessness. Why? Because, by definition, insofar as any statement about the "Absolute" or "God" does not touch the world of human experience, to that extent it cannot be verified in any sensible way. Thus have the analytical philosophers devastatingly criticized the metaphysical affirmations of the modern philosophical tradition represented by Hegel and Kant; and thus do the theological dualists on the contemporary scene fall under the critical axe of the same verifiability test. If, for example, the claim is made that Christ rose from the dead, but in the suprahistorical realm of *Geschichte*, not in the empirical realm of *Historie*, one has every right to ask: "What precisely do you *mean* by the realm of *Geschichte* and how do you know anything — much less a resurrection — goes on there?" A supra-experiential realm is, *ex hypothesi*, untestable, and therefore, like my orange hippopotamus mentioned earlier, irrelevant as a theological concept. It may (and does) tell us much about the theologians who rely upon it (particularly, that they fervently wish to avoid criticism from secular historians!), but it tells us nothing whatever about the truth-value of alleged events of a *geschichtliche* character. We know (or can know) whether a resurrection occurred in this world, and we know (or can know) whether God was incarnated in this world; but about a realm beyond all human testability, we can know nothing. To theological dualisms, Wittgenstein's final proposition has precise applicability: "Whereof one cannot speak, thereof one must be silent."

Existential affirmations, however, would seem to fall within the sphere of verifiable meaning, since they (unlike dualistic assertions) treat of "existence" rather than of "essence." What of this area of modern philosophy, which forms an even more important element than Dualism in the make-up of anti-inerrancy views of Scripture?

One must understand, first of all, that the assertions of Existentialism are

---

36. Tillich, *Dynamics of Faith* (New York: Harper Torchbooks, 1958), p. 95.

not simply statements about verifiable, existent things or events; rather, they are specialized philosophical claims about the nature of man's existence in the universe, i.e., they are genuinely metaphysical affirmations. Consider such basic tenets of the existentialist world-view as the following: "Truth cannot be found in abstract propositions." "Truth is discovered in responsible decision." "Personal encounter is the only sure avenue to truth." "The subject-object distinction must be transcended."[37] Such beliefs as these are very definitely claims as to the nature of the world and of man's relationship to it, and as such deserve analytical inspection in the same way as other truth-claims.

And what is the result when existentialist affirmations are subjected to verifiability tests? An excellent illustration has been provided in Rudolf Carnap's examination of the following typical argument in Heidegger's *Was Ist Metaphysik?*:

> What is to be investigated is being only and — *nothing* else; being alone and further — *nothing*; solely being, and beyond being — *nothing. What about this Nothing?* . . . *Does the Nothing exist only because the Not, i.e., the Negation, exists?* Or is it the other way around? *Does Negation and the Not exist only because the Nothing exists?* . . . We assert: *the Nothing is prior to the Not and the Negation.* . . . Where do we seek the Nothing? How do we find the Nothing? . . . We know the Nothing. . . . *Anxiety reveals the Nothing.* . . .That for which and because of which we were anxious, was "really" — nothing. Indeed: the Nothing itself — as such — was present. *What about this Nothing? — The Nothing itself nothings.*

This argument, asserting the primacy of existence (the "Nothing") over essence ("the Negation and the Not") and the necessity of embracing it through personal recognition of estrangement ("anxiety"), is shown by Carnap to consist of analytically meaningless "pseudo-statements," whose "non-sensicality is not obvious at first glance, because one is easily deceived by the analogy with . . . meaningful sentences." To assert that "the rain rains" is meaningful; but to argue that "the Nothing nothings" is something else again! "Even if it were admissible to introduce 'nothing' as a name or description of an entity, still the existence of this entity would be denied in its very definition, whereas [Heidegger] goes on to affirm its existence."[38] In point of fact, all the basic metaphysical affirmations of Existentialism, in purporting to unfold the very heart of existent reality, overreach themselves and arrive not at reality but at nonsense.

The fundamental cause of meaninglessness in Existentialism lies in its convictions that the subject-object distinction must be overcome and that "I-thou" personal encounter must be substituted for propositional truth. One can certainly appreciate the historical factors that gave rise to these affirmations: the breakdown of idealistic philosophy, the coldness of "dead-orthodox"

---

37. Cf. Jean-Paul Sartre, *Existentialism and Human Emotions* tr. Frechtman and Barnes (New York: Philosophical Library, 1957).
38. Rudolf Carnap, "The Elimination of Metaphysics through Logical Analysis of Language," in *Logical Positivism*, ed. Ayer, pp. 69-73. Carnap's paper originally appeared in German in Vol. II of *Erkenntnis* (1932).

theology (cf. Kierkegaard's *Attack upon "Christendom"*), the depersonalization of Western man in modern technological, scientific society, and the anxieties produced by decades of hot and cold wars. But appreciation of existentialist motives must not obscure the fundamental fact that meaningful thought absolutely requires the subject-object distinction, and that questions of truth cannot even be formulated apart from propositions. "Bohr has emphasized the fact that the observer and his instruments must be presupposed in any investigation, so that the instruments are not part of the phenomenon described but are used."[39] The absolute necessity of the subject-object distinction is the source of the riotous humor in Robert Benchley's story of his experience in a college biology course: he spent the term carefully drawing the image of his own eyelash as it fell across the microscopic field! If in any investigation — whether in science or in theology — the observer loses the distinction between himself and his subject matter, the result is complete chaos: not a "transcending of the subject-object barrier," but a necessary fall into pure subjectivity. The more perceptive existentialists have indeed seen this; Sartre, for example, asserts that what all existentialists, atheistic and Christian, "have in common is that they think that existence precedes essence, or, if you prefer, that subjectivity must be the starting point."[40] Such subjectivity, however, is utterly nontestable; and utterances concerning "estrangement," "existential anxiety," and "nothingness" stand outside of meaningful discourse.[41]

Like logic itself, both the subject-object distinction and propositional thinking must be presupposed in all sensible investigations. Why? Because to argue against their necessity is to employ them already! When one asserts: "Personal encounters, not propositions, yield truth," one is in fact stating a proposition (though a meaningless one), and is implying that there is sufficient distinction between "truth" and those who claim to possess it to warrant a clarifying statement on the subject! Existentialism's passionate attempt to dissolve subject-object boundaries and to escape from propositions about reality to reality itself is thus bound to fail and necessarily to arrive at nonsense. Of objective propositional truth, as of logic itself, one must say what Emerson said of Brahma: "When me they fly, I am the wings."[42]

39. Victor F. Lenzen, *Procedures of Empirical Science* ("International Encyclopedia of Unified Science," I/5; Chicago: University of Chicago Press, 1938), p. 28. That the Heisenberg Indeterminacy Principle does not in any sense break the subject-object distinction has been shown by Lenzen and by many others.

40. Sartre, *op. cit.*, p. 13.

41. To avoid misunderstanding, I must anticipate myself by pointing out here that my argument does *not* negate a "Christian existentialism" (Christian subjectivity) *founded upon testable, objective considerations* (specifically, upon an inerrant Scripture); indeed, I myself have made much use of genuine Christian-existential categories (e.g., in my Strasbourg thesis for the degree of Docteur de l'Université, mention Théologie Protestante, 1964). But it is this very idea of an objective basis for existential subjectivity that the contemporary philosophical and theological existentialists decry; and this is the reason for my above-stated counter to subjectivistic Existentialism. Apart from an objective foundation, all existentialism is analytically meaningless.

42. Cf. my *Chytraeus on Sacrifice* (St. Louis, Missouri: Concordia, 1962), p. 27.

The Analytical Meaninglessness of a
"Non-Inerrant Inspired Scripture"

Our study to this point has yielded the following conclusions: (1) Biblical inerrancy is under severe attack in our time not because of the discovery of empirical data militating against the view, but because of the climate of philosophical opinion presently conditioning Protestant theology. (2) The current theological Zeitgeist, as pertains to the issue of biblical authority, is governed by existentialistic and dualistic aprioris. (3) The fundamental axioms of both Dualism and Existentialism are analytically meaningless. From these conclusions, it is but a short step to the central claim of this paper: that the current attempt to maintain a divinely inspired but non-inerrant Bible is as analytically nonsensical as are the dualistic and existential assumptions upon which the attempt rests. We shall proceed to make this point through an examination of four major anti-inerrancy inspiration-claims; these four positions, it is believed, cover the gamut of non-verbal-inspiration views in contemporary Protestantism.

(I.) "Holy Scripture is inspired, not in conveying inerrant propositions about God and the world, but in acting as a vehicle for true Christian existential experience." This is, in substance, the position taken by Bultmann and by those who follow in his train. For Bultmann, "self-understanding of one's existence" arises from the kerygma of the primitive church; for the "post-Bultmannians," who, like Günther Bornkamm, Kaesemann, Fuchs, and Ebeling, are engaged in a "new quest of the historical Jesus," this "self-understanding" arises from a correlation between our personal existential situation and Jesus' own self-understanding of *His* existence.[43] But both Bultmann and his former disciples accept in general the same critical presuppositions and existential aprioris; for both, inerrancy is a hopeless, pre-existential identification of truth with propositions instead of with vital existential experience.

This approach to biblical inspiration is seen, on analysis, to be completely unverifiable and therefore nonsensical. For what is meant by "Christian existential experience"? and what gives one any reason to suppose that the Bible will serve instrumentally in promoting it? To determine what "Christian existential experience" is, one would have to define it in propositional terms (but "propositions" are ruled out in the original statement of the view!), and one would have to set up criteria for distinguishing truly salvatory experience from non-salvatory experience, and the Bible from other, non-existentially pregnant religious works (but all objective tests are ruled out by the existential refusal to employ the objective-subjective distinction!). Thus one is left in a morass of untestable subjectivity.

C. B. Martin, in discussing this problem of "a religious way of knowing"

---

43. Cf. the essays in Helmut Ristow & Karl Matthiae, eds., *Der Historische Jesus und der kerygmatische Christus* (Berlin: Evangelische Verlagsanstalt, 1961). For a thoroughgoing critique of such views, see Carl F. H. Henry (ed.), *Jesus of Nazareth: Saviour and Lord* (Grand Rapids, Michigan: Eerdmans, 1966), to which I contribute a chapter titled, "Toward a Christian Philosophy of History" (pp. 225-40).

asks how one can know whether someone has a direct experience of God — or how the believer himself can know if he has this direct experience. Martin correctly points out that the claim to immediate existential experience on a believer's part is not analogous to experience claims in general, and is *per se* analytically meaningless.

> In the case of knowing a blue sky in Naples, one can look at street signs and maps in order to be sure that this is the really blue sky in question. It is only when one comes to such a case as knowing God that the society of tests and check-up procedures that surround other instances of knowing, completely vanishes. What is put in the place of these tests and checking procedures is an immediacy of knowledge that is supposed to carry its own guarantee.[44]

In actuality, however, "tests and checking procedures" for truly Christian existential experience have not "vanished"; they have been obliterated by those who refuse to take the objective fact of an inerrant Bible seriously. It is only a Bible capable of standing the acid test of objective verifiability that will provide the "map" of God's blue sky of religious truth. And apart from such a map, the domain of immediate religious experience will forever remain a *terra incognita* of confusion and meaninglessness.

(II.) "Holy Scripture is inspired, not in its scientific or historical statements, but in the theological truths it conveys." Relatively few Lutherans on the American scene are prepared to move fully into the Bultmannian position on Scripture represented by anti-inerrancy argument (I). The more usual approach among American Lutheran theologians who would bring the Church out of "captivity" to verbal inspirationism is to argue for a distinction between the religious and the non-religious content of the Bible: the former is indeed inspired and fully reliable, while the latter is subject to the human fallibility which besets all of man's undertakings.[45]

The problem here is two-fold: first, how do we distinguish the religious from the historical-scientific (including the sociological and the moral) element in the Scriptures and, second, how do we show that the "theological" affirmations of the Bible are indeed inspired of God? The first of these questions we postpone temporarily — for consideration in the next section of this paper, where it will be shown that a dichotomy between "sacred" and "secular" is antithetical to the very heart of the Biblical faith. The second question alone, however, sufficiently reveals the meaninglessness of anti-inerrancy argument (II.). For here, obviously, one again encounters Dualism: a split between eternity (the theological element in the Bible: the *Heilsgeschichte*) and time (the scientific-historical content of Scripture: *Historie*).

An effort is being made to free the Bible from secular criticism; in effect, the proponents of this view argue, "It doesn't matter what historical

---

44. C. B. Martin, "A Religious Way of Knowing," in *New Essays in Philosophical Theology*, ed. Flew and Macintyre, p. 83. See also my *Shape of the Past*, pp. 257-311.
45. This is the general position espoused in *Dialog*; see above, our text at notes 4 and 5.

and scientific errors, or what internal contradictions, are discovered in the Bible; its theological truth stands firm!" But note well: every theological "truth," to the extent of its isolation from empirical reality, becomes unverifiable and therefore meaningless. As one approaches the realm of idealistic "Absolutes," refutability does indeed become less and less possible, but this chimerical advantage is achieved by the corresponding loss of meaningless relevance. The (theoretical) possibility of proving a claim *wrong* is the *sine qua non* for the claim's meaningfulness, since those assertions which are so separated from the world that they are devoid of testability are a waste of time to discuss, except in psychological or sociological terms. The theologian who pleads for a "theologically inspired," historically errant Bible pleads a meaningless case, for insofar as theological truths are removed from the world of testable experience, nothing at all can be said of their truth-value. Like the "eternal truths" of Tantrism, such "theological truths" of Christianity might as well remain unexpressed. In avoiding the necessary offense of defending the Bible's historical and scientific content, the dualistic theologians have succeeded in rendering the Bible utterly irrelevant.

It should, moreover, be a sobering thought to those who have accepted the above-described dualistic approach in principle to be reminded that, carried to its logical conclusion, such dualism will eventually necessitate the denial of infallibility *even to the "theological" content of Scripture.* Why? Because the "theological," just like the "historical-scientific," element of the Bible was conveyed to human agents (the biblical writers) and therefore (on the dualistic apriori) must also have been touched by human fallibility. Martin Scharlemann overlooks this point completely when he argues:

> The very limitations of the individual authors in terms of language, geographical, historical, and literary knowledge testify to the specifics of divine revelation. This is part of the "scandal" of the Bible. An insistence on its "inerrancy" is often an attempt to remove this obstacle. The use of the term almost invariably results in a docetic view of the Bible and so tends to overlook the fact that our Sacred Scriptures are both divine and human documents.[46]

Actually, if one is to avoid all "docetism," the inevitable conclusion is that even in its theological affirmations the Bible is touched by the fallibility of its human writers (or perhaps *especially* in its theological affirmations, since these evidently constitute the major part of the Bible??).

Paul Tillich does not blink at the consequences of such a consistent (though, as we have seen, meaningless!) dualism; for him, *everything* in the Bible must in theory at least stand under judgment. Nothing on earth can be identified fully with Being Itself which constitutes the only true "ultimate concern." This is Tillich's "Protestant principle": "The only infallible truth of faith, the one in which the ultimate itself is unconditionally manifest, is that any truth of faith stands under a yes-or-no judgment."[47] Thus the Bible loses even theologically normative force; and what then constitutes the basis of "yes-or-no judgment" in religion? Clearly, as Professor Gordon Clark has

---

46. M. Scharlemann, *op. cit.*, p. 14.
47. Tillich, *Dynamics of Faith*, p. 98.

argued in reference to Barth's theology, one must then accept as a norm or canon, "something or other external to the Bible"; and "since this external norm cannot be a wordless revelation, for a wordless revelation cannot give us the necessary information, it must be secular science, history, or anthropology."[48] The result is a reduction of special revelation to a vague and secularistic "natural revelation," which lands us again in the hopeless maze of unreconstructed Modernism. From the heights of the Unconditioned we are plummeted to the depths of a world lacking any inspired word from God. Such is the inevitable effect of analytically nonsensical revelational dualisms.

(III.) "Holy Scripture is inspired, not as a conveyor of infallible information, but insofar as it testifies to the person of Our Lord and Savior Jesus Christ." Tillich himself employs this approach when he identifies (but symbolically only, to be sure) the "yes-or-no judgment" on all things human with "the Cross of the Christ." But it is especially the contemporary Lutheran anti-inerrantists who present argument (III.), since they — in spite of Reu's impeccable historical case[49] — hold that Luther himself took this position. Writes M. Scharlemann: Biblical "knowledge is not a matter of acquiring information but of being confronted with God Himself as He is revealed in His Son."[50] Robert Schultz expresses his "hope that Lutheran theologians generally will move back through the accumulated traditions of verbal inspiration and reappropriate Luther's dynamic insight that the Scripture is that which teaches Christ."[51]

Argument (III.) incorporates the existential element from argument (I.) and the dualistic element from argument (II.) — thus acquiring a double dose of analytical meaninglessness. The argument must be regarded as dualistic if it is not to avoid condemnation for simple circularity: the "Jesus Christ" spoken of must be a *geschichtlicher* "Christ of faith," not a *historischer* "Jesus of history," for the latter would be describable propositionally and subject to inerrancy tests — which obviously would defeat the whole point of the argument. The idea here, as in argument (II.), is to raise biblical inspiration beyond the level of historical, scientific judgment by focusing it upon a Christ-figure who stands above the realm of verifiability. But, as emphasized in analyzing argument (II.), such supraempirical claims by definition pass into irrelevant nonsense; and, as we shall see in the next section of this paper, a "Christ" of this kind is theologically nonsensical as well, for the biblical Christ entered fully into the empirical sphere, subjecting Himself to the full "offense" of verifiability.

The existential side of argument (III.) is pointed up in its anti-"informational" character; scriptural inspiration allegedly leads to confrontation

48. Gordon H. Clark, *Karl Barth's Theological Method* (Philadelphia: Presbyterian and Reformed Publishing Co., 1963), p. 224.
49. M. Reu, *Luther and the Scriptures* (Columbus, Ohio: Wartburg Press, 1944), reprinted in *The Springfielder*, XXIV (August, 1960). Cf. my review of W. J. Kooiman's *Luther and the Bible*, in *Christianity Today*, VI (February 16, 1962), 498.
50. M. Scharlemann, *op. cit.*, p. 11.
51. Robert C. Schultz, "Scripture, Tradition and the Traditions: A Lutheran Perspective," *Dialog*, II (Autumn, 1963), 281.

with Christ, not to theological data. But, as we saw in our discussion of argument (I.), meaningful "confrontation" is possible only on the basis of verifiable data — for otherwise, there is no way of knowing whether one has engaged in a real confrontation at all! Particularly in the realm of religion it is desperately important to know the difference (to speak irreverently but precisely) between Christ-in-the-heart and heartburn. Apart from an objectively reliable, inerrant biblical description of Christ, the result is always, on the part of sinful man, the creation of subjective Christs to fit one's needs. This has, in fact, been the tragic history of twentieth-century theology: the creation of God in our philosophical or cultural image instead of the straightforward acceptance of His portrait of us and of His salvation for us as presented in Holy Writ.[52]

Schultz is, we fear, unaware of the ghastly implications of his position when he expresses the hope "that Lutherans will once again find themselves bound to all in Scripture and tradition that teaches Christ, compelled to change all that is contrary to Christ, free to use creatively everything that does not matter, as well as to create new tradition."[53] What, we ask, will serve as the criterion for determining what in Scripture is "contrary to Christ" and "does not matter", for setting the pattern of scriptural "change", for the "creative use" of the "unimportant" in the Bible? Obviously not the biblical Christ Himself, who was concerned about the inerrancy even of scriptural jots and tittles! The theological criterion has clearly become an existential Christ-in-the-heart, who, because of his non-propositional, analytically indefinable character, can take on, chameleonlike, the qualities of his spokesman. Perhaps we are not as far away as we think from the *Deutsche Christen* of the Third Reich, whose "Christ" conveniently supported all aspects of their demonic ideology. It is well not to forget that from analytical meaninglessness, as from logical contradiction, *anything* can be "deduced," depending on the predilections, conscious or unconscious, of the deducer.

(IV.) "Holy Scripture *is* inerrant, but in its intent — in its dynamic ability to fulfil God's purposes — not in its static accord with objective scientific or historical fact." Here we consider an argument which would not deserve attention were it not for its deceptive quality. Argument (IV.) in reality says nothing which has not already been expressed more directly in

---

52. When we do subject ourselves fully to the biblical testimony concerning Christ, we find, note well, that we must simultaneously accept the plenary inspiration and inerrancy of *all* of Scripture — for this was the belief of the biblical Christ Himself. This fact has been emphasized by numerous writers across the centuries; for a succinct marshalling of the evidence for it, see Pierre Marcel, "Our Lord's Use of Scripture," in *Revelation and the Bible*, ed. Carl F. H. Henry (Grand Rapids, Michigan: Baker Book House, 1958), pp. 119-34. Moreover, to employ kenotic arguments in an effort to lessen the binding force of Jesus' attitude toward Scripture is to board a vehicle whose logically inevitable destination is theological solipsism, since a Jesus who accommodates to the first-century thought world in one respect cannot be assumed to have stated any absolutes in other respects; thus all of Jesus' words lose binding force if His view of Scripture is not held to be normative.
53. Schultz, *loc. cit.*

37

the preceding three arguments. However, it conceals its analytic meaninglessness under the guise of the word "intent."

The question, of course, is not whether the Bible infallibly or inerrantly achieves the purposes for which God intended it; the orthodox Christian would be the last to deny this. The question is simply: How does one determine God's intent? Only two answers are possible: from an inerrant revelation, or from a source or sources external to special revelation. The former answer is hardly what the proponent of argument (IV.) wants; his purpose in stating the argument is to move away from propositional inerrancy to an "inerrancy" which will focus on "theological" considerations, or on "existential experience," or on "personal encounter with Christ" — i.e., on the existential-dualistic affirmations of arguments (I.), (II.), and (III.). Scripture is "inerrant" only when it achieves the purpose which *he* (the non-plenary inspirationist) accepts as appropriate to it.

Thus, again, we encounter the analytical nonsense of Dualism and Existentialism, and the subtle importation of non-revelational considerations by which revelation is judged. In point of fact, only God's Word is capable of indicating God's intent; and if this Word is not propositionally inerrant and perspicuous, man will never know the Divine intent in general — to say nothing of His intent as regards Holy Writ itself! But a study of the totality of Scripture confirms the historic claim of the Church that God intended by His special revelation to convey the truth of Christ within the solid framework of, and confirmed by, the entire truth of an infallibly inspired Bible.[54]

In our discussion of arguments (III.) and (IV.), we have referred in passing to Christ's view of the Bible and the Bible's own attitude toward itself. These references lead us quite naturally to a theological evaluation of non-inerrancy views of scriptural inspiration. We have found that analytically such views are nonsensical; it now remains for us to see that from the standpoint of biblical theology also they are without any genuine meaning.

The Theological Meaninglessness of a "Non-Inerrant Inspired Scripture"

Advocates of the anti-inerrancy positions discussed in the preceding sections of this paper are united in their contention that the Bible itself, and Christ its Lord, present a "dynamic," "personalized" view of truth which is irreconcilable with the propositional, objectively historical approach to truth characteristic of plenary inspirationists. Emil Brunner, for example, asserts: "In the time of the apostles as in that of the Old Testament prophets, divine revelation always meant the whole of the divine activity for the salvation of the world. Divine revelation is not a book or a doctrine."[55] Fre-

---

54. On the Bible's view of itself, see B. B. Warfield's classic essays published under the title, *The Inspiration and Authority of the Bible* (Philadelphia: Presbyterian and Reformed Publishing Company, 1948). This volume is a new edition of Warfield's *Revelation and Inspiration,* published by Oxford University Press and now out-of-print.
55. Emil Brunner, *Revelation and Reason,* tr. Olive Wyon (Philadelphia: Westminster Press, 1946), p. 8.

quently appealed to in support of this contention is Albrecht Oepke's article in Kittel's *Woerterbuch,* where one is told that in the Bible "revelation is not the communication of rational knowledge" but rather "Yahweh's offering of Himself in mutual fellowship."[56] Though James Barr's revolutionary book, *The Semantics of Biblical Language,* has decisively shown that Neo-Orthodox, "biblical-theology-movement" apriori, rather than linguistic objectivity, lies at the basis of such articles as Oepke's,[57] the general question remains as to whether the biblical view of revelation is anti-objective, anti-propositional. It is worthwhile noting that if the latter is the case, then the Bible, like many of its modern interpreters, will pass into the never-never land of analytical meaninglessness, for its content will be devoid of testability; like the Scriptures of the Eastern religions, its "truth" will be "known" only to those who read it through the glass of prior belief — and it will say nothing to all those who, not having had an (indefinable, unverifiable) experience in relation to it, are understandably wary of such "experiences"!

But in fact the Bible does not operate within an existential-dualistic frame of reference. Fundamental to the entire biblical revelation are the twin convictions that subjective truth is grounded in and verifiable through objective truth, and that the eternal has been made manifest in the temporal.

Consider such prominent Old Testament events as Gideon and the fleece (Judges 6) and Elijah on Mount Carmel (I Kings 18). Gideon, realizing how easy it is to deceive oneself in matters of subjective religious assurance, asks an objective sign from God by which he can know that the Lord will deliver Israel from her enemies. God willingly complies, not once but twice: first, dew falls on Gideon's fleece but not on the surrounding ground; second, dew falls on the ground but not on the fleece. The point? Gideon, like any spatio-temporally bound member of the human race, was incapable of knowing by subjective, existential immediacy that the voice within him was God's voice; yet he had to know, for the lives of others as well as his own safety depended upon his ability to make a true religious judgment. In this quandary, God provided Gideon with external evidence — in concrete, empirical terms — showing that it was indeed He who spoke within Gideon's heart.

Elijah was faced with a common religious problem — one which existential immediacy is totally unable to solve. This is the problem of conflicting religious claims. The "false prophets" said one thing to the people; Elijah said another. How were the people to know who was proclaiming God aright and who was the idolater? An objective test was the only way of ridding the situation of endless confusion and meaningless claims. So Elijah gave the false prophets the opportunity to demonstrate the "reality" of their god through his ability to perform an act of divine power on earth. The inability of the false prophets' truth-claim to hold up under such a test,

---

56. *TWNT,* III, 575 (art. ἀποκαλύπτω).
57. Barr takes Oepke as "a very bad example" of the absorption of philology by theological apriori in the *TWNT.* He shows that Oepke's ἀποκαλύπτω article "is assimilated to modern theological usage to a degree that the actual linguistic material will not bear" (*The Semantics of Biblical Language* ([London: Oxford University Press, 1961], p. 230).

when coupled with Yahweh's positive response to the identical test, provided the needed ground for belief in the true God.

Such examples could be multiplied in the Old Testament, but let us now turn to our Lord's own attitude toward religious verifiability. A close look at a frequently misunderstood event in His public ministry will be especially revealing. In all three Synoptic Gospels (Matt. 9; Mark 2; Luke 5) Jesus' healing of the palsied man is recorded in similar detail; here is the Marcan account:

> And again he entered into Capernaum after some days; and it was noised that he was in the house. And straightway many were gathered together, insomuch that there was no room to receive them, no, not so much as about the door; and he preached the word unto them. And they come unto him, bringing one sick of the palsy, which was borne of four. And when they could not come nigh unto him for the press, they uncovered the roof where he was; and when they had broken it up, they let down the bed wherein the sick of the palsy lay. When Jesus saw their faith, he said unto the sick of the palsy, Son, thy sins be forgiven thee. But there were certain of the scribes sitting there, and reasoning in their hearts, Why doth this man thus speak blasphemies? Who can forgive sins but God only? And immediately when Jesus perceived in his spirit that they so reasoned within themselves, he said unto them, Why reason ye these things in your hearts? Whether is it easier to say to the sick of the palsy, Thy sins be forgiven thee; or to say, Arise, and take up thy bed, and walk? But that ye may know that the Son of man hath power on earth to forgive sins; (he saith to the sick of the palsy,) I say unto thee, Arise, and take up thy bed, and go thy way into thine house. And immediately he arose, took up the bed, and went forth before them all; insomuch that they were all amazed, and glorified God, saying, We never saw it on this fashion.

It is generally assumed that the answer to Jesus' question, "Is it easier to say, Thy sins be forgiven, or Take up thy bed and walk?" is "Take up thy bed and walk." Quite the opposite is the case. Perhaps it is easier to restore a sick man to health than to forgive sin, but Jesus' question has to do, not with acts but with *claims;* Jesus asks, not "Which is easier?" but "Which is easier *to say?*" Clearly it is easier to *claim* to be able to forgive sin than to be able to restore a palsied man to health miraculously, for the former is a theological affirmation which cannot *per se* be subjected to verification.

So what does our Lord do? Does He leave His forgiveness claim in the realm of the unverifiable, as have numerous religious leaders through the ages? By no means; he connects the theological claim with an empirical claim whose verifiability is not only possible but inevitable. The argument thus runs: "You do not believe that I can forgive sins. Very well; I cannot show you that directly. But if I show you that I can, by my Divine power, remedy the empirical sickness that connects with the sin problem, will you have any reason left for denying my power to work in the theological sphere?" The empirical, objective healing of the palsied man was performed that men might "know that the Son of man hath power on earth to forgive sins" — a fact that, had our Lord not coupled it with an objective test, could

40

have been dismissed as meaningless and irrelevant by those who had doubtless heard such claims many times before. In precisely the same way does the New Testament present Christ's resurrection as the objective ground for belief in the theological significance of His death on the Cross.[58]

The picture of the biblical conception of truth drawn from the foregoing passages is in no way altered by Jesus' affirmations, "I am the Truth" (John 14:6), and "Everyone who is of the truth hears my voice" (John 18:37), or by any other "personalized" references to truth in the Bible. Of course such statements are part of the scriptural revelation; plenary inspirationists have never denied their existence or importance. The question is not whether truth is ever conceived of personally in the Bible, but whether it is *only* conceived of personally there. We contend that the biblical view of truth requires subjective (existential, if you will) truth to be grounded in objective, empirical facticity — for only then can existential truth be distinguished from existential error. Jesus' claim to be the Truth hardly warrants the conclusion that the facticity of His earthly acts, or the precise veracity of His words, is unimportant. Quite the contrary: It is the truth of His acts and words that drives us to commit our lives to Him as the only final answer to man's quest for Truth.

The biblical conception of truth not only stands over against analytically nonsensical existentialisms; it categorically opposes the equally meaningless notion of a dualistic split between the "theological" and the "historical/empirical" or between "personal encounter" and "objective facticity." Here, indeed, we find ourselves at the very heart and center of the Christian faith: the doctrine of Incarnation. According to biblical teaching, the Old Testament revelation typologically introduces, and the New Testament writings express the fulfillment of, the genuine Incarnation of God in human history. The Prologue of John's Gospel summarizes this superlative teaching in the simple words: ὁ λόγος σὰρξ ἐγέντο. As the Ecumenical Creeds of the Church consistently testify, this Incarnation was in every sense a real entrance of God into the human scene; the gap between eternity and time was fully bridged in Christ.

The soteriological necessity of this act has often been stressed through Christian history,[59] but at the same time the epistemological need for the Incarnation ought never to be forgotten. Apart from empirical confrontation with God in Christ, man's religious aspirations and conceptions would have forever remained in the realm of unverifiable meaninglessness. This is why throughout the New Testament the Apostles place such powerful stress on having "seen with their eyes" and "touched with their hands" the incarnate Word.[60] The biblical message recognizes finite man's need to "try the spirits" representing diverse religious claims and ideologies; and the only meaningful test is objective verifiability: "Every spirit that confesseth that Jesus Christ is come in the flesh is of God" (I John 4:1-3).

In biblical religion it is impossible to conceive of theological truth divorced

---

58. See I Cor. 15, and cf. my University of British Columbia lectures (*op. cit.*).
59. One thinks immediately of Anselm's *Cur Deus Homo?* and Aulen's *Christus Victor*. Cf. my *Chytraeus on Sacrifice* (*op. cit.*).
60. See, e.g., I John 1:1-4, where existential "joy" (v. 4) is grounded in objective empirical contact with the incarnate Christ (vs. 1-3). Cf. also John 20:24 ff.

from historical, empirical truth; this divorce would destroy the whole meaning of Incarnation. The theological truths of Scripture are thus inextricably united with earthly matters, and the truth of the one demands the truth of the other. The Bible recognizes as fully as does analytical philosophy that to speak of "theological truth" or of "existential encounter with God" apart from empirical veracity is to speak nonsense. When Bishop Wand asserts that "there is no external guarantee of inspiration,"[61] he is asserting just such nonsense, for without the "external guarantee" of empirical facticity, "inspiration" becomes no more than an emotive plea — on the same level with the innumerable and conflicting immediacy claims to inspiration by religious fanatics.

Even Beegle, in his recent attempt to demolish biblical inerrancy, admits that "subjective truth cannot occur without some minimal amount of objective truth";[62] but here he gives his whole case away. For what amount of objective truth is "minimal?" The Bible declares, as does analytic philosophy, that only where objective truth is unqualifiedly present can one avoid meaninglessness on the subjective side. Thus the "minimum" is unrestricted objective truth, which, in the case of the Christian revelation, means nothing less than an inerrant Bible. For wherever the Scripture were to err objectively, there doubt would be warranted subjectively; and wherever the words of Scripture were to carry historically or scientifically erroneous ideas, there the reader would have every right to reject the theological affirmations, which, in the very nature of God's revelation, are inextricably entwined with empirical facts.[63]

And here, like it or not, we arrive at verbal inspiration, for, as contemporary linguistic analysis has so fully demonstrated, every genuine word carries genuine meaning and influences the context in which it is used. Therefore, each "jot and tittle" of Scripture has an impact, however slight, on the totality of the Bible; and this impact must be either for good or for ill. On the basis of the thoroughgoing incarnational theology of the Bible, we can affirm that the verbal impact is always veracious, not only theologically but also in all other aspects touched. For, in the final analysis, the biblical theology that centers on Christ the incarnate Word knows no distinction between "other aspects of life" and the religious: biblical truth is holistic, and its claim to theological validity is preserved from meaninglessness by its verifiability in the empirical domains that it touches.[64]

---

61. J. W. C. Wand, *The Authority of the Scriptures* (London: Mowbray, 1949), p. 61.
62. Beegle, *op. cit.*, p. 191.
63. The fallacy of "minimum" objective facticity has been implicitly recognized in Kaesemann's damning criticism of Bultmann's claim that Christian existential experience requires only the "thatness" of Jesus as a historical person — the mere fact that he existed. Says Kaesemann (representing the "post-Bultmannian" reaction in contemporary European theology): Such minimal "thatness" will reduce the Christian gospel to a Gnostic redeemer myth and docetism.
64. I am not arguing (note well) that empirical verifiability of the historical and scientific content of Scripture automatically produces subjective *commitment* to the truth of its religious claims. The Pharisees could (and doubtless many of them did) refuse to believe that Jesus was able to forgive sin even after he had healed the palsied man. However, only where objective verifiability is

A Final Clarification and Caveat

It has been not infrequently argued by those who would move Lutheranism away from the inerrancy view of biblical inspiration that the Lutheran Church is fortunate in lacking explicit statements on verbal inspiration in its historic creeds. We are informed that it is to our advantage that, unlike the Calvinists, our creeds contain no assertions concerning "the entire perfection" and "infallible truth" of Scripture.[65] Therefore, the argument continues, we are free to embrace fully, without loss of intellectual integrity, the non-propositional, non-verbal view of inspiration which has become so popular in recent years.

The analytical discussions comprising the bulk of this paper should have prepared us to see the fallacy in this superficially attractive line of reasoning. Let us see what the last of the Reformation Lutheran Confessions, the *Formula of Concord*, does say on the subject of biblical inspiration. The *Formula's* position in this matter is drawn from Luther:

> [Luther] diesen Unterschied ausdrücklich gesetzt hat, dass alleine Gottes Wort die einige Richtschnur und Regel aller Lehre sein und bleiben solle, welchem keines Menschen Schriften gleich geachtet, sondern demselben alles unterworfen werden soll.

> Hoc discrimen (inter divina et humana scripta) perspicue posuit, solas videlicet sacras litteras pro unica regula et norma omnium dogmatum agnoscendas, iisque nullius omnino hominis scripta adaequanda, sed potius omnia subiicienda esse.

> Luther explicitly made this distinction between divine and human writings: God's Word alone is and should remain the only standard and norm of all teachings, and no human being's writings dare be put on a par with it, but everything must be subjected to it.[66]

Here, it is true, there is no reference to infallibility or inerrancy. Yet the Scriptures are declared to be the "only standard and rule," to which all other writings must be "subordinated." Clearly, the Bible is held to stand in judgment over all other books — in all fields — and no man is permitted to judge the Scripture in any particular. Such a view of biblical authority differs in no way from the verbal inspiration position set out in this paper.

And, indeed how could it, if Luther and the theologians of the Confessions understood the implications of scriptural inspiration? We have seen that the incarnational theology of the Bible demands the plenary truth of Scripture — that the "historical-empirical" elements in the Bible must be regarded as no less veracious than the "theological" truths intimately bound up with them and epistemologically dependent upon them. Though the Lutheran fathers were

---

present can genuine faith be distinguished from blind faith. To engage in the existentialists' "leap of faith" is to topple headlong into the domain of analytic meaninglessness, where one man believes in "Christ" and another in a pantheon of six-headed monsters! Only biblical inerrancy preserves biblical faith from condemnation as nonsensically irrelevant.

65. These phrases appear in the *Westminster Confession of Faith*, chap. i, sec. 5.
66. *F. C.* (Sol. Dec.), Summary Formulation, 9.

not acquainted with the technical concept of analytic meaninglessness, they understood the Bible too well to believe that it would retain its theological value if its truthfulness in other particulars were impugned. The writers of the Lutheran Confessions did not face the epistemological issue of biblical reliability that we face today, but they knew full well that to allow the Scriptures to fall under *any* kind of negative criticism would tear the foundation out of all meaningful theology. That "the Word was made flesh" gripped them too powerfully to permit their losing the objective veracity of God's revelation.

Today the winds of philosophical change are veering away from existentialistic and dualistic world-views. The analytical tradition has delivered mortal body-blows to these metaphysical *Weltanschauungen*. And within the realm of analytical philosophy itself, every year that goes by sees greater stress placed upon "words," "language," and "propositions."[67] How unfortunate it would be if now, when the presuppositions of the anti-verbal inspirationists have been thoroughly undermined along with the aprioris of Existentialism and Dualism, and a new era of appreciation for the verbal proposition is on the horizon, Christians in the Reformation tradition should sell their biblical heritage for a mess of outdated philosophical pottage. In the Bible and in the Christ to whom it testifies God has given a $\pi\lambda\acute{\eta}\rho\omega\mu\alpha$ of meaningfulness. May we not lose it in chasing the phantoms of analytical nonsensicality.

---

67. The analytical stage is now being occupied particularly by the "linguistic analysts," such as the "ordinary language philosophers" Ryle and Toulmin. Here also is to be classed the work of the later Wittgenstein (the posthumous *Philosophical Investigations*).

II.

LUTHERAN HERMENEUTICS AND HERMENEUTICS TODAY

"Le problème de l'hermèneutique est, depuis plusieurs années à côté de celui du 'Jésus historique,' le problème le plus souvént traitê au sein de la théologie protestante." So wrote Jesuit theologian René Marlé as he observed the Protestant scene in 1963.[1] The last two years have marked an even greater intensification of interest in the hermeneutic question, as is well evidenced by the appearance this year of an American counterpart to Gerhard Ebeling's *Zeitschrift für Theologie und Kirche*, the first volume of which is titled *The Bultmann School of Biblical Interpretation: New Directions?*[2] The latest issue of *Dialog* is appropriately devoted to "Biblical Interpretation," and there we find Samuel Laeuchli of the Garrett Theological Seminary noting the crucial nature of the present hermeneutic quest: "After even a superficial study of the questions involved, one comes rather soon to one's senses, realizing that in this pertinent debate a great deal is at stake — the meaning of scriptural language, the possibility of a theological discipline, and above all, the task of preaching and teaching in the church and to the world."[3]

Laeuchli is not exaggerating: the very possibility of the theological enterprise and the continuance of evangelical proclamation depend squarely upon the church's response to current hermeneutic issues. Because hermeneutics is no longer seen as an isolated and rather prosaic subbranch of exegetical theology but as the focal point of all the theological disciplines — as the key to the overall relation of Word and faith,[4] the church that takes a misstep here may well find itself fatally committed to heresy or to irrelevance. Thus it behooves us in all seriousness to examine the approaches to the hermeneutic task being advocated today and to compare them with Scripture and with the hermeneutical heritage of the Reformation.

---

1. René Marlé, *Le Problème théologique de l'herméneutique: Les grands axes de la recherche contemporaine* (Paris: Editions de l'Orante, 1963), p. 7.
2. James M. Robinson, et al., *The Bultmann School of Biblical Interpretation: New Directions?* Vol. I of *Journal for Theology and the Church* (New York: Harper Torchbooks, 1965).
3. Samuel Laeuchli, "Issues in the Quest of a Hermeneutic," *Dialog*, IV (Autumn 1965), 250.
4. Cf. especially Gerhard Ebeling's programmatic essay, "The Significance of the Critical Historical Method for Church and Theology in Protestantism," which appeared in *Zeitschrift für Theologie und Kirche*, XLVII (1950), 11ff., when the journal was reestablished under Ebeling's editorship; the same essay may be consulted in Ebeling's *Wort und Glaube* (Tübingen: J. C. B. Mohr, 1960), pp. 12ff., and in its English translation, *Word and Faith* (Philadelphia: Fortress Press, 1963), pp. 27 ff.

The present essay endeavors to provide such a comparison, with special reference to the Lutheran hermeneutic. It is this essayist's conviction that far too little of present hermeneutic discussion takes into account the church's past wrestlings with interpretive problems. How readily we forget Bernard of Chartres' sage words: "Nous sommes comme des nains assis sur les épaules de géants. Nous voyons donc plus de choses que les Anciens, et de plus lointaines, mais ce n'est ni par l'acuité de notre vue, ni par la hauteur de notre taille, c'est seulement qu'ils nous portent et nous haussent de leur hauteur gigantesque."[5] The insights of the Reformation, above all, must not be neglected in our contemporary hermeneutic quest, for that epoch wrestled most tenaciously and heroically with the core problems of biblical interpretation and application.

Our first task will be to obtain a clear picture of the mid-20th-century hermeneutic stance in Protestantism. Next we shall observe the manner in which the contemporary hermeneutic movement understands Luther's approach to Scripture; and this in turn will lead to a re-examination of the Lutheran hermeneutic. Finally we shall take a hard doctrinal and epistemological look at the current hermeneutic orientation and pose the unavoidable question of confessional limits as regards the employment of interpretive methodology.

The Leitmotiv of Contemporary Hermeneutics

Is it possible to arrive at any single characterization of Protestant hermeneutics today? The bewildering variety of theological approaches both in Europe and in America would seem to militate against any unified hermeneutic theme. Bultmann's successor at Marburg, Werner Georg Kümmel, sees no less than five distinct orientations in European New Testament scholarship, not counting "orthodox" Barthians and Bultmannians:[6] (1) conservatives (e.g., Karl Heinrich Rengstorf of Münster), (2) Heilsgeschichte scholars (e.g., Kümmel himself), (3) the post-Bultmannian group (including Ernst Fuchs, Gerhard Ebeling, Hans Conzelmann, Ernst Käsemann, and Günther Bornkamm, as well as the more individualistic Heinrich Ott), (4) the Pannenberg school, led by the young Mainz theologian Wolfhardt Pannenberg, and (5) independents, whose views defy group categorization (e.g., Ethelbert Stauffer, Helmut Thielicke, and Oscar Cullmann). And if these several groupings were not sufficiently intimidating, we can remind ourselves that they leave out contemporary American theological thought entirely! Yet I do believe that a single hermeneutic orientation can be traced in current theology. To find it we must set forth the hermeneutic thrust of individual European and American theologians and then observe the common thread binding them together. Our survey, though necessarily cursory, will endeavor to render faithfully the hermeneutic perspective of the views discussed; references to primary and secondary literature will offer avenues for further study to those wishing it.

---

5. Quoted in Etienne Gilson, L'Esprit de la philosophie médiévale, 2d ed. (Paris: Librairie Philosophique J. Vrin, 1944), p. 402.
6. Kümmel presented this typology in discussion with Carl F. H. Henry; see the latter's "European Theology Today," Faith and Thought: Journal of the Victoria Institute, XCIV (Spring 1965), 9-91, especially p. 12.

Rudolph Bultmann

We begin with Rudolf Bultmann, whose preoccupation with hermeneutics has probably been the single most important factor in bringing about the overwhelming current interest in the subject. Bultmann sets forth his hermeneutical position most clearly in his essay, "Is Exegesis Without Presuppositions Possible?"[7] His answer: Though exegesis must not presuppose its results, it can never dispense with the method of historical-critical research (including the nonmiraculous view of the universe that sees "the whole historical process as a closed unity") or with an existential "life relation" between Scriptural text and the interpreter himself; thus all Biblical interpretation involves a necessary circularity (the so-called "hermeneutical circle" embracing text and exegete), and no exegesis can properly be regarded as "objective."[8]

> The validity of Bultmann's hermeneutics depends on whether or not he is right when he says that to speak of God is simultaneously to speak of oneself. That is, hermeneutics — when its object is to understand the meaning of Christian faith in the Bible — deals with history, and one cannot interpret history validly from some distant, disengaged vantage point. . . . We can now see in what terms Bultmann is willing to speak of the Bible as authoritative: the Bible is authoritative only in so far as it communicates the claim (*Anspruch*) of God on me and thus leads me to radical obedience in faith. It is authoritative in so far as it calls into question my previous self-understanding and leads me to a new self-understanding — from seeing myself as one who must and perhaps can make his own way to seeing myself as a sinner before God who by God's now occurring act of grace has been given new life with an openness to the future.[9]

Karl Barth

Barth roundly condemns Bultmann's claim that before interpreting Scripture one has to "put on the armor" of Heidegger's existential philosophy. Implicitly in his *Church Dogmatics* and explicitly in his *Rudolph Bultmann: Ein Versuch ihn zu verstehen*,[10] Barth sets himself against such a hermeneutic

7. Rudolf Bultmann, "Ist voraussetzungslose Exegese möglich?" *Theologische Zeitschrift*, XIII (1957), 409-17; English translation in *Existence and Faith: Shorter Writings of Rudolf Bultmann*, ed. Schubert M. Ogden (New York: Meridian Living Age Books, 1960), pp. 289-96.
8. Cf. on Bultmann's circularity principle Armin Henry Limper, "Hermeneutics and Eschatology: Rudolf Bultmann's Interpretation of John, Chapters 13-17" (unpublished Ph.D. dissertation, The Divinity School, University of Chicago, 1960), and John Warwick Montgomery, "The Fourth Gospel Yesterday and Today," *Concordia Theological Monthly*, XXXIV (April 1963), 203-205.
9. Jackson Forstman, "Bultmann's Conception and Use of Scripture," *Interpretation*, XVII (1963), 459-61. The same point is made in greater detail and with even more force in chap. i ("Qu'est-ce que l'"objectivité'?") of André Malet, *Mythos et logos: La pensée de Rudolf Bultmann*, Lettre-préface de R. Bultmann (Genéve: Labor et Fides, 1962), pp. 5-19. Cf. also Friedebert Hohmeier, *Das Schriftverständnis in der Theologie Rudolf Bultmanns*, in Arbeiten zur Geschichte und Theologie des Luthertums, XIII (Berlin und Hamburg: Lutherisches Verlagshaus, 1964).
10. Karl Barth, *Rudolf Bultmann: Ein Versuch ihn zu verstehen* (Zollikon-Zürich: Evangelischer Verlag, 1952).

— which for him is nothing less than a return to the Old Liberalism. Barth rejects the Bultmannian notion of a normative *Vorverständnis* brought to Scripture from the outside; the interpreter, says Barth, must allow the Bible to act as a "catalyst" on his powers of comprehension, thereby modifying and refining the preconceptions he brings to the reading of Scripture.[11]

Yet, as the Italian scholar Riverso has cogently shown, Barth never succeeded in completely ridding his own theology of existential-dialectic elements.[12] Thus he is as willing as Bultmann to admit that neutral investigation of *Historie* will never yield a resurrected Christ (for Barth the "objectivity" of the *heilsgeschichtliche* Resurrection is discovered only in the faith relation).[13] Barth's position, we are told, "disposes of many difficulties arising from the intellectualist bedevilment of the concept of faith, and sets it clearly in the context of existential encounter and response. . . . Although the New Testament message is often formulated 'Jesus is the Christ,' the Object of faith is not doctrinal propositions about Jesus, but the divine presence or objectivity encountered in Him."[14] Since truth is conceived as personal encounter with the Christ of Scripture and not as the propositional affirmations of the Bible, the biblical writers "can be at fault in every word, and have been at fault in every word, and yet according to the same scriptural witness, being justified and sanctified by grace alone, they have still spoken the Word of God in their fallible and erring human word."[15] Not urlike Bultmann, Barth asserts: "The Bible is God's Word so far as God lets it be His Word, so far as God speaks through it."[16] Well recognizing the ecumenical implications of this view for dialog with Roman Catholicism, Robert McAfee Brown declares that Barth "delivers us from what can be a very perverse notion of *sola Scriptura* that would assert that we go to the Bible and to the Bible alone, as though in the process we could really bypass tradition. He delivers us from a kind of Biblicism that is content to rest simply with a parroting of the vindication,

11. See the excellent comparative treatment of Bultmann and Barth on the problem of hermeneutical *Vorverständnis* by Jesuit L. Malevez, "Exegèse biblique et philosophie," *Nouvelle Revue Théologique*, LXXVIII (Nov.-Dec., 1956), 897-914, 1027-42; English translation as Appendix II to Malevez, *The Christian Message and Myth: The Theology of Rudolf Bultmann* (Westminster, Md.: Newman Press, 1958), pp. 168-212.
12. Emmanuele Riverso, *La teologia esistenzialistica di Karl Barth: Analisi, interpretazione e discussione del sistema* (*Napoli, 1955*). Bouillard agrees, though for various reasons he is not happy with the flat characterization of Barth as an "existentialist": "Certes, cette théologie [de Barth] offre des aspects existentialists (au sens trés large de ce mot): son auteur lui-même en convient [D. III, 4 viii; *Bultmann*, p. 38]" — Henri Bouillard, *Karl Barth*, III (Paris: Aubier, 1957), 298-99.
13. See John Warwick Montgomery, "Karl Barth and Contemporary Theology of History," *The Cresset*, XXVII (Nov. 1963), 8-14.
14. James Brown, *Kierkegaard, Heidegger, Buber and Barth: Subject and Object in Modern Theology* (New York: Collier Books, 1962), pp. 145-46.
15. Karl Barth, *Church Dogmatics* (Edinburgh: T. & T. Clark, 1936-), I, Part 2, 529 to 30.
16. *Ibid.*, I, Part 1, 123. For an excellent discussion of this and related passages in Barth's *Church. Dogmatics* see Robert D. Preus, "The Word of God in the Theology of Karl Barth," *Concordia Theological Monthly*, XXXI (Feb. 1960), 105-15.

'the Bible says.' "[17] And the eminent Jesuit theologian Gustave Weigel perceptively notes that for Barth

> Scripture is the word of God, not in the sense that its propositions are spoken by God, but in the sense that the vision of the men who wrote the words points efficaciously to the transcendent Lord God. Barth does not give an exegesis of the Scriptures, but gives the existentialist meaning of the Biblical narratives.[18]

In Barth's approach to biblical interpretation, then, the "hermeneutical circle" of text and interpreter remains unbroken in spite of his opposition to Bultmann, and it is only through the existential dynamic of the hermeneutic situation that a fallible book becomes God's Word and revelatory. Only when we see this fully can we appreciate Oscar Cullmann's recent about-face: his refusal any longer to support the Barthian hermeneutic that would give philological and historical exegesis merely a preliminary role to theological interpretation proper. Cullmann observes that Barth is especially exposed to the danger of uncontrolled theological speculation "à cause de la richesse de sa pensée," and in order to avoid this danger of allowing the existential situation or theological tradition to engulf the clear teaching of Scripture, Cullmann now opts for objective philological treatment of the text throughout all exegetical operations.[19]

Post-Bultmannians

The most influential movement in European theology today is variously called "post-Bultmannianism" and "the New Hermeneutic." Bultmann's satisfaction with the mere "thatness" of the historical Jesus — his unwillingness to

---

17. Robert McAfee Brown, "Scripture and Tradition in the Theology of Karl Barth," in Leonard J. Swidler, ed., *Scripture and Ecumenism: (Protestant, Catholic, Orthodox and Jewish* (Pittsburgh: Duquesne University Press, 1965), p. 42.
18. Gustave Weigel, *A Survey of Protestant Theology in Our Day* (Westminster, Md.: Newman Press, 1954), p. 33. Weigel's remarks on p. 30 are also to the point here: "Barth especially is interested in a return to the reformers, not to the content of their teaching, but merely to their starting point. Against the liberals, Barth and Brunner go back to the Bible as the Word of God, and they free the theological enterprise from the chains of philological method in order to achieve the true meaning of the Scriptures, which philology cannot detect. Against the Orthodox, the Neo-Orthodox reject any Biblicism whereby verbal inspiration or literal inerrancy condemn the theologian to make affirmations that have nothing to do with God. Seemingly, therefore, the Neo-Orthodox are a Center theology, but a closer examination of their thought has led many critics to believe that they are basically liberals in a strange guise. In America Neo-Orthodoxy in the Barthian manner is not popular, though his work is sufficiently known. The paradoxical character of such thought is bewildering because the constant linking of 'Yes' and 'No,' with no possibility of bringing them into some kind of unified synthesis, leaves the student dizzy."
19. Oscar Cullmann, "La nécessité et la fonction de l'exégèse philologique et historique de la Bible," in Jean Boisset, et al., *Le Problème biblique dans le Protestantisme* (Paris: Presses Universitaires de France, 1955), pp. 131-47. Cullmann here disavows the Barthian position on "theological exegesis" that he advocated in "Les problèmes poses par la méthode exégétique de l'école de Karl Barth," *Revue d'Histoire et de Philosophie Religieuses*, VIII (Jan. -Feb. 1928), 70-83.

pursue the historical question beyond the perspective of the early church's interpretation of Jesus — has impelled a number of his students to engage in a hermeneutic quest for a more meaningful conjunction of the Jesus of history with the Christ of the early church. Wide differences exist among the post-Bultmannians (e.g., between Fuchs and Ott), but they are united in their endeavor to connect faith and history hermeneutically. Though they have departed from their master in many respects, they all maintain the centrality of Bultmann's "hermeneutical circle" and his conviction that an objective identification of the biblical text with God's Word is a manifestation of unfaith. Thus Ernst Käsemann writes:

> In New Testament language we are driven to test the spirits even within Scripture itself. We cannot simply accept a dogma or a system of doctrine but are placed in a situation vis-à-vis Scripture which is, at the same time and inseparably, both responsibility and freedom. Only to such an attitude can the Word of God reveal itself in Scripture; and that Word, as biblical criticism makes plain, has no existence in the realm of the objective — that is, outside our act of decision.[20]

Gerhard Ebeling is doubtless the most influential spirit of the New Hermeneutic. For him systematic theology has as its subject matter "the word event itself, in which the reality of man comes true," and by "word event" is meant "the event of interpretation";[21] theology, then, has its source in the hermeneutic circle embracing biblical text and existentially grounded interpreter.[22] In reviewing Ebeling's *Das Wesen des christlichen Glaubens*,[23] James M. Robinson uses the term "neo-liberalism" to describe his position and notes that "although Ebeling devotes chapters to most of the traditional doctrines, he would not refer to these as the objects of faith. Faith is not to be bifurcated into the believer and his beliefs on the analogy of the scientist and his objects of study, that is, the subject-object pattern of scientific epistemology is not applicable for faith."[24] Marlé offers in much the same terms a fuller analysis of Ebeling's conscious break with the hermeneutic of orthodox Protestantism:

> For him, the fundamental error of Protestant orthodoxy (and doubtless, in his view, the error of all orthodoxy) has been to consider the Word of God independently of its actualization in preaching — to make it in some way an object instead of seeing a movement there. That is why, moreover, orthodoxy could not recognize the peculiarly theological importance

20. Ernst Käsemann, *Exegetische Versuche und Besinnungen*, I (2d ed.; Göttingen: Vandenhoeck und Ruprecht, 1960), 232-33; English translation in Käsemann's *Essays on New Testament Themes*, in Studies in Biblical Theology, No. 41 (London: SCM Press, 1964), p. 58.
21. Gerhard Ebeling, *Theologie und Verkündigung; Ein Gespräch mit Rudolf Bultmann*, in Hermeneutische Untersuchungen zur Theologie, I (Tübingen: J. C. B. Mohr, 1962), 14 to 15. Cf. James M. Robinson and John B. Cobb, Jr., eds., *The New Hermeneutic*, in New Frontiers in Theology, II (New York: Harper & Row, 1964), *passim*.
22. Ebeling discusses the hermeneutical circle in his *Wort and Glaube*, p. 337.
23. Gerhard Ebeling, *Des Wesen des christlichen Glaubens* (Tübingen: J. C. B. Mohr, 1959); trans. R. G. Smith, *The Nature of Faith*, (London: Collins, 1961).
24. James M. Robinson, "Neo-Liberalism," *Interpretation*, XV (Oct. 1961), 488.

of hermeneutics. For hermeneutics is precisely that which permits the Word of God to be truly Word, in other words to attain its meaning, by conjoining with the one to whom it is addressed. . . . The [Protestant] perspective was transformed from the day when hermeneutics was no longer regarded as the simple application of rules external to the reality concerned, but as the way of disclosing that reality from the inside. According to Ebeling, the role of Heidegger and of Bultmann has been determinative in this regard. For both — and Ebeling resolutely follows in their wake — hermeneutics expresses a relationship to reality, allowing that reality to express itself, indeed, to realize its meaning.[25]

In Ernst Fuchs the "dynamic" (vs. orthodox propositional) concept of the Word seems to attain its zenith. By a hermeneutical principle Fuchs means the situation in which one places something to see what it really is, thereby allowing it to display its meaning; so, for example, to find out what a cat is, put it in front of a mouse.[26] Scripture, then, cannot be interpreted objectively; it must be placed into dynamic, existential relation with its theological interpreter. Instead of being objectified, the Word actively objectifies everything else while forever remaining subject. "Freedom for the Word" is manifested not in reliance on objective history or on a propositionally inerrant text but in a staking of everything on the Word of love.[27] Fuchs's hypostatizing of language is but a logical outcome of the post-Bultmannian rejection of the subject-object distinction, but it gives to his writings such an air of mystical unreality that he is much less frequently quoted than his confrère Ebeling. Marlé devotes but three sentences to him (in the last footnote of his book); for those surprised at his neglect of Fuchs — especially for those students of Fuchs who would see in him the most profound theologian of the New Hermeneutic — Marlé must confess that he has found in Fuchs "much obscurity, a multitude of viewpoints more rapidly touched on than given depth treatment, and a most abstract terminology, the original force of which has escaped us."[28]

Heinrich Ott, Karl Barth's successor at Basel, rejects "the so-called 'subject-object schema' and the view that all thinking and language to a very great extent necessarily have an objectifying character";[29] he goes so far as to assert that "the objective mode of knowledge is entirely inappropriate to historical reality because there are no such things as objectively verifiable facts, and,

---

25. Marlé, pp. 88-89.
26. Ernst Fuchs, *Hermeneutik* (Bad Cannstatt: R. Müllerschön, 1954), pp. 103-18.
27. See Fuchs, "Was wird in der Exegese interpretiert?" in his *Zür Frage nach dem historischen Jesus, in Gesammelte Aufsätze,* No. 2 (Tübingen: J. C. B. Mohr, 1960), pp. 286 ff.; trans. Andrew Scobie, *Studies of the Historical Jesus,* in Studies in Biblical Theology, No. 42 (London: SCM Press, 1964), pp. 84 ff. A semipopular work directly reflecting Fuchs's hermeneutic approach is Heinz Zahrnt, *Es begann mit Jesus von Nazareth* (Stuttgart: Kreuz-Verlag, 1960); trans. J. S. Bowden, *The Historical Jesus* (New York: Harper & Row, 1963).
28. Marlé, p. 139.
29. Heinrich Ott, "Was ist systematische Theologie?" *Zeitschrift für Theologie und Kirche,* LVIII, Beiheft 2 (Sept. 1961), p. 32; English translation in James M. Robinson and John B. Cobb, Jr., eds., *The Later Heidegger and Theology,* in New Frontiers in Theology I (New York: Harper & Row, 1963), 93.

secondly, that all true knowledge of history is finally knowledge by encounter and confrontation."[30] Ott's attempt to repristinate Heidegger theologically will be evident from these existential (and virtually solipsistic) assertions that intentionally eliminate the possibility of an objective Biblical hermeneutic.[31]

The practical exegetical consequences of the post-Bultmannian hermeneutic can be seen in the work of Hans Conzelmann and Günther Bornkamm. Conzelmann regards the New Testament writers as free reshapers of the Jesus tradition; thus Luke's own existential stance produces a "subordinationist" portrait of Jesus, and Luke "deliberately takes the 'today' [Luke 4:21] which is expressed in this passage [Mark 2:19] as belonging to the past, and builds up the picture of Jesus' whole career on the basis of this historical interpretation."[32] Discrepancies and historical-geographical blunders are rife in Luke's Gospel, for Conzelmann does not hold to any kind of propositional inspiration. A single example will suffice:

> The locality of the Baptist becomes remarkably vague. Luke can associate him neither with Judea nor with Galilee, for these are both areas of Jesus' activity. Yet on the other hand there has to be come connection, so the Baptist is placed on the border. It is obvious that Luke has no exact knowledge of the area, and this is why he can make such a straightforward symbolical use of localities.
>
> He creates a further discrepancy by introducing a motif of his own: in place of the Pharisees and Sadducees he puts the ὄχλοι [Luke 3:7].[33]

Günther Bornkamm's *Jesus of Nazareth*[34] leaves one in little doubt as to the effect of the New Hermeneutic on biblical theology. In a penetrating review of this book, Otto Piper of Princeton writes:

> The English translation has been hailed by some American scholars as "the best presentation of Jesus that we have" and as an "event in the

---

30. Heinrich Ott, *Die Frage nach dem historischen Jesus und die Ontologie der Geschichte* (Zürich: EVZ-Verlag, 1960); English translation in Carl E. Braaten and Roy A. Harrisville, eds., *The Historical Jesus and the Kerygmatic Christ* (New York: Abingdon, 1964), p. 148. Readers of the present essay may be interested to learn that an orthodox Reformation counterweight to the Braaten-Harrisville symposium has recently been published under the title, *Jesus of Nazareth: Saviour and Lord* (Grand Rapids: Mich.: Eerdmans, 1966). Carl F. H. Henry is the editor, and this essayist provides a chapter titled, "Toward a Christian Philosophy of History" (pp. 225-40).

31. For a valuable insight into Ott's most recent thinking, see Robert W. Funk's report of the Second Drew University Consultation on Hermeneutics (April 9-11, 1964), in which Ott participated; the report was published under the title "Colloquium on Hermeneutics," *Theology Today*, XXI (Oct. 1964), 287-306. Funk succinctly summarizes Ott's position as follows: "Ott continues to attempt to mediate between Barth and Bultmann, as he did in his early works. He has increasingly taken his cues from the later Heidegger in endeavoring to work out a theological program which transcends the subject-object dichotomy and is thus nonobjectifying in character." (p. 289)

32. Hans Conzelmann, *The Theology of Saint Luke*, trans. Geoffrey Buswell (London: Faber and Faber, 1960), pp. 170-71.

33. *Ibid.*, p. 20.

34. Bornkamm, *Jesus of Nazareth*, trans. Irene and Fraser McLuskey (New York: Harper & Row, 1960).

intellectual history of our time." May this reviewer be forgiven for dissenting from the views of his esteemed colleagues. . . .

This new position . . . does not differ in principle from Bultmann's. Though faith is not necessarily to be understood in existentialist terms, nonetheless the theologian has already arrived at the knowledge of the religious truth before he opened his New Testament, and consequently everything in the Gospels that is not fit to illustrate this truth is *a priori* doomed to be rejected.[35]

Paul J. Achtemeier, in evaluating the post-Bultmannian "New Quest," finds the whole movement riddled with unexamined and perilous *a prioris;* it is in fact a revival of the ancient heresy of Docetism.

We have, in short, the anomalous fact that the new quest of the historical Jesus is being carried on by a group of men who would have to regard any valid historical fact about Jesus of Nazareth as threatening the purity of the Christian faith. That the renewed search is carried on within a perspective that contains such a strange contradiction would seem to indicate that the movement, as now conceived, can hardly reach conclusive results.[36]

This antipathy to objective data among the post-Bultmannians is quite understandable in the light of our preceding discussion: these theologians are simply working out the logical implications of the hermeneutical circle — the "dynamic interaction" of text and interpreter — that appears in varying degrees in virtually all of contemporary theology.

American Lutheranism

Leaving the European scene,[37] we hasten on to America, particularly to the Lutheran theological situation in our own country. Is the same non-

---

35. Otto A. Piper, "A Unitary God with Jesus as His First Theologian," *Interpretation,* XV (Oct. 1961), 473-74. For further evidences of Bornkamm's aprioristic exegesis, see Bornkamm, G. Barth, and H. J. Held, *Tradition and Interpretation in Matthew,* trans. Percy Scott (London: SCM Press, 1963).
36. Paul J. Achtemeier, "Is the New Quest Docetic?" *Theology Today,* XIX (Oct. 1962), 364.
37. It will be noted that we have not discussed the hermeneutics of those European theologians whom Kümmel considers conservative or independent (see above, the text at note 6). If more space were at our disposal, we could show that even the most orthodox of these theologians balk at an unqualified, objective identification of the historical Scripture with God's Word. For Kümmel and the *Heilsgeschichte* school, as for the positions we have discussed above, divine revelation "exists only in response" (quoted in Carl F. H. Henry, *Faith and Thought: Journal of the Victoria Institute,* XCIV, 34) and must not be viewed propositionally. Rengstorf and the "conservatives" seem to use the Holy Spirit as a kind of *deus ex machina* to bolster an epistemologically weak hermeneutic (cf. Karl Heinrich Rengstorf, *Die Auferstehung Jesu,* 4th ed. (Witten Ruhr: Luther-Verlag, 1960), p. 109). Stauffer properly recognizes the necessity of an objective treatment of the Gospel records (see Ethelbert Stauffer, *Jesus and His Story,* trans. Richard and Clara Winston (New York: Knopf, 1960)) but handles most of the theological concepts of the Bible as mythical motifs (cf. Krister Stendahl's comments in the text at note 52 below). Pannen-

propositional, nonobjective view of biblical interpretation in evidence here? The answer is very definitely, "Yes." Examples could be multiplied; we shall restrict ourselves only to the more prominent. As early as 1948 Joseph Sittler endeavored to reorient Lutherans from a verbal, "static" approach to the Bible, to a "dynamic," "instrumental" understanding of God's Word.

> All verbal forms, all means of communication through speech, prove too weak for this massive bestowal [of Revelation]. . . . We must ask after the Word of God in the same way faith asks after Jesus Christ. That is to say, that the Word of God *becomes* Word of God for us. . . . To assert the inerrancy of the text of scripture is to elevate to a normative position an arbitrary theological construction.[38]

Martin Heinecken has consistently approached the problem of biblical interpretation from the standpoint of Kierkegaard's existentialism. In *The Moment Before God,* Heinecken's most influential book, truth is identified with paradoxical subjectivity, faith is understood as blind "encounter with the un-known," and the objective historical accuracy of the biblical text is considered totally irrelevant to Christian commitment.

> It is thus impossible to find an objective certain basis for the revelation of God in Christ. Again, Kierkegaard's prophetic insight is apparent in the controversies waged over the inspiration, inerrancy, and infallibility of the Bible. Fundamentalists, who staked everything on a repudiation of higher criticism, have definitely lost the battle. As far as any merely historical facts can be established with a degree of certainty, the com-posite character of many of the books of the Bible is established. Yet the witness of faith is not thereby affected. . . . A very radical critic of the Bible may really be a "believer" if he makes the proper distinctions and does not try to bolster with irrelevant argument that which must be "believed" in a transformation of existence.[39]

That the "dynamic" (as opposed to "propositional") view of Scripture is now quite well established in Lutheran theological circles in the United States is evident from the 1963 symposium volume, *Theology in the Life of the*

---

berg and Thielicke, though their theologies are a healthy corrective to the current existential-dialectic mainstream, draw the line at inerrant Biblical authority. And Cullmann, whose theology is perhaps the most attractive of all, while categorically refusing to view the resurrection of Christ (or any link in the temporal sequence of salvation history) as mythical, nonetheless regards the Fall and the ultimate Eschaton as biblical myths (see, on Cullmann, Jean Frisque, *Oscar Cullmann: Une théologie de l'historie du salut* [Tournai, (Belgique:) Castermann, 1960], and the critical remarks in Gustaf Wingren, *Creation and Law,* trans. Ross Mackenzie [Edinburgh: Oliver and Boyd, 1961], *passim*).

38. Joseph Sittler, *The Doctrine of the Word* (Philadelphia: Muhlenberg Press, 1948), pp. 62-63, 68 (Sittler's italics).

39. Martin J. Heinecken, *The Moment Before God* (Philadelphia: Muhlenberg Press, 1956), p. 262. In his Foreword the author writes: "It has been asserted that this book is not so much about Kierkegaard as it is an expression of my own views. This is cheerfully admitted" (p. 7). "Cheerfully" is hardly *le mot juste,* however, since the vital objectifying elements in Kierkegaard are totally neglected in Heinecken's interpretation of him.

Church, to which 14 members of the Conference of Lutheran Professors of Theology contributed essays. In the chapter dealing with "The Bible," Warren Quanbeck of Luther Seminary considers hopelessly outmoded the conviction of Protestant orthodoxy that Scripture is " a collection of revealed propositions unfolding the truth about God, the world, and man" and that "because the Holy Spirit was the real author of Scripture, every proposition in it was guaranteed infallible and inerrant, not only in spiritual, but in secular matters."[40] For Quanbeck, biblical exegesis requires the hermeneutic assumption that "since human language is always relative, being conditioned by its historical development and usage, there can be no absolute expression of the truth even in the language of theology. Truth is made known in Jesus Christ, who is God's Word, his address to mankind. Christ is the only absolute."[41]

The very recent introduction of the post-Bultmannian New Hermeneutic into the American theological scene is doing much to reinforce and deepen the theological stance represented by such older Lutheran theologians as Sittler, Heinecken, and Quanbeck. The focal center of the "young Turks" is *Dialog*, the Lutheran theological journal begun in 1962 under the editorship of Carl E. Braaten of the Lutheran School of Theology in Chicago. Two other members of the editorial staff whose frequent contributions set the tone of the journal are Roy A. Harrisville of Luther Seminary and Robert W. Jenson of Luther College. Significantly, Braaten wrote his doctoral dissertation on Martin Kähler (1835-1912), who "with apparently equal justification can be viewed as a forerunner of either Karl Barth or Rudolf Bultmann"[42] and whose "influence cuts across such varied theologies as those of Tillich, Barth, Brunner, and Bultmann."[43] In a Foreword to Braaten's partial translation of Kähler's *Der sogenannte historische Jesus und der geschichtliche, biblische Christus,* Paul Tillich makes the revealing assertion: "I do believe that one emphasis in Kähler's answer is decisive for our present situation, namely, the necessity to make the certainty of faith independent of the unavoidable incertitudes of historical research."[44] Braaten agrees, and stresses the fact that Kähler rejected the objective approach to biblical interpretation characteristic of Protestant orthodoxy:

> Kähler felt that the orthodox definition of faith involving the sequence of *notitia, assensus,* and *fiducia* led to an intellectualistic regimentation of the *ordo salutis.* Volitional assent to intellectual information about God and Christ was made a prerequisite of saving faith. This information was to be found in the Bible and was secured by the doctrine of verbal inspiration. This attempt of Protestant Orthodoxy to provide a threshold of objectivity over which a person must pass to enter the household of faith was particularly offensive to Kähler. . . . [For him] the Bible is nothing less than the Word of God to those who believe in

---

40. *Theology in the Life of the Church*, ed. Robert W. Bertram (Philadelphia: Fortress Press, 1963), p. 23.
41. *Ibid.,* p. 25.
42. Martin Kähler, *The So-called Historical Jesus and the Historic, Biblical Christ,* trans. and ed. Carl E. Braaten (Philadelphia: Fortress Press, 1964), p. 2.
43. *Ibid.,* p. 33.
44. *Ibid.,* p. 12.

Christ. . . . With Kähler's christological view of biblical authority it was possible to arbitrate the painfully fruitless discussion about whether everything in the Bible or only parts of it are the Word of God. The first alternative can be set aside by a *reductio ad absurdum.*[45]

Harrisville, who has flatly stated in a *Dialog* article, "we admit to the discrepancies and the broken connections in Scripture,"[46] is the co-editor with Braaten of two volumes that endeavor through translations of current German theological articles to introduce American theologians to post-Bultmannian trends. In the second of these anthologies,[47] Harrisville himself writes a paper in which he, like his European counterparts, rejects the subject-object distinction in hermeneutics and history and classes attempts to operate with an objective text as throwbacks to the liberal "life of Jesus" era.[48] Jenson, a critic of the present essayist for his belief in plenary inspiration,[49] likewise blurs the hermeneutic task by interlacing biblical text with "dogmatic tradition" and with "the live questions of our present existence"; thus, for him, "even the profoundest reading and understanding of the Bible will not in itself give us a message to proclaim," and "at the moment when we must speak, Scripture provides no guarantee that we will speak rightly."[50]

And now, what of the question with which this section began? How can the numerous positions here described be related to one another? We might point out the clear historical connections; for example, Heinz Kimmerle has shown that Wilhelm Dilthey, on whom Martin Heidegger and Bultmann based their existentialisms, derived his hermeneutic from the later Friedrich Schleiermacher[51] — thus a chain is forged from the subjective psychologism of Schleiermacher (from which Ritschlian modernism grew) to the post-Bultmannian

---

45. *Ibid.,* pp. 17-18, 31.
46. Roy A. Harrisville, "A Theology of Rediscovery," *Dialog,* II (Summer 1963), 190. Harrisville's book, *His Hidden Grace: An Essay on Biblical Criticism* (New York: Abingdon, 1965), is an attempt to make the higher criticism of Scripture palatable if not attractive to clergymen schooled in classical Lutheran theology.
47. Cited in note 30 above. The first is Carl E. Braaten and Roy A. Harrisville, *Kerygma and History: A Symposium on the Theology of Rudolf Bultmann* (New York: Abingdon Press, 1962).
48. Harrisville, "Representative American Lives of Jesus," *The Historical Jesus and the Kerygmatic Christ,* pp. 172-96.
49. Robert W. Jenson, "Barth Weak on Scripture?" *Dialog,* I (Autumn 1962), 57-58; this is a comment on my report, "Barth in Chicago: Kerygmatic Strength and Epistemological Weakness," *Dialog,* I (Autumn 1962), 56-57.
50. Jenson, "An Hermeneutical Apology for Systematics," *Dialog,* IV (Autumn 1965), 269, 274. Jenson has specialized in Barth; see his *Alpha and Omega: A Study in the Theology of Karl Barth* (New York: Thomas Nelson, 1963).
51. Cf. James M. Robinson, "Hermeneutic Since Barth," in his *The New Hermeneutic,* pp. 70-71. Kimmerle is a student of the Dilthey critic Hans-Georg Gadamer, who, though he is trying to give an "ontological turn" to hermeneutics by concentrating on linguistic understanding rather than existential psychology, nevertheless (like Dilthey) takes the hermeneutical circle for granted, asserting that "historic tradition can only be understood by recalling the basic continuing concretizing taking place in the continuation of things." (*Wahrheit und Methode: Grundzüge einer philosophischen Hermeneutik* [Tübingen: J. C. B. Mohr, 1960], p. 355).

New Hermeneutic. And we have already noted the dependence of Barth as well as Bultmann on Martin Kähler, whose distinction between *Geschichte* and *Historie* places biblical theology in a nonobjective frame of reference. But such historical connections, though they evidence a relationship among the positions we have discussed, do not tell us precisely what that relationship is.

On Dec. 30, 1957, at the annual meeting of the Society of Biblical Literature, a symposium was held on "Problems in Biblical Hermeneutics." Two papers at that symposium, both presented by advocates of the new approach in biblical study, set forth in bold strokes the core connections among the views we have been treating. Let us hear first from Lutheran Krister Stendahl of Harvard:

> Recent studies by Käsemann, Dahl, Bornkamm, Stauffer, and others have reopened the question about the historical Jesus and tried to indicate the necessity of overcoming our defeatism at this point. This has great significance for historical studies but for the problem of interpretation in terms of hermeneutics it seems to remain a fact that by and large we have to approach Jesus in the traditions about him, not the traditions about him in the light of factual historical information. . . .
>
> This state of affairs has a tendency to cut two ways: It has led to the strange situation where modern biblical studies deal with the traditional theological concepts of incarnation, miracles, redemption, justification, election, and all the rest in a language which causes some old liberals to shiver and leads the listeners to many modern preachers to believe that the liberal era of doubt and disbelief is finally overcome once and for all. Yet the preacher as well as the scholar knows — or should know — that he is expounding *traditions*, the faith of the Church in Christ, while people might think that he is telling them the simple facts about Jesus of Nazareth. In the long run it must become clear that the situation which has allowed this kind of double talk and has made it possible to capitalize on the distance between "sender" and "receiver," is actually based on an insight into the nature of the biblical material which is more radical in its positivism than that of the liberals.[52]

Thus modern biblical hermeneutics has shifted its concern from Scripture as a record of objective fact to Scripture as a compendium of traditions reflecting the faith stance of the writers. It has in consequence become possible to use traditional biblical-theological terminology without committing oneself to the veracity of the events or interpretations involved; and this admitted "double talk" is actually more radical than the old liberalism.[53]

Another speaker at the SBL symposium, J. Coert Rylaarsdam of the University of Chicago Divinity School, has rendered contemporary theology,

---

52. Krister Stendahl, "Implications of Form-Criticism and Tradition-Criticism for Biblical Interpretation," *Journal of Biblical Literature*, LXXVII (March 1958), 34-36.

53. A good example of this nonfactual, "dramatic-mythical" treatment of traditional biblical concepts is provided by the Norwegian Lutheran New Testament scholar Ragnar Leivestad in his *Christ the Conqueror; Ideas of Conflict and Victory in the New Testament* (London: SPCK, 1954).

liberal and conservative, an immense service by spelling out explicitly the radical and unbridgeable chasm separating the hermeneutics of Reformation orthodoxy from the hermeneutics of 20th-century Protestantism. The following paragraphs cannot receive too close attention:

> For orthodoxy the forms and processes of revelation were summed up in the contents of the Bible and in the form of events it reported. The Bible was called "the objective Word of God," or "the Word of God written." It was revelation, rather than faith's testimony to revelation. The paradox between revelation and biblical history was wiped out in like manner. Orthodoxy not only said God revealed himself in history, but also that there was a bit of history which was revelation. To be sure, this bit of history was set apart, not subject to the laws of history in general, and so, in a sense, irrelevant for it. But, chronologically and materially, revelation was history. The Nile turned into real blood; and every first-born son in Egypt really died. This may or may not be so; but for orthodoxy the meaning of revelation depended on it. There was no gap between fact and faith. Fact demanded faith and the dependence of faith on fact is not paradoxical, but absolute. The integrity and factual accuracy of the Bible is the guarantee for the history on which faith rests.

> The most distinctive feature of the current theological emphasis is its dynamic view of revelation. This is not only true of its neo-orthodox wing; it is equally true of the successors of liberalism; or, for that matter, in such Jewish theologians as Buber and Heschel. Revelation is not a static form with a stable content, subject to descriptive analysis; it is a dynamic action, existentially apprehended, the source of faith and inspired response. Revelation, *per se*, is not subject to analysis. Deeply aware of the conditionedness of all forms, material and intellectual, contemporary theology shies away from equating any of them with revelation. Relativism, long with us, plays a more radical role than ever before. Forms may be the media of revelation; they are an inevitable outcome of it. They can serve as a cue to its meaning; but, as such, forms are never revelation. To use the technical term, there is a paradoxical relationship between the action of God, which is revelation, and all objective structures and processes that are patient of descriptive analysis.[54]

Here we have not only a clear and precise statement of the classical Protestant hermeneutic stance but also a lucid description of the ideological thread uniting contemporary hermeneutical positions from Barth to the post-Bultmannians. For orthodoxy the Bible in its entirety is God's objective revelation, and both the events and the interpretations comprising it are veracious; faith accepts and is grounded in the propositional validity of the scriptural text, and all sound exegesis of the Bible must proceed from this presuppositional base. For contemporary hermeneutics, however, the text of Scripture cannot be understood as objective, historically veracious revelation separated from the exegete (the subject-object distinction); an existential-dialectical relation between text and interpreter (the hermeneutical circle) has to be

---

54. J. Coert Rylaarsdam, "The Problem of Faith and History in Biblical Interpretation," *Journal of Biblical Literature*, LXXVII (March 1958), 27-29.

assumed; and since God's revelation can never be equated with the Scriptural text, hermeneutical affirmations will necessarily have a paradoxical quality, and relativism will "play a more radical role than ever before." In brief, for orthodox Protestantism the Bible has stood as an unblemished historical revelation, objectively distinguishable from its interpreters, who in order to understand it must allow it to interpret itself apart from the existential orientations reflected in church tradition or in the mind-set of the exegete; but for 20th-century hermeneutics the Bible, as a fallible witness to revelation, cannot be qualitatively distinguished from its interpreters, past or present, and to understand it we must recognize the relativistic dialectic that connects us as interpreters with the text we endeavor to interpret.

Luther's Hermeneutic in Fiction and in Fact

Having obtained a detailed picture of the contemporary Protestant hermeneutic scene, we can now benefit from a historical analysis of Reformation Lutheranism's interpretive approach to Holy Writ. Our particular concern is to discover whether the confessional roots of Lutheranism encourage, permit, or reject the existential-dialectic hermeneutics of present-day Protestant (not excluding Lutheran) thought. Since a theological wedge is frequently driven today between Luther and the representatives of classical Lutheran orthodoxy,[55] emphasis will be placed here on Luther himself. This is not to say that we agree with the stereotyped criticisms of the much maligned orthodox theologians; indeed, criticism of them is but the first step toward criticism of Luther and of the Confessions, for as C. S. Lewis well noted in reference to the 19th-century Tübingen-school attack on Paul as a perverter of Jesus' teachings:

> In the earlier history of every rebellion there is a stage at which you do not yet attack the King in person. You say, "The King is all right. It is his Ministers who are wrong. They misrepresent him and corrupt all his plans — which, I'm sure, are good plans if only the Ministers would let them take effect." And the first victory consists in beheading a few Ministers: only at a later stage do you go on and behead the King himself.[56]

But considerations of space prohibit our dealing here with the hermeneutics of classical orthodoxy. Presumably, in any case, it will be granted that if Luther manifests a thoroughgoing "orthodox" hermeneutic, his orthodoxist followers are deserving of no more condemnation than he is.

At present, however, the advocates of the modern hermeneutical stance have no interest in criticizing Luther; quite the opposite, for they claim that he is a forerunner of the very interpretive approach they are supporting. So

---

55. See Jaroslav Pelikan, *From Luther to Kierkegaard* (St. Louis, Mo.: Concordia Publishing House, 1950), *passim,* and cf. the present essayist's editorial Introduction to *Chytraeus on Sacrifice* (St. Louis, Mo.: Concordia Publishing House, 1962).

56. C. S. Lewis' Introduction to J. B. Phillips, *Letters to Young Churches* (New York: Macmillan, 1948), p. 10.

for many years it has been fashionable to associate Luther with Kierkegaard, the theological father of existentialism.[57] Along the same line, Sittler unfavorably compares the hermeneutic of Protestant orthodoxy with "Luther's dialectical understanding of the Word":

> The post-Reformation theologians did not understand the Scriptures in this way. They failed sufficiently to ponder the fact that the Bible, when it speaks of revelation, points beyond itself to an event to which it bears witness, but which is not the Bible itself. Luther's theological concern was directed toward this event, this divine self-disclosure, to which the Bible is a singular and incomparable witness. But Luther did not equate Scripture with the divine event.[58]

Luther's Christological approach to the Bible is supposed to have freed him from static, plenary inspiration and given him an existentially dynamic hermeneutic; thus Quanbeck interprets Luther's view:

> The apprehension of the Bible in static or mechanical terms is necessarily inadequate. The reader must approach it as a dynamic and personal message in which he is himself existentially involved in order to experience its purpose and power. . . .
>
> Luther's view of the authority of Scripture differs greatly from that of the Middle Ages. For the Occamist theologian, Scripture is authoritative because every word in it has been inspired by the Holy Spirit. This is true of the Lutheran scholastics also, with the significant difference that, standing on Luther's shoulders, they rejected the four-fold interpretation and insisted on the historical sense of Scripture. Luther stands apart from both groups. Scripture is his authority because it reveals Jesus Christ, because in it God speaks His Word of judgment and grace.[59]

(Note here that the proportion is created: Medieval exegesis is to Luther's exegesis as the propositional, plenary inspiration of Lutheran orthodoxy is to an existential hermeneutic. We shall see very shortly how the terms of this proportion must be exactly reversed!) This same general evaluation of Luther is shared by a recent student of his Galatians commentary who claims that, in contrast to Calvin, Luther's "interpretations tend to be subjective, directed toward the individual, existential life of the believer"; accordingly Luther's hermeneutic principles can "lead to an extreme — to a subjectivism (as in Schleiermacher or Bultmann) which stresses the religious feeling or the

---

57. See, for example, Heinecken, *The Moment Before God*, passim.
58. Sittler, pp. 34-35. Sittler relies here on Philip S. Watson, *Let God Be God* (London: Epworth Press, 1947), a secondary source of generally high quality, which, however, leaves something to be desired in its treatment of Luther's doctrine of the Word. A more recent work presenting essentially the same interpretation of Luther's biblical hermeneutic is Willem Jan Kooiman, *Luther and the Bible*, trans. John Schmidt (Philadelphia: Muhlenberg Press, 1961).
59. Warren A. Quanbeck, "Luther's Early Exegesis," in Roland H. Bainton, et al., *Luther Today* in Martin Luther Lectures, I (Decorah, Iowa: Luther College Press, 1957), pp. 92, 99.

existential (personal) dimensions of subjective faith over against the object of faith, thus losing what Prenter calls Luther's 'realism'."[60]

For most of contemporary biblical scholarship, however, as Rylaarsdam has made clear, stress on "the existential (personal) dimensions of subjective faith over against the object of faith" is anything but an "extreme." Thus no time has been lost in endeavoring to bring Luther into the very midst of the Bultmannian and post-Bultmannian hermeneutic camp. Bultmann's interpreters have consistently claimed that in him "one sees in unmistakable outlines the shadow of Luther,"[61] for just as Luther saw the inadequacy of man's moral efforts toward salvation, so (we are told) Bultmann sees the inadequacy of man's "intellectual" efforts to "justify himself" by way of a propositionally inerrant Scripture.[62]

The post-Bultmannian advocates of the New Hermeneutic have been especially vocal in claiming Luther as their spiritual father. The following comment by Käsemann is typical:

> Neither miracle nor the canon nor the Jesus of history is able to give security to our faith. For our faith there can be no objectivity in this sense. That is the finding which New Testament scholarship has made plain in its own fashion. But this finding is only the obverse of that acknowledgment which Luther's exposition of the third article of the Creed expresses.[63]

Ebeling has made Luther one of his specialties; his *Habilitationsschrift* in fact dealt with the Reformer's hermeneutics.[64] We are therefore justified in including a rather long quotation from Ebeling — a quotation which shows with crystal clarity how Luther has been drawn into the orbit of the non-propositional, existential, circular, "word-event" hermeneutic:

> The fundamental problem for him is not a verbal description of God but the exposure of man's existence before God; that is to say, the proclamation of God's judgment over man. With this we are not brought into the horizon of metaphors. The linguistic use of metaphors has now quite another task with reference to the subject-matter of theology, namely, to bring man into the real situation, where the subject-matter itself occurs. . . . This understanding of language is not defined from the point of view of signification but from the viewpoint of the word-event which

60. Thomas D. Parker, "The Interpretation of Scripture. I. A Comparison of Calvin and Luther on Galatians," *Interpretation*, XVII (Jan. 1963), 68, 75. Interestingly enough, Sittler, in his *Doctrine of the Word*, takes a diametrically opposite tack by claiming that Calvin as well as Luther maintained Sittler's dialectic-existential view of the Word (pp. 27-32).
61. So argues Robert Scharlemann in "Shadow on the Tomb," *Dialog*, I (Spring 1962), 22-29.
62. André Malet concludes his detailed treatment of Bultmann with this analogy (pp. 394-96).
63. Käsemann, *Exegetische Versuche und Besinnungen*, I, 236.
64. *Evangelische Evangelienauslegung. Untersuchung zu Luthers Hermeneutik* (1942). Cf. his article, "Die Anfänge von Luthers Hermeneutik," *Zeitschrift für Theologie und Kirche*, XLVIII (1951), 172-230. Ebeling is responsible for the article on Luther's theology in the third edition of *Die Religion in Geschichte und Gegenwart*, IV (Tübingen: J. C. B. Mohr, 1960), 495-519.

must be accounted for and which, in turn, enables such accountability. The hermeneutical result is, therefore, that the very word as such is of hermeneutical importance and is able to illumine, to bring about clarity, and to give life. The hermeneutical task can only consist of the fact that we devote ourselves to the service of the word-event in such a way that the word becomes truly word, and that it occurs as pure word in the fullness of its power. Luther's thesis on the Bible as *sui ipsius interpres* must be understood along this line.[65]

For Ebeling's Luther, then, the hermeneutical focus does not lie in "verbal description" or in "signification," nor is the Scripture objectively Word; rather, in order for the Word to become "truly" Word, we must "devote ourselves to the service of the word-event." Marlé expresses amazement at how Ebeling has been able to give Luther "une étonnante actualité";[66] quite so: in the above passage Luther is practically indistinguishable from his contemporary interpreter.[67]

Says Ebeling at an earlier point in the article from which the above extended passage was quoted: "We can by no means short-circuit the hermeneutics of the Reformation and pass it off as a mere precursor of modern historico-critical hermeneutics."[68] To which we respond with a hearty "Amen"! Therefore let us by analysis of primary sources determine what in fact Luther's attitude was toward the interpretation of the biblical text. Is he properly to be aligned with the contemporary dialectical-existential approach, or does he view the Scripture in another way?

The issue here is emphatically not whether Luther's own existential experiences (his realization of justification by grace through faith, his *Anfechtungen*, etc.) played a role in his biblical exegesis. Certainly they did — as they do for all readers of God's Word. The question is rather whether Luther considered his experiences to conjoin with the scriptural text in a dialectic manner so that, in the terms of the contemporary hermeneutical circle, each could legitimately work upon the other, and "God's Word could truly become God's Word." Granted that psychological or sociological conditions often led the sensitive Luther to an interest in certain passages of Holy Writ; granted even that on occasion his existential stance colored the Scripture he was endeavoring to understand. But *in principle* did he consider such "word-event" situations to be self-validating, or did he believe that Scripture

---

65. Gerhard Ebeling, "The New Hermeneutics and the Early Luther," *Theology Today*, XXI (April 1964), 45-46.
66. Marlé p. 80.
67. Robert Scharlemann has recently performed a parallel operation on the great Lutheran theologian of classical orthodoxy, Johann Gerhard. In *Thomas Aquinas and John Gerhard* (New Haven: Yale University Press, 1964) Scharlemann characterizes Gerhard's doctrine of Creation as "the dialectic of obedience" and his doctrine of Redemption as "the dialectic of the court." As Ebeling's Luther comes to sound like Ebeling, so Scharlemann's Gerhard speaks the language of Scharlemann. Contrast Edmund Smits, "The Lutheran Theologians of the 17th Century and the Fathers of the Ancient Church," *The Symposium on Seventeenth Century Lutheranism: Selected Papers*, I (St. Louis Mo.: The Symposium on Seventeenth Century Lutheranism, 1962), 1-31.
68. Ebeling, "The New Hermeneutics and the Early Luther," p. 35.

properly stood over his existential life as an objectively inerrant revelation, proclaiming factual truth to him in judgment and in grace?

Further, the issue of Luther vis-à-vis contemporary hermeneutics does not turn on his employment of Christological exegesis or of the justification principle or of the basic Law-Gospel distinction. That Luther uses these interpretive approaches to Scripture (and sometimes even over-uses them!) no one acquainted with the Reformer's exegetical writings will deny. But this does not commit Luther to a dialectic, experiential hermeneutic. It would do so only if Luther saw these principles as legitimately arising out of existential experience. Does he? Or does he believe that they arise solely from the objective, perspicuous text of an infallible Scripture?

One could attempt to answer these key questions by *catenae* of Luther quotations derived from the overwhelming riches of the Weimar Ausgabe. But in order to avoid the damning epithet of "proof-texter" and in order to see the issues in the historical context of Luther's life, we shall observe how he employed Scripture in the three major theological controversies of his career: his battle with Roman Catholic ecclesiocentrism, with Erasmian humanism, and with Zwinglian sacramentarianism.

At Worms Luther was presented with clean-cut alternatives: recanting his position, which patently ran counter to the *de facto* (shall we say existential?) church teaching of his day, or suffer the ban of the Holy Roman Empire. Not an easy choice. A coward would have recanted; a *hybris*-motivated man would have set the power of his personal existential experience over against the tradition of the church. Luther was neither; his refusal to compromise truth showed that he was no coward, and the total subjection of his existential decision to the Word of Scripture evidenced his humility. Listen to his confession:

> Unless I am convinced by the testimonies of the Holy Scriptures or evident reason (for I believe in neither the Pope nor councils alone, since it has been established that they have often erred and contradicted themselves), I am bound by the Scriptures that I have adduced, and my conscience has been taken captive by the Word of God; and I am neither able nor willing to recant, since it is neither safe nor right to act against conscience. God help me. Amen.[69]

This earth-shaking testimony has become so familiar to us that we neglect to see what precisely it says. If no other statement from Luther were available, his confession at Worms would be sufficient to establish his hermeneutical stance in contradiction to the current dialectic movement. For Luther says: (1) My conscience — my existential life — has been taken captive by the Word (here clearly identified with the Holy Scriptures); thus Luther, even at the most formidable time of his life, refused to succumb to the temptation of placing personal experience on the same level as God's Word or of giving it any kind of dialectic relation with Scripture (thereby allowing it to become a le-

---

69. *D. Martin Luthers Werke,* 7, (Weimar: Hermann Böhlaus Nachfolger, 1897), 836-38; hereafter cited as *WA.* Cf. Gordon Rupp's excellent treatment of this incident: *Luther's Progress to the Diet of Worms,* 2d ed (New York: Harper Torchbooks, 1964), pp. 96 ff.

gitimate basis for his theological stand). (2) The testimonies of the Holy Scriptures are sure — unlike Pope and councils who err and contradict themselves; thus for Luther the objectively inerrant, noncontradictory character of Scripture was taken for granted, in diametric contrast to the objectively fallible judgments of the church. (3) Evident reason is legitimately to be employed in reaching theological truth; thus Luther was no subjectivistic irrationalist who in existential fashion considers an objective, propositionally perspicuous Bible to be an offense to faith.[70]

Indeed, in Luther's biblical opposition to the Roman Catholicism of his day, we can see exactly the opposite proportion to that suggested by Quanbeck.[71]

Instead of

$$\frac{\text{Medieval exegesis}}{\text{Luther's exegesis}} = \frac{\text{Orthodox hermeneutics}}{\text{Contemporary hermeneutics}}$$

we have

$$\frac{\text{Medieval exegesis}}{\text{Luther's exegesis}} = \frac{\text{Contemporary hermeneutics}}{\text{Orthodox hermeneutics}}$$

Why? Because the Romanism Luther so vehemently opposed consciously permitted a dialectic interrelation between Scripture and existential situation, thereby allowing the latter to influence the interpretation of the former. Beryl Smalley, the foremost specialist on medieval biblical scholarship, has made clear how, during its formative period, medieval exegesis allowed "present needs" to swallow up the objective message of Scripture:

> The Latin Fathers, followed by the assistants of Charlemagne, made Bible study serve their present needs. They retained both the literal sense and textual criticism, but only as a basis for the spiritual interpretation. First and foremost the Scriptures were a means to holiness. *Lectio divina* formed one side of the ascetic triangle: reading, prayer, contemplation. Equally vital was its role in upholding the faith. The long line of commentators who developed the spiritual senses were not only contemplatives but men of action. They built up the church, defending her doctrines against pagans, Jews and heretics. They rallied her to the defense of the Christian State under Charlemagne. They supported the Gregorian reform against the secular power. They set forth the duties of clergy and laity.
>
> They subordinated scholarship meanwhile to mysticism and to propaganda. It was natural in troubled times, when chroniclers were

---

70. The ghost of this perennial stereotype of "Luther the existential irrationalist" has been well laid by two recent publications: Robert H. Fischer, "A Reasonable Luther," in *Reformation Studies: Essays in Honor of Roland H. Bainton*, ed. Franklin H. Littell (Richmond, Va.: John Knox Press, 1962), pp. 30-45, 255-56; and B. A. Gerrish, *Grace and Reason: A Study in the Theology of Luther* (Oxford: Clarendon Press, 1962).
71. See above, the text quotation corresponding to note 59.

beginning their paragraphs not 'Eo tempore . . .,' but 'Ea tempestate.
. . .' The decline of biblical scholarship is less surprising than its
endurance. The wonder is that even in a minor degree it survived, as a
thread, if a slender thread, in the skein that ran from the Alexandrians to
the Victorines.[72]

As "early medieval and many twelfth-century commentators had digressed 'an-
agogically,' " and as the 13th century displayed a "growing interest in things
present," so Smalley predicts that in the exegesis of the later Middle Ages "secular interests and naturalism will increase."[73] In this prediction Smalley is
quite correct. Torrance has recently shown that Thomas Aquinas, whose theological exegesis so deeply colored the thought patterns of the later medieval
church, accepted the "hermeneutical circle"[74] and was unaware of the degree
to which he allowed "ecclesiastical tradition" to outweigh the authority of the
Scriptural message:

> St. Thomas had a giant mind, to which there have been few equals, but
> his own immense intellectual powers laid him open to great temptations.
> His prior understanding of human experience, of the intellect and the
> soul, his masterful interpretation of Aristotelian physics, metaphysics,
> and psychology proved too strong and rigid a mould into which to pour
> the Christian faith. It is philosophy that tends to be the master, while
> theology tends to lose its unique nature as a science in its own right in
> spite of the claims advanced for it. In so far as the contents of theology
> surpass the powers of scientific investigation they are to be accepted as
> revealed truth but in the end the authority of ecclesiastical tradition
> outweighs in practice the authority of sacred scripture so that interpreta-
> tion of revealed truth is schematized to the mind of the church.[75]

The schematization "of revealed truth to the mind of the church" becomes
more and more characteristic of Roman biblical hermeneutics as the medieval

---

72. Beryl Smalley, *The Study of the Bible in the Middle Ages* (Oxford: Blackwell,
    1952), p. 358.
73. *Ibid.*, pp. 372-73. On the wide influence of the "fourfold" scheme of Biblical
    interpretation on medieval exegesis see Harry Caplan, "The Four Senses of
    Scriptural Interpretation and the Mediaeval Theory of Preaching," *Speculum,*
    IV (1929), 282-90.
74. For primary evidence, see *Summa Theol.*, 2.2, q.8, a.1, ad 2; and cf. T. F.
    Torrance, "Scientific Hermeneutics According to St. Thomas Aquinas," *The
    Journal of Theological Studies,* XIII (Oct. 1962), 287-88. Unhappily, Tor-
    rance does not see that when church tradition submerges the biblical text in
    Thomas' hermeneutic, this is due not to "deficiencies" in his application of the
    hermeneutical circle but to the very nature of the circle itself, wherein text
    and interpreter are placed in dialectical relation to each other. A valuable
    contrast with Thomas' exegesis is provided by the objectively textual approach
    of Athanasius, who was so highly regarded both by Luther (cf. Gustaf Aulén,
    Christus Victor: An Historical Study of the Three Main Types of the Atonement,
    trans. A. G. Hebert [London: SPCK, 1931]) and by the theologians of classical
    Lutheran orthodoxy (cf. David Chytraeus, *On Sacrifice: A Reformation
    Treatise in Biblical Theology,* trans. and ed. John Warwick Montgomery [St.
    Louis: Concordia Publishing House, 1962]); see T. E. Pollard, "The Exegesis of
    Scripture and the Arian Controversy," *Bulletin of the John Rylands Library,*
    XLI (1958-1959), 414-29.
75. Torrance, p. 289.

period draws to a close, and it reaches a high degree of refinement in such Counter-Reformation interpreters of the Bible as Sixtus of Siena.[76] And it was precisely this existential accommodation of objective scriptural teaching to "the mind of the church" that Luther opposed at Worms and throughout his career. For him, unlike both medieval Roman and contemporary Protestant hermeneutics,[77] the objective message of God's written Word must stand forever over the corporate and the individual conscience — judging them, not in any sense being judged by them.

Likewise in dealing with the Renaissance humanists of his day Luther stood firm: Scripture speaks as clearly against the ability of the human will in salvation as it does against any form of traditional work-righteousness. Luther's opposition to Erasmus was squarely based on his convictions that whenever Scripture speaks it speaks with absolute authority and clarity, that propositional assertions of truth can, and must, be drawn from the biblical revelation, and that the literal meaning of the scriptural text must be accepted unless the biblical context itself (not any external influence) forces a metaphorical interpretation. Listen to the following typical passages from *De servo arbitrio,* which expressly spell out the distance separating Luther from the nonpropositional, existentially oriented hermeneutics of contemporary Protestantism:

> If you [Erasmus] are referring to essential truths — why, what more irreligious assertion could a man possibly make than that he wants to be free to assert precisely *nothing* about such things? The Christian will rather say this: "So little do I like sceptical principles, that, so far as the weakness of my flesh permits, not merely shall I make it my invariable rule steadfastly to adhere to the sacred text in all that it teaches, and to assert that teaching, but I also want to be as positive as I can about those non-essentials which Scripture does not determine; for uncertainty is the most miserable thing in the world." . . . What is this newfangled religion of yours, this novel sort of humility, that, by your own

76. John Warwick Montgomery, "Sixtus of Siena and Roman Catholic Biblical Scholarship in the Reformation Period," *Archiv für Reformationsgeschichte,* LIV/2 (1963), 214-34.

77. Present-day Roman Catholic scholars, it is worth noting, are exceedingly pleased to see the Protestant move toward dialectic Scriptural interpretation, for such a move opens up the possibility that Protestants, in accepting as legitimate the dynamic force of church tradition in interpreting the Bible, will once again listen to the voice of Rome. Readers may be interested in comparing with the earlier-cited contemporary Lutheran approaches to Scripture, "New Shape," Roman Catholic Eduard Schillebeeckx's paper, "Exegesis, Dogmatics and the Development of Dogma," which begins: "The religion of revelation is essentially a dialogue, a meeting between man and the living God," and which sees Christian doctrine as dynamically drawn by the church from the Scriptural *sensus plenior,* not as "formally theological deductions from New Testament data" (*Dogmatic vs Biblical Theology,* ed. Herbert Vorgrimler [London: Burns & Oates, 1964], pp. 115-45). Cf. also Lutheran Wilhelm H. Wuellner's unpublished doctoral dissertation, "The Word of God and the Church of Christ: The Ecumenical Implications of Biblical Hermeneutics" (University of Chicago Divinity School, 1958); and for a different evaluation John Warwick Montgomery, "Evangelical Unity in the Light of Contemporary Orthodox Eastern — Roman Catholic — Protestant Ecumenicity," *The Springfielder,* XXX (Autumn 1965), 8-30.

example, you would take from us power to judge men's decisions and make us defer uncritically to human authority? Where does God's written Word tell us to do that?[78]

The notion that in Scripture some things are recondite and all is not plain was spread by the godless Sophists (whom now you echo, Erasmus) — who have never yet cited a single item to prove their crazy view; nor can they. And Satan has used these unsubstantial spectres to scare men off reading the sacred text, and to destroy all sense of its value, so as to ensure that his own brand of poisonous philosophy reigns supreme in the church. I certainly grant that many passages in the Scriptures are obscure and hard to elucidate, but that is due, not to the exalted nature of their subject, but to our own linguistic and grammatical ignorance. . . . . Who will maintain that the town fountain does not stand in the light because the people down some alley cannot see it, while everyone in the square can see it?[79] Let this be our conviction: that no "implication" or "figure" may be allowed to exist in any passage of Scripture unless such be required by some obvious feature of the words and the absurdity of their plain sense, as offending against an article of faith. Everywhere we should stick to just the simple, natural meaning of the words, as yielded by the rules of grammar and the habits of speech that God has created among men; for if anyone may devise "implications" and "figures" in Scripture at his own pleasure, what will all Scripture be but a reed shaken with the wind, and a sort of chameleon? There would then be no article of faith about which anything could be settled and proved for certain, without your being able to raise objections by means of some "figure." All "figures" should rather be avoided, as being the quickest poison, when Scripture itself does not absolutely require them.[80]

The objective, propositional reliability and clarity of the biblical text was also Luther's fundamental hermeneutic assumption in his battles with the sacramentarians over the Real Presence of Christ's body and blood. Here — on what has always been one of the key points of Lutheran doctrine — the lines are most decisively drawn between Luther and the modern Protestant hermeneutics. For Luther is so convinced of the verbal soundness and objective perspicuity of the original text of the Bible that he is willing to center his whole defense of his Lord's Supper doctrine on the five words τουτό ἐστιν τὸ σωμά μου. His book, *That These Words of Christ, "This Is My Body," etc., Still Stand Firm Against the Fanatics*, begins with a penetrating historical survey of the devil's successes in destroying the clear testimony of the church through corrupting the interpretation of the Bible. In the Middle Ages, Satan "had some of his followers in the Christians' schools, and through them he stealthily sneaked and crept into the holy Scriptures"; then Scripture became "like a broken net and no one would be restrained by it, but everyone made a hole in it wherever it pleased him to poke his snout, and followed his own opinions, interpreting and twisting Scripture any way he pleased."[81] And now, says Luther, even

78. Martin Luther, *De servo arbitrio*, WA, 18, 604-605.
79. *Ibid.*, 606.
80. *Ibid.*, 700-701.
81. Martin Luther, "That These Words of Christ, 'This Is My Body,' etc., Still Stand Firm Against the Fanatics" in *Word and Sacrament III*, ed. Robert H. Fischer, Vol. XXXVII in *Luther's Works*, American Edition, ed. Jaroslav

with the restoration of the Gospel and the Scriptures, the *Schwärmer* perverts God's Word by refusing to stand under the literal force of its eucharistic message; again and again Luther comes back to this same argument — the words of Scripture must be taken as simple and literal truth:

> Here let the judge between us be not alone Christians but also heathen, Turks, Tartars, Jews, idolaters, and the whole world: whose responsibility is it to prove his text? Should it be the Luther who asserts that Moses says, "In the beginning the cuckoo ate the hedge sparrow," or the person who asserts that Moses says, "In the beginning God created the heavens and the earth"? I hope the decision would be that Luther ought to prove his text, since in no language does "God" mean the same as "cuckoo." Well, away creeps Luther to the cross, grieved that he cannot prove that "God" means "cuckoo." For anyone who ventures to interpret words in the Scriptures any other way than what they say, is under obligation to prove this contention out of the text of the very same passage or by an aricle of faith. But who will enable the fanatics to prove that "body" is the equivalent of "sign of the body," and "is" the equivalent of "represents"? No one has brought them to this point up to now.[82]

Luther's encounters with tradition-oriented Romanists, rationalistically inclined humanists, and spiritualistic Protestants leave no doubt as to his standard of religious authority, the degree to which he subjected himself to it, or his approach to its interpretation. For Luther the canonical[83] Scripture was in its entirety God's inerrant Word, and its clear propositional teachings stood in judgment over all other writings. Thus one does not have to look far in Luther to discover such unqualified assertions as the following:

> I have learned to ascribe the honor of infallibility only to those books that are accepted as canonical. I am profoundly convinced that none of these writers has erred. All other writers, however they may have distinguished themselves in holiness or in doctrine, I read in this way: I evaluate what they say, not on the basis that they themselves believe that a thing is

---

Pelikan and Helmut T. Lehmann (Philadelphia: Fortress Press, 1961), pp. 13-14. This is perhaps the best edited and translated volume thus far published of the American Edition of Luther's writings.

82. *Ibid.,* p. 32. "His [Luther's] exegesis sought to derive the teachings of the Scriptures from the particular statements of the Scriptures rather than from the *a priori* principles of a theological system. Not even to his own theological speculation, therefore, would Luther consciously accord the status of an *a priori* principle that would dictate his exegesis, even though it cannot be denied that in his exegetical practice he sometimes operated with such *a priori* principles. Hence he was unwilling to have his doctrine of the ubiquity of the body of Christ, which was compounded of exegetical and speculative elements, lay down the terms for his exegesis of 'This is My Body' " (Jaroslav Pelikan, *Luther the Expositor,* companion volume to *Luther's Works,* American Edition [St. Louis, Mo.: Concordia Publishing House, 1959], p. 141).

83. It should be unnecessary to mention that Luther's early rejection of the General Epistle of James and some other Scripture portions stemmed from his (fallacious) criterion of *canonicity,* not from any weakness in his doctrine of *inspiration.*

true, but only insofar as they are able to convince me by the authority of the canonical books or by clear reason.[84]

The Holy Scriptures are assuredly clearer, easier of interpretation, and more certain than any other writings, for all teachers prove their statements by them, as by clearer and more stable writings, and wish their own treatises to be established and explained by them. But no one can ever prove a dark saying by one that is still darker. Therefore, necessity compels us to run to the Bible with all the writings of the doctors, and thence to get our verdict and judgment upon them; for Scripture alone is the true overlord and master of all writings and doctrines on earth. If not, what are the Scriptures good for? Lets us reject them and be satisfied with the books of men and human teachers.[85]

And here we arrive — in language no less than in substantive content — to the confessional statements of Lutheranism, where we read:

... wie D. Luther ... diesen Unterschied ausdrücklich gesetzt hat, dass alleine Gottes Wort die einige Richtschnur und Regel aller Lehre sein und bleiben solle, welchem keines Menschen Schriften gleich geachtet, sondern demselben alles unterworfen werden soll.

Hoc discrimen (inter divina et humana scripta) perspicue posuit, solas videlicet sacras litteras pro unica regula et norma omnium dogmatum agnoscendas, iisque nullius omnino hominis scripta adaequanda, sed potius omnia subiicienda esse.[86]

The Lutheran Confessions, then, in harmony with and in dependence on Luther himself, categorically refuse to allow "dialectic relations" between Scripture and any human teacher or writing whatever; the Bible judges man's total existential life — it is not intertwined with it in "hermeneutical circle" or "word-event."[87]

---

84. "Defense Against the Ill-tempered Judgment of Eck," WA, 2, 618. This passage and many others like it demonstrate, as I have argued elsewhere, that unless we make the clumsy blunder of equating "verbal inspiration" with traditional Romanist mechanical inspiration (the "dictation theory"), "it is difficult to feel . . . that Luther, if he lived today, would not in fact consider 'verbal inspiration' the biblical view most congenial to his own" (review of *Luther and the Bible* by Willem Jan Kooiman, *Christianity Today*, VI, [Feb. 16, 1962], 498).

85. "An Argument in Defense of All the Articles of Dr. Martin Luther Wrongly Condemned in the Roman Bull," WA, 7, 308 ff. In the preceding paragraph of this work Luther asserts his belief that the Scriptures "never yet have erred" and quotes Augustine as holding the same conviction. Two excellent treatments of Luther's Scriptural position that reinforce the case we have been presenting are Lewis W. Spitz, Sr., "Luther's *Sola Scriptura*," *Concordia Theological Monthly*, XXXI (Dec. 1960) 740-45; and Douglas Carter, "Luther As Exegete," *Concordia Theological Monthly*, XXXII (Sept. 1961), 517-25.

86. FC SD, Summary Formulation, 9. For an English translation, see Essay I, the text at note 66.

87. Emile Léonard properly interprets Art. V of the Augsburg Confession with this understanding: "Il est bien vrai que, parmi les spiritualistes, Sébastien Franck professait que la Parole agit *ohne Mittel*, sans instrument, et que Schwenckfeld soutenait une doctrine semblable dans son traité *Vom Lauf des Wortes Gottes* (1527). Mais la pointe de l'article était autant contre le catholicisme, avec sa conception d'un Saint-Esprit (incarné dans l'Eglise) indépendant du texte de la Parole" (*Histoire Générale du Protestantisme*, I [Paris: Presses Universitaires de France, 1961], 158).

Moreover, as Luther derived his Christological theme ("the whole Scripture is about Christ alone everywhere")[88] from Scripture itself, so the Lutheran Confessions ground their justification principle in a verbally perspicuous and totally authoritative Scripture:

> It is surely amazing that our opponents are unmoved by the many passages in the Scriptures that clearly attribute justification to faith and specifically deny it to works. Do they suppose that this is repeated so often for no reason? Do they suppose that these words fell from the Holy Spirit unawares."[89]

Never do the Confessions view the central doctrine of justification as arising independently of Scripture or from an existential "life relation" with Scripture — nor do they ever (in accord with a reprehensible modern practice) employ the doctrine as a means of devaluating the literal truth of some portions of Scripture. To the contrary, they recognize full well that apart from the perspicuously inscripturated "words of the Holy Spirit" the fundamental Christian truth of justification could not be sustained at all.

A Perplex in Perspective

The hermeneutic of Luther and of the Lutheran Confessions stands, then in irreconcilable opposition to the existential-dialectic hermeneutic of contemporary Protestant theology. To make of Luther a forerunner of Bultmann — or of Ebeling, Fuchs, or Ott — is almost ludicrous. As I have written elsewhere of the Luther-Bultmann analogy:

> The parallel is, of course, fallacious and "constructed" (cf. the old saw: What does an elephant and a tube of toothpaste have in common? Answer: Neither one can ride a bicycle). Whereas Luther turned from moral guilt to confidence in the *objective* facts of Christ's death for his sin and resurrection for his justification, Bultmann turns from his intellectual doubts to *subjective* anthropological salvation — a direct about-face from the objective Gospel Luther proclaimed.[90]

The contemporary hermeneutic is, as we have seen, a repristination of the very approach to the Bible Luther opposed throughout his career. Luther con-

---

88. Luther, *Vorlesung über den Römerbrief*, 1515-16, ed. J. Ficker (4th ed.; Leipzig, 1930), p. 240. Philip S. Watson in lectures on "The Theology of *Sola Scriptura*" (Chicago Lutheran Theological Seminary, Summer 1961) defended Luther's Christological reading of the Old Testament by noting that an entire play can properly be read in terms of its final act; this is quite true, but it should be stressed that Luther could *legitimately* do this (while many modern theologians cannot) because he was fully convinced that the entire Bible is the work of a single "Playwright," whose perspicuous composition warrants such interpretation. For a typical attempt by a contemporary mediating theologian to maintain a Christological view of the Bible, see Nels F. S. Ferré, "Notes by a Theologian on Biblical Hermeneutics," *Journal of Biblical Literature*, LXXVIII (1959), 105-14, and Howard M. Teeple's devastating critique: "Notes on Theologians' Approach to the Bible," *Journal of Biblical Literature*, LXXIX (1960), 164-66.
89. Ap. IV 107 f.
90. John Warwick Montgomery, *The Shape of the Past: An Introduction to Philosophical Historiography* (Ann Arbor, Mich.: Edwards, 1963), pp. 159-60.

stantly strove to maintain the objective purity of the biblical message over against all adulterations of God's Word with human opinions. Existential-dialectic approaches to Scripture invariably produce such adulterations, for by interlocking text and interpreter into a "word-event" relationship uncontrolled by the subject-object distinction, they permit — if they do not actually encourage — the absorption of the scriptural teaching into the existential-cultural situation of the interpreter. Instead of God's Word re-creating man in God's image, man re-creates God's Word in his own image.

Commenting on the Second Drew University Consultation on Hermeneutics, which so well reflects today's perplex in biblical interpretation, Robert Funk perceptively wrote:

> Neo-orthodoxy taught that God is never object but always subject, with the result that third generation neo-orthodox theologians have been forced to wrestle with the non-phenomenal character of God. They are unwilling to settle for God as noumenon (perhaps as a legacy of theologies of history, and perhaps as the result of a radical empiricism), which means that for them God does not "appear" at all. . . .
>
> It is possible on this circumspective view to see why the question of non-objectifying speaking and thinking in theology is a crucial problem, and yet why it refuses to come into focus: it touches upon a root question, viz., can or how can one speak meaningfully of God, but it is also difficult to address in an ordered and logical way because it is not apparent what "logic" is appropriate to the question.[91]

Here the chasm between Luther and the 20th-century hermeneutic yawns the widest, for Luther was never in doubt as to the "logic" appropriate to divine-human communication: It was and would always remain the logic of the Scriptural address. For Luther and for confessional Lutheranism, over against the *finitum non capax infiniti* tradition common both to idealistic philosophy and to classical Calvinism, God is indeed capable of "appearing" in the human situation and of making His will known to man in univocal language. When the contemporary hermeneutic reaches the nadir of "non-objectifying speaking and thinking in theology," it simply betrays its refusal to accept what for Luther was axiomatic to all theology: God is able to speak absolute, objective truth to man in man's language, and the Bible is that inerrant discourse. Luther's Christological principle in biblical hermeneutics has implications few modern Lutherans wish to face; for just as Luther refused to limit the Incarnation or the Real Presence through rational speculation about what God could or could not do, so he would have had no patience with our endeavors to limit revelation to God's "acts" (as distinguished from His Scriptural word), to the "doctrinal" content of Scripture (over against its "non-theological" material), or to the "spiritual" in the Bible. The God of Luther and of confessional Lutheranism has never been tongue-tied.

The 20th-century hermeneutic perplex in theology is a reflection of the general cultural confusion of the epoch. Smalley, it will be remembered,[92] commented that the decline of medieval hermeneutics "was natural in troubled

---

91. Funk, pp. 303-304.
92. See above, the text quotation corresponding to note 72.

times." Certainly we today begin our chronicles with *Ea tempestate*, and the chaos of hot and cold wars has unsettled us to the point where subjective relativism — the bias against the objective absolutes — has come to dominate even the field of theology, where there is least justification for it.[93]

Ironically, nontheological disciplines have in recent years been far more successful than theology in recovering ground lost to "nonobjectivistic" thinking. In spite of the popular view that Einsteinian physics and Heisenberg's Indeterminacy Principle have obliterated the subject-object distinction in favor of an "existential dynamism" in science, "Bohr has emphasized the fact that the observer and his instruments must be presupposed in any investigation, so that the instruments are not part of the phenomenon described but are used."[94] In philosophy, the existential tide that has conditioned so much of the twentieth century theology is receding under the impact of powerful analytical and linguistic criticism which has shown that dialectic-existential affirmations, owing to their subjective non-testability, are technically meaningless.[95] How remarkably like a modern philosophical-linguistic analyst is Luther when he says that he should send the nonpropositional Erasmus off to Anticyra — a health resort for the mentally ill — since Erasmus necessarily *asserts* that he finds *no satisfaction in assertions!*[96]

In the historical field also, the presuppositions of existentialism are being seriously questioned. The Dilthey tradition of subjective historiography (which has so profoundly colored biblical scholarship from Barth and Bultmann to the post-Bultmannians) is incapable of sustaining the criticisms directed at it by analytically trained philosophers of history. So, for example, J. W. N. Watkins, reflecting the new drive toward objectivity in historical study, has little patience with the idea that "to understand Ghengis Khan the historian must be someone very like Ghengis Khan" and points out that historical truth is determined not by the historian's subjective "temperament and mentality" but by his inductive examination of factually objective evidence.[97]

A recent literary tour de force has particularly well evidenced the growing self-awareness by belletristic scholars of the ghastly results of existential

93. See John Warwick Montgomery, "Ascension Perspective," *The Cresset*, XXIV (May 1961), 17-19.

94. Victor F. Lenzen, *Procedures of Empirical Science*, Vol. I, No. 5 in *International Encyclopedia of Unified Science* (Chicago: University of Chicago Press, 1938), p. 28.

95. In my paper, "Inspiration and Inerrancy: A New Departure," *Evangelical Theological Society Bulletin*, VIII (Spring 1965), 45-75 (reprinted as Essay I in the present volume), I have applied the insights of analytical philosophy to the question of biblical authority; noninerrancy inspiration claims for the Bible (particularly those by contemporary Lutherans both outside and inside The Lutheran Church — Missouri Synod) are there seen to be philosophically nonsensical and theologically at variance with the biblical epistemology.

96. WA 18, 603-605.

97. J. W. N. Watkins, "Philosophy of History: Publications in English," in *La Philosophie au milieu du vingtième siècle*, ed. Raymond Klibansky, 4 vols., 2d ed. (Firenze, 1961-62), III, 159, 174. On the implications of analytical historiography for theology of history, see my chapter, "Toward a Christian Philosophy of History," in Carl F. H. Henry's symposium, *Jesus of Nazareth: Saviour and Lord*, pp. 225-40.

"life relation" thinking in literary criticism. Frederick C. Crews of the English Department at the University of California (Berkeley), in *The Pooh Perplex* has "analyzed" A. A. Milne's perennial children's classic, *Winnie the Pooh*,[98] through assuming the guise of "several academicians of varying critical persuasions"[99] Here we have a series of hilarious examples of what invariably happens when interpreters create an "existentially dynamic" relation between themselves and their text. "Harvey C. Window," author of a casebook significantly titled, *What Happened at Bethlehem*, writes on the "paradoxical" in Pooh; for him "all great literature is more complex than the naive reader can suspect," the literal meaning is to give way to "multivalent symbolism," and when the events of the book do not fit his paradoxical categories, they are reinterpreted until they do so. "P. R. Honeycomb," a poetical contributor to the "little magazines" who engages in "intensely personal criticism," brings his existential stance to bear on the text: "In wondering what I shall set down next in these notations, I am reminded of Heisenberg's Uncertainty Principle. The only thing that is certain is that I am uncertain what to set down next, and in this I typify the whole modern age and the collision of elementary particles in particular, a fact I find peculiarly comforting." "Myron Masterson," a distinguished "angry young man" for the past 20 years, writes on "Poisoned Paradise: The Underside of Pooh," employing as his guides Karl Marx, St. John of the Cross, Friedrich Nietzsche, Sacco and Vanzetti, Sigmund Freud, and C. G. Jung; he rejects those finicky "experts" who have said that "there exist differences of opinion among these thinkers," for, after all, "each of them has helped to shape my literary and moral consciousness." "Woodbine Meadowlark," a perpetual graduate student romantically overwhelmed by the *Angst* of existence, paints a poohological picture in exact conformity with his world view:

> The most perfect emblem of ignorance is contained in the "Woozle" scene, which gives us Pooh and Piglet (ethereal, pure-hearted Piglet, the real hero of the book) wandering helplessly in circles, following their own darling little tracks and misconceiving their goal ever more thoroughly as they proceed. Is this not the very essence of modern man, aching with existential *nausée* and losing himself more deeply in despair as his longing for certainty waxes?

"Simon Lacerous," editor of the feared quarterly, *Thumbscrew*, describes Pooh as "Another Book to Cross Off Your List" and terminates his acid analysis by completely losing the subject-object distinction between the book and himself; indeed, to use Fuchs' terminology (but hardly in a manner to please Fuchs), the poohological word has "objectified" its interpreter: "The more I think about it, the more convinced I become that Christopher Robin not only hates everything I stand for, he hates me personally." Finally, "Smedley Force," a spokesman for "responsible criticism," completely submerges the text by his interest in literary antecedents, conjectural emendations, and the "discovery"

---

98. In a theological paper such as this it seems only right to cite the eminent Latin translation of Pooh: *Winnie ille Pu,* trans. Alexander Lenard (Novi Eboraci: Sumptibus Duttonis, 1960).
99. Frederick C. Crews, *The Pooh Perplex* (New York: Dutton Paperbacks, 1965).

of errors and inconsistencies in the book. Such endeavors, he is convinced, place us "on the threshold of the Golden Age of POOH!"[100]

The fervent desire to avoid just such a "golden age of Pooh" has led more and more literary critics to stop running in hermeneutical circles (the *Doppeldeutigkeit* is intentional) and to seek objective canons of interpretation. The result can be seen in such a superlative study as Elder Olson's "Hamlet and the Hermeneutics of Drama,"[101] where, over against all existential blendings of text and interpreter, Olson defines a perfect interpretation as "one which is absolutely commensurate in its basic, inferential, and evaluative propositions with the data, the implications, and the values contained within the work." Theologians should carefully ponder Olson's essay, for, just as he notes that the only alternative to this objective approach is "an endless succession of free improvisations on Shakespearean themes," so modern theology has offered ample evidence that the dialectic hermeneutic yields but a parallel series of unrestrained improvisations on God's Word.

Even in the theological field (where an oddly conservative temperament seems to encourage the persistence of liberal folly long after it has been rejected in other areas of knowledge!) there is evidence that hermeneutics is awaking from an enchanted sleep of half a century. Thus, as we have seen earlier,[102] Cullmann has disengaged himself from Barth's "theological exegesis." More significant yet is James Barr's demonstration that the dialectic "revelation through history" approach of the Neo-Orthodox "biblical theology movement" has colored with theological *a priori* even such an ostensibly reliable work as Kittel's *Wörterbuch*. Albrecht Oepke, who in the *Wörterbuch* claims that "revelation is not the communication of rational knowledge,"[103] is taken by Barr as "a very bad example" of the absorption of philology by modern theological presuppositionalism.[104] In his inaugural address at Princeton in December 1962 Barr drew the lines even sharper:

> God can speak specific verbal messages, when he wills, to the men of his choice. But for this, if we follow the way in which the Old Testament represents the incidents, there would have been no call of Abraham, no Exodus, no prophecy. Direct communication from God to man has fully as much claim to be called the core of the tradition as has revelation through events in history. If we persist in saying that this direct, specific communication must be subsumed under revelation through events in his-

---

100. With considerable difficulty, I have restrained myself from giving a sampling of Marxist and psychoanalytic interpretations of Pooh and of equally fascinating literary analyses based on specialized hermeneutic principles.

101. Elder Olson, "Hamlet and the Hermeneutics of Drama," *Modern Philology,* LXI (Feb. 1964), 225-37.

102. Note 19 above and corresponding text.

103. Albrecht Oepke, "ἀποκαλύπτω ," *Theologisches Wörterbuch zum Neuen Testament,* ed. Gerhard Kittel, III (Stuttgart: Verlag von W. Kohlhammer, 1938), 575.

104. Barr shows that Oepke's article "is assimilated to modern theological usage to a degree that the actual linguistic material will not bear" (James Barr, *The Semantics of Biblical Language* [London: Oxford University Press, 1961], p. 230).

tory and taken as subsidiary interpretation of the latter, I shall say that we are abandoning the Bible's own representation of the matter.[105]

From philosophical theology severe criticisms are beginning to be voiced against the epistemological sloppiness of existentially immediate truth claims and against the strangely illogical argument, so frequently heard today, that to expect any kind of objective grounding for Christian affirmations is to exhibit unfaith.[106]

In short, the hermeneutic of Luther and of the Lutheran Confessions can hardly be regarded as obscurantist today. In its insistence that "sensus literalis sive historicus . . . solus tota est fidei et theologiae Christianae substantia,"[107] it stands with the most advanced and clearheaded of contemporary scholarship.

But a far more powerful reason than scholarship *per se* impels us to hold on to the Lutheran hermeneutic. We have seen that the central doctrines of the Lutheran faith, such as justification and the Real Presence, were derived from Scripture through the application of this hermeneutic. To the extent that we move away from the literal sense and plain meaning of Scripture, to that very extent we undermine the salvatory doctrines Scripture proclaims and our church has so courageously preached. Desertion of the Lutheran hermeneutic by the introduction of nonverbal, nonpropositional, noninerrant conceptions of the Bible is, though we may not wish to see it, the ancient Calvinist *finitum non capax infiniti* heresy rearing its head;[108] and the result will be the eventual loss of the Real Presence and possibly even (as in Calvinistic modernism) the disappearance of any genuine Incarnation.[109] And to substitute a dialectic-existential "event of interpretation" for the objective message of *sola Scriptura* is to fall back into the subjectivistic evils of Pietism, to which more than one critic of Bultmann has attributed his theological failings.[110]

Moreover, let us not deceive ourselves into thinking that hermeneutics and biblical inspiration are distinct problems or that hermeneutical decisions have no necessary bearing on our doctrine of inspiration. A few years ago, outside our circles, an exceedingly important paper was published with the

---

105. James Barr, "The Interpretation of Scripture. II. Revelation Through History in the Old Testament and in Modern Theology," *Interpretation,* XVII (April 1963), 201-202.
106. See, for example, Frederick Ferré, *Language, Logic and God* (New York: Harper & Row, 1961), especially pp. 94-104; and several papers in *New Essays in Philosophical Theology,* ed. Antony Flew and Alasdair Macintyre, (London: SCM Press, 1955), especially C. B. Martin, "A Religious Way of Knowing" (pp. 76-95), and Ronald W. Hepburn, "Demythologizing and the Problem of Validity." (pp. 227-42).
107. *WA,* 14, 560.
108. So John R. Lavik criticizes Joseph Sittler's dialectic view of inspiration (*The Christian Church in a Secularized World* [Minneapolis: Augsburg, 1952], pp. 72-73).
109. This should be carefully observed especially by those who assert that the hermeneutic of propositional inerrancy deserves the pejorative epithet "Calvinist-fundamentalist."
110. See, e.g., Reginald H. Fuller, *The New Testament in Current Study,* rev. ed. (London: SCM Press, 1963), p. 30.

title "Hermeneutics as a Cloak for the Denial of Scripture";[111] in it the author demonstrated by example how a nonliteral, nonobjective hermeneutic can sap the meaning out of Scripture so as actually to deny its inspiration. Whenever we reach the point of affirming on the one hand that the Bible is infallible or inerrant and admitting on the other hand to internal contradictons or factual inaccuracies within it, we not only make a farce of language, promoting ambiguity, confusion, and perhaps even deception in the church; more reprehensible than even these things, we in fact deny the plenary inspiration and authority of Scripture, regardless of the theological formulae we may insist on retaining.

And if church history can teach us anything, it should teach us that seemingly minute problems of biblical hermeneutics (such as the historicity of Jonah and the leviathan) never remain minute. The decisions made on the "small" problems govern subsequent decisions on larger issues. Scripture is a seamless garment, and when the threads are unraveled at one place, soon the entire fabric gives way. From Jonah to the Resurrection is as short a distance as our Lord Himself placed between them.

Permissiveness in regard to the basic hermeneutic of Lutheranism is the surest way of introducing permissiveness throughout our doctrinal spectrum. Why? Because all doctrine (and this includes the contents of the creeds and confessions) derives from Scripture, and vagueness in biblical interpretation will most definitely yield, sooner or later, vagueness in the understanding of confessional teaching.[112] Let us not soon forget this fact, for more powerful churches than ours have in an unbelievably short time and in our own experience passed doctrinally into a "golden age of Pooh" through hermeneutic contamination.

And if, having reached the end of this somewhat involved essay, we hesitate in our commitment to the Lutheran hermeneutic of literal sense and objective perspicuity, doubtless we can benefit from some maieutic advice. First let us hear from Luther as he stresses the eschatological merit of his hermeneutic as compared with the interpretive approach of the subjectively oriented Schwärmer:

> Even supposing that our text and interpretation were uncertain or obscure — which it is not — as well as their text and interpretation, you still have this glorious, reassuring advantage that you can rely upon our text with a good conscience and say, "If I must have an uncertain, obscure text and interpretation, I would rather have the one uttered by the lips of God himself than one uttered by the lips of men. And if I must be deceived, I would rather be deceived by God (if that were possible) than by men. For if God deceives me, he will take the responsibility and make amends to me, but men cannot make amends to me if they have deceived me and led me into hell."[113]

111. J. Barton Payne, "Hermeneutics as a Cloak for the Denial of Scripture," *Evangelical Theological Society Bulletin,* III (Fall 1960), 93-100.
112. Marlé stresses the related point that hermeneutic issues bear directly on interconfessional dialog and ecumenical discussion (pp. 97-102). Here also an unambiguous hermeneutic is mandatory.
113. Martin Luther, "Confession Concerning Christ's Supper," *Word and Sacrament III,* p. 305.

Finally we shall listen to Gilbert Murray, one of the greatest classicists of our century, who, like Luther, had confidence in words.

> [We must] pause before thinking that it is a simple matter to understand and interpret even a book in our own language and belonging to our own civilization, not to speak of one removed from us by great gulfs.
>
> And yet, as I said, we do it. It is a question, I suppose, of caring and of taking pains. I am often struck, when I read controversial literature about Homer, say, or Plato, to notice how comparatively small a part of the field the controversy covers. If you take the whole of what Plato or Homer means to one of the disputants, and the whole of what he means to the other, nine-tenths of the two wholes coincide. And they often coincide in the most important and essential things, those which are felt and do not particularly claim to be talked about. In the language of the stage, the great things "carry" — across the footlights, and across the ages.[114]

Perhaps the καιρός has come for The Lutheran Church — Missouri Synod to take stock of herself: to see that she does not become enmeshed in a hermeneutic perplex when the interpretive task is, like most profoundly spiritual things, disarmingly simple: to bow to the full authority of God's Word that it may carry across the footlights to our darkling age.

---

114. Gilbert Murray, *The Interpretation of Ancient Greek Literature; an Inaugural Lecture Delivered Before the University of Oxford, January 27, 1909* (Oxford: Clarendon Press, 1909), p. 18.

Part Two

Doctrine, Ethics and the Church

III.

THEOLOGICAL ISSUES AND PROBLEMS OF BIBLICAL INTERPRETATION NOW FACING THE LUTHERAN CHURCH - MISSOURI SYNOD

If an Unidentified Flying Object suddenly disgorged a Martian whose task it was to obtain a concise description of the state of our Church, what would the Creature from Outer Space discover? In my opinion, he would have quite a job on his hands, for the Lutheran Church-Missouri Synod today presents an ambivalent and in many ways confused face both to its members and to those who observe it from the outside. When I was studying for my theological doctorate at Strasbourg, I had an interesting conversation with a priest who was taking his doctorate in the Roman Catholic theological faculty there — and whose thesis topic was the Missouri Synod! I asked him why, with so many Protestant denominations available, he had chosen to study our particular Church, and he said that in Europe many Roman Catholics consider Missouri to be the one Protestant body that still maintains a strict Reformation position and knows what it believes. Later, however, I learned that this priest had delimited his subject to Missouri's *earlier* theological history; his contact with the more recent theological situation in our Church had left him with a much less clean-cut impression of our stance.

Confusion as to where Missouri stands today is by no means restricted to priests and Martians. Within our Church increasing numbers of people are deeply and sincerely troubled over a ferment which they only vaguely understand. Numerical growth in membership continues; we read that "for the 21st consecutive year the Lutheran Church-Missouri Synod had the highest numerical gain in membership among all Lutheran bodies in North America, the National Lutheran Council has reported in its annual statistical summary."[1] Yet economically the Synod is facing real difficulties, and the common explanation that "churches cannot stand prosperity" rings hollow when we read that "as of August 12 the Wisconsin Evangelical Lutheran Synod had exceeded by $600,000 its $4 million goal for the expansion of its educational institutions."[2] So disturbed are many pastors and entire districts over current theological confusions in our Church that some district presidents have with greatest difficulty restrained local churches from putting contributions into escrow until doctrinal fidelity is demonstrated in certain quarters. The Ebenezer Thankoffering is receiving only half-hearted support from those who

---

1. *The Lutheran Witness Reporter*, August 21, 1966, p. 6.
2. *Ibid.*, p. 7.

are convinced that the Synod should put its house in order before attempting further expansion.

For the layman especially such considerations as these are a source of perplexity and heartache. By definition the layman is not theologically trained, and so is generally by-passed in discussions of the issues at stake. Indeed, contrary to the fundamental biblical teaching of the priesthood of all believers, the layman is often given the impression that theology is the business of seminary professors and that the ordinary churchman should simply listen to the voice of those better fitted to speak than himself. Personally, I am irrevocably opposed to such an approach — even though (or perhaps because?) I myself am a seminary professor. I believe that Lutheran Protestantism will survive only as long as Luther's aim in translating the Bible continues: to permit any ploughboy to hear Christ's word. If the Bible does not speak clearly to every layman — if the laity are not capable of distinguishing God's truth from heresy and error — then we had better hie ourselves back to the bosom of the Roman Church without delay, for one pope is far preferable to a legion of seminary professors. To paraphrase an eminently sound aphorism: theology is too important a business to leave to the theologians.

This paper is therefore written neither for UFO pilots, theologians, or even pastors; it is directed to believing Lutheran layman who want to know what the theological issues are that presently trouble the Church, and who are convinced that the Bible is a clear book that reveals God's unambiguous message to all who read it in faith. Our procedure is a straightforward one: to outline the contrasting positions now taken in Synod on major theological issues, so that laity may arrive at their own conclusions in light of Scripture itself. The issues to be discussed are seven in number: the authorship of biblical books; the factuality of the Genesis accounts; the historicity of Jonah; the person and work of Christ; immortality and resurrection; the moral law in the Christian life; and the inspiration of Scripture. In each case, two radically different treatments of the issue will be described; these could roughly be designated "liberal" and "conservative," but in order to avoid unfortunate connotations, we shall simply label them "A" and "B". This will eliminate the prejudicial emphasis introduced into discussions where the liberal position has been called "evangelical confessionalism" and the conservative view "scholastic confessionalism."[3] Indeed, since (for the record) my own position is the conservative one, and I have labeled it "B" and not "A", lay teachers familiar with letter-grading can hardly regard my method as bigoted! After discussing the seven doctrinal issues individually, we shall conclude with an analysis of the larger questions of biblical interpretation that underlie the theological problems now facing our Christian communion.

---

3. These terms were introduced by F. Dean Lueking in his book, *Mission in the Making* (St. Louis: Concordia Publishing House, 1964), and have been extensively employed by Walter R. Bouman in his essay, "The Teaching of Religion: A Theological Analysis," in John S. Damm (ed.), *The Teaching of Religion: Twenty-second Yearbook* (River Forest, Illinois: Lutheran Education Association, 1965).

THE THEOLOGICAL ISSUES

1. The Authorship of Biblical Books

In 1753, during the so-called "Enlightenment" or century of Rationalism, a French physician by the name of Jean Astruc published a book in which he conjectured that the different names for God in Genesis 1 (*Elohim*) and 2 (*Jehovah*) were the result of a rough combination of early sources into a single narrative. Thus commenced the "documentary" or "higher" criticism of biblical books, which endeavored to discover the "real" origins of scriptural material. Portions of the Bible especially affected by this method have been the Pentateuch (the first five books of the Old Testament),[4] Isaiah, the Gospels, and the Pauline epistles. Pentateuchal criticism argues that the alleged Mosaic writings of the Old Testament actually originated from diverse strands (the most common theory being the 4-document, or J-E-P-D hypothesis of Graf, Kuenen, and Wellhausen) and that these documents did not attain their present form until well after Moses' time (generally the final editing is attributed to the post-Exilic period, during the time of Nehemiah). Documentary critics regard the Book of Isaiah as actually the product of two or more authors (I Isaiah, chaps. 1-39; Deutero-Isaiah, chaps. 40 ff.; Trito-Isaiah, chaps. 56 ff.), and consider only the first part of the book to have been written by Isaiah of Jerusalem; in this way it becomes possible to explain the prophecies in the second half of the book as having been written "at the time when these latter were being fulfilled."[5]

Gospel criticism follows the so-called "form-critical method" (*formgeschichtliche Methode*) of Dibelius and Bultmann, and holds that the four Gospels are the end product of a process of oral tradition about Jesus that was shaped and freely altered by the early Church according to its own needs; the form critics are convinced that the New Testament records yield not an "objective" picture of Jesus drawn by the Apostles and Evangelists themselves, but a portrait reflecting the beliefs and varied life-interests of the first and second century Church. As for the Pauline epistles, the higher critics attribute only some of them to the Apostle: the Pastoral Epistles (I and II Timothy and Titus) are almost never regarded as Paul's writings; Ephesians is generally considered non-Pauline; and some critics (e.g., MacGregor and Morton) go so far as to reject all claims to Pauline authorship in the New Testament with the exception of Romans and Galatians.

Considerable variation in emphasis is possible within the authorship positions just described, and it would be unfair to imply that all of these documentary views are uniformly held by Position A in our Church. But Position A does agree in principle with the underlying conviction of the higher critics: that the Christian faith is in no way impugned if one attributes biblical writings to prior authors or later editors, even when the Bible itself makes specific statements as to authorship. Two illustrations of Position A

---

4. The Book of Joshua is often involved also, so the term Hexateuch is common as well.
5. H. H. Rowley, *The Growth of the Old Testament* (London: Hutchinson's University Library, 1950), p. 90.

will suffice — the first in reference to a typical Old Testament authorship issue, the second in regard to a New Testament matter:

> Some [faculty members at Concordia Seminary, St. Louis] believe that the New Testament writers accepted the tradition that Moses was the author and writer of the entire Pentateuch. Others on the faculty contend that this evidence is not decisive. They hold that when Christ or the New Testament writers speak of Moses or the Law of Moses in reference to the Pentateuch, the question of authorship is not the subject under discussion. The speakers or writers are simply employing the language of the audience as convenient references, much as a person today might refer to a piece of English literature saying "As Shakespeare said in Hamlet . . ." without thereby entering into a discussion whether Shakespeare, Marlowe, Bacon, or any other contemporary may have been the actual author. They point out that had Jesus or the New Testament writers introduced the question of authorship they would have confused the point under discussion.[6]

> A careful examination of the Gospel tradition reveals that even within a single work, such as the Gospel of Luke, a variety of theological viewpoints can be found. . . . Not only are we confronted with a variety of theologies in the New Testament, but beneath these theologies we encounter a number of Christian communities whose doctrinal viewpoints were certainly not uniform.[7]

Position B, in contrast, holds that whenever a Bible book makes authorship claims, or whenever one biblical writer speaks about the authorship of another portion of Scripture, or whenever our Lord refers to biblical authors, these statements must be taken as factually true and as establishing the provenance of the writings beyond all doubt. Advocates of Position B point out that any other view of the matter does not take Scripture seriously, casts doubt on the Scripture's own claim to contain God-inspired truth throughout, and (in the case of our Lord) introduces a real problem as to the perfection of His knowledge and therefore as to His very Deity. Position B categorically rejects the argument that Jesus would have limited Himself to fallacious contemporary views on Old Testament authorship in the interests of larger questions, for then Jesus would have been guilty of the basic moral error of letting the end

6. Letter of 27 May 1963 from President Alfred O. Fuerbringer to the Effingham-Altamont Circuits, Central Illinois District of the Lutheran Church-Missouri Synod. The quoted material is taken from Dr. Fuerbringer's reply to the question: "Do all members of the faculty insist that it is a false doctrine to deny that Moses wrote the first five books of the Bible?"

7. Richard J. Gotsch, "New Testament Theology and Church Unity," *American Lutheran*, XLVIII (December, 1965), 14. For a fuller development of the same theme, see Gotsch's essay, "The Study and Interpretation of the New Testament" (mimeographed), presented as a closed seminar paper at the Concordia Teachers College, River Forest, Illinois, on November 1, 1965. Professor Dr. N. S. Tjernagel, author of *Henry VIII and the Lutherans*, has recently prepared a critique of the eight seminar papers delivered in closed sessions at River Forest from September 27 to December 6, 1965; of Gotsch's essay, he writes: "What a pity that the author should so far downgrade the New Testament as to say merely that 'It is the word of men, entirely and completely' and that he should repudiate the historic Lutheran faith in the divine inspiration of Holy Scripture."

justify the means; and, had he so limited himself here, how could we possibly know that He did not limit Himself at some — or even all — other points of His teaching? For Position B, Jesus meant precisely what he said when he preached: "Had ye believed Moses, ye would have believed me: for he wrote of me. But if ye believe not his writings, how shall ye believe my words?" (John 5:46-47).

On scholarly as well as theological grounds, Position B rejects the documentary methods of Position A. Such considerations as the following are especially pertinent: (1) Documentary theories are not based on objective textual evidence; unlike the "lower" or "textual" critics who work with actual manuscript sources, the higher critics limit themselves to literary judgments which, by their very nature, involve a high degree of personal subjectivity. The earliest copies of all our Bible books (including the Dead Sea scroll Isaiah) do not present the assumed fragments or supposed sources alleged by the critics; they display the same holistic texts we have today. The documentalist thus ironically builds his theories without documents, and the resultant hypotheses of one critic often differ wildly from those of another — a clear sign that something very unscientific is going on. Critics cannot agree where one "source" begins and another leaves off, and (to take one example) there are Pentateuchal theorists such as Morgenstern who have divided the Mosaic writings to the point of K and K_1 documents. Position B listens carefully to the results of such a survey as H. F. Hahn's:

> This review of activity in the field of Old Testament criticism during the last quarter century has revealed a chaos of conflicting trends, ending in contradictory results, which create an impression of ineffectiveness in this type of research. The conclusion seems to be unavoidable that the higher criticism has long since passed the age of constructive achievement.[8]

(2) The use of parallel critical methods in other academic fields has proven so unfruitful that these techniques have been largely discredited outside of biblical scholarship. Today it is held that (as one of my Cornell classics professors put it), "If the *Iliad* and *Odyssey* were not written by Homer, they were written by someone of the same name about the same time!" H. J. Rose waxes eloquent on the Homeric authorship issue: "The chief weapon of the separatists has always been literary criticism, and of this it is not too much to say that such niggling word-baiting, such microscopic hunting of minute inconsistencies and flaws in logic, has hardly been seen, outside of the Homeric field, since Rymar and John Dennis died."[9] As to the continued presence of "such niggling word-baiting" in biblical criticism, Yamauchi of Rutgers has stated at the close of a recent lecture which has been expanded into an exceedingly important monograph:[10] "If we applied the criterion of 'Divine

---

8. Herbert F. Hahn, *The Old Testament in Modern Research* (rev. ed.; Philadelphia: Fortress Press, 1966), p. 41.

9. H. J. Rose, *Handbook of Great Literature from Homer to the Age of Lucian* (London: Methuen, 1934), pp. 42-43.

10. Edwin Yamauchi, *Composition and Corroboration in Classical and Biblical Studies* ("International Library of Philosophy and Theology. Biblical and Theological Studies"; Philadelphia: Presbyterian and Reformed Publishing Company, 1966); the lecture which formed the basis of this monograph was

Names' [the *Elohim* vs. *Jehovah* argument on Genesis 1 and 2] to Ugaritic, Egyptian, or Arabic texts, we would see that the principle was not valid. I could multiply examples for all the other criteria of the documentary hypothesis."

(3) The rationalism involved in post-dating Isaiah's prophecies so as to make them follow the events predicted is foreign to all legitimate scholarship. Such presumptive judgments of what God can or cannot do is not incidental to higher criticism and to its views of biblical authorship, as one can see from the use of the same method in post-dating Gospel material: it is widely held that Matthew, Mark, and Luke must have been written or edited after the destruction of Jerusalem in A.D. 70, for otherwise Jesus' "predictions" of the fall of the city (Matt. 24; Mark 13; Luke 21) would be inexplicable! And sheer rationalism is likewise the basis of the view that the early Church painted a variegated New Testament picture of Jesus in accord with the "variety of theological viewpoints" reflected in its own diverse faith-experience; in point of fact, the New Testament writers claim primary source contact with Jesus and precise accuracy and consistency in describing what He objectively said and did (Luke 1:1-4). The Gospel writers tell us that it was *Jesus* who determined *their* message — in diametric contrast to the view so often heard today that the early Church was responsible for freely shaping our picture of Jesus.

(4) Position B notes the bizarre results when the direct affirmations of Pauline authorship in the New Testament are questioned. Macgregor and Morton employed "the literary style" of Romans and Galatians as a computer criterion for testing the authorship of the other New Testament letters claiming to be Pauline, and concluded that none of the latter were actually written by Paul. Subsequently, Macgregor and Morton's book on the subject was itself subjected to computer analysis using parallel criteria, and it was likewise "proven" that their work was actually the product of multiple authorship![11]

2. The Factuality of the Genesis Accounts

Position A, in regarding the Pentateuch as a developmental product of Near Eastern literary sources, quite naturally takes a negative or neutral view

---

read at the 20th Annual Convention of the American Scientific Affiliation on August 24, 1965. For a lucid overview of the scholarly fallacies in the documentary method, see Gleason L. Archer, Jr., °A *Survey of Old Testament Introduction* (Chicago: Moody Press, 1964), pp. 73-165 (especially pp. 96-100). HERE AND ELSEWHERE IN THE NOTES, ASTERISKS IDENTIFY MATERIALS WHICH LAYMEN WILL FIND TO BE OF PARTICULAR VALUE FOR FURTHER STUDY.

11. See *Christianity Today*, IX (February 26, 1965), 588; and cf. Cameron Dinwoodie, "Notes on the Use of Computing Machines in New Testament Literary Research, *New College Bulletin* [University of Edinburgh, Scotland], ½ (1964), 18-25. For an excellent general overview of the biblical authorship position historically maintained in the Missouri Synod, see the articles on "Higher Criticism" by Walter R. Roehrs, and "Isagogics" by William F. Arndt, in the *Lutheran Cyclopedia*, ed. Erwin L. Lueker (St. Louis: Concordia Publishing House, 1954), *in loco*. Both Roehrs and Arndt advocate the position we have designated "B."

as to the historicity of the early narratives in the Book of Genesis. Creation, Fall, and Flood accounts can be found in other Near Eastern literatures, and in certain respects these parallel the biblical material; if the Pentateuch was formed by literary accretion as were nonbiblical Near Eastern mythological and religious writings, then why should we place a higher historical value on the former than on the latter?

In the case of Genesis 1 and 2, advocates of Position A would persuade us to consider historical only those aspects of the text that do not parallel Near Eastern myth and that do not clearly violate the assured results of modern evolutionary investigations.[12] When one approaches the biblical Creation stories in this way, he arrives at a single and simple teaching: that God created the world and cares for each of his creatures. Indeed, the absolutely disharmonious character of the Genesis 1 and 2 narratives leads to this very conclusion:

> How can both of these accounts be literally true? Is it plausible that God was pleased to give us these mutually exclusive accounts, to show us that we cannot probe behind the exact "how" of man's creation, that according to God's will this is supposed to remain a mystery? . . .

> What then is the result of this investigation? Is it possible to conclude from the basic differences between Genesis 1 and Genesis 2 that it was not God's intention to provide us with details concerning the "how" of creation or the mystery of man's origin? It may well be that He simply wanted us to accept the truth *that* He fashioned the universe and *that* He created man. He also wanted us to realize that creation was not an end in itself, rather it was to demonstrate *how much God cared* for the people He had made.[13]

The account of the Fall of man in Genesis 3 is treated similarly by Position A. Parallels between the biblical story of the Fall and extrabiblical Near Eastern mythology (for example, "the snake symbolism of the local Canaanite fertility cultus"[14]) are employed as sufficient ground for holding

12. A defense of the amoeba-to-man evolutionary view held by Position A was given at Valparaiso University on October 21-22, 1965 by Professors Kreckeler and Bloom of the University (authors of a biology text advocating a thorough-going evolutionary orientation) and by Professor Walter R. Bouman of River Forest. The historic Missouri Synod stand on the question was presented by Professors Paul Zimmerman, John Klotz, and Wilbert H. Rusch, Sr. An expanded version of Professor Rusch's presentation was subsequently published under the title, °"Analysis of So-called Evidences of Evolution," in the *Creation Research Society* 1966 *Annual*, III (May, 1966), 4-15, and also in °*Essays from the Creationist Viewpoint* (1966), to which Zimmerman and Klotz also contribute (address for obtaining this latter publication: 435 Pine Brae, Ann Arbor, Michigan).

13. Alfred von Rohr Sauer, "The Interpretation of Genesis One and Two" (mimeographed paper dated October 8, 1965 and employed in class instruction at Concordia Seminary, St. Louis), pp. 3-4 (italics Sauer's). This same general approach to Genesis 1-2 is advocated by Martin Scharlemann in a recent "Gnomon" column in *The Lutheran Scholar* (April, 1966, pp. 24-25), and by Walter Wegner in his article, "Creation and Salvation: A Study of Genesis 1 and 2," *Concordia Theological Monthly*, XXXVII (September, 1966), 520-42.

14. Norman C. Habel, *The Form and Meaning of the Fall Narrative: A Detailed Analysis of Genesis 3* (St. Louis: Concordia Seminary Print Shop, 1965), p. 35.

that the Genesis 3 account has the literary form of "a 'symbolic' narrative or religious story which was culturally relevant and legitimate for the Israelite congregation at the time of the author. In other words, it is not necessary to demand that from our perspective of the nature of history every action or speech corresponds precisely to the specific stages or incidents (*ipsissima acta*) in the first revolt or the very words (*ipsissima verba*) involved on that occasion."[15] What, then, is the resultant teaching of Genesis 3 after the symbolism is identified? Simply the fact of man's universal sinfulness, extending back in time to the beginnings of the race.

Position A handles the Genesis narrative of the Flood analogously: the existence of stories of a world-wide deluge in Near Eastern mythologies allow us to regard the Noah account as a literary device (possibly based on an impressive local flood) employed to teach a theological lesson. What lesson? The fundamental biblical theme of Law and Gospel: that God brings radical judgment to bear on man's sinfulness, but also that He saves from destruction all who (like Noah) believe His promises.

Whereas Position A is satisfied to derive general theological lessons from Genesis, Position B insists on the historicity of the events which give rise to the lessons. Thus advocates of Position B hold that Genesis 1-2 (while not of course employing the constantly changing terminology and explanatory constructs of science) does provide a factually accurate description of God's creative activity; Genesis 3, a true historical account of how our first parents fell into sin; and Genesis 6-8, a veracious narrative of a deluge which once inundated the whole earth. On scholarly grounds alone, Position B is convinced that Position A lacks sufficient support: the documentary fragmentation of Genesis is highly subjective (as we noted in the last section); the existence of parallels between extra-biblical Near Eastern mythology and the Genesis accounts in no way proves that the latter are also mythological (one can equally well argue that the Near Eastern myths are pale approximations to and reflections of the historical narratives in Scripture!); evolutionary theory still remains exactly that — a theory[16] — and one plays an exceedingly dangerous

---

15. *Ibid.*, p. 33. See the appendix to the present essay for additional discussion of Professor Habel's paper, especially with reference to the principles of biblical interpretation he employs.

16. Chemist Anthony Standen's words are worth pondering: "By far the most sweeping, and by far the best, of the great generalizations of biology is the Theory of Evolution, if it can be called a theory that has by no means been tested by experiment. . . . "The missing link" . . . is a most misleading phrase, because it suggests that only one link is missing. It would be more accurate to say that the greater part of the entire chain is missing, so much that it is not entirely certain whether there is a chain at all. With every new discovery of a fossil man or subman, the genealogical tree gets more complicated until it begins to resemble chain mail, with a great many links still missing. Any prudent, unprejudiced layman would conclude, 'It may be that the biological origin of man will eventually become as clear as that of the horse, or the elephant, or it may be that it will not. Let us wait and see.' Biologists are not so cautious. They have an unshakeable faith in What Science Is Going To Do Some Day" (*Science Is a Sacred Cow* [New York: Dutton, 1950], pp.

game to regard a theory as so certain that it is allowed to become a determining element in interpreting and evaluating scriptural material; geologic evidence of a world-wide catastrophe in ancient times is too powerful to permit a cavalier attitude toward the Genesis Flood as a historical reality.[17]

Position B is not concerned with the factuality of the Genesis narratives simply for academic reasons, however. Adherents of this view are convinced that the "symbolical" approach of Position A is theologically destructive not only to Genesis but to scriptural understanding in general. To allow the factuality of biblical material to be judged by extra-biblical considerations (such as ancient mythologies and modern scientific speculations) is in effect to say that Scripture does not speak a clear message in its own right. Thus God's special revelation through inspired writers disappears: the Bible becomes a chameleonic reflection of its sinful human environment instead of God's absolute word of truth to man's situation. Moreover, if we hold that extra-biblical considerations are required to tell us what is truly factual in Scripture, do we not end up believing as factually true only the biblical affirmations that have passed the extra-biblical test or that are incapable of being so tested? The factuality of God's word waits on the investigation and testing of it by external, non-revelational considerations! One thus reduces "the whole counsel of God" to generalizations such as "God created the world" and "God works through Law and Gospel" (which, hopefully, are too general to be touched by extra-biblical judgments!). The result is a constriction of the factual content of the Bible to a limited number of theological aphorisms — and even these float free of the historical grounding that they require. Specifically: Why do we consider Genesis factual when it says *that* God created the world if we regard it as speaking only in symbolic terms as to *how* He made the world? Why do we believe that Genesis 3 speaks factual truth as to the Fall of all men into sin if we come to the conclusion that the story itself is "symbolical"? Why do we hold with the Genesis writer to God's preserving grace toward His creatures if we believe that He did not factually save Noah and family from the universal deluge and put the rainbow in the sky as an everlasting testimony? If the "details" of Scripture (whatever they are!) can be regarded as "symbolic," why can't the supposed "theological message" associated with them be non-factual also? But such a view of Scripture, Position B insists, is totally misinformed: Scripture is not to be judged from the outside; *it* does the judging (as the *Formula of Concord,* para. 1, specifically states); and the Bible is true not merely in the general theological principles it elucidates, but in every word and event it contains. As Jesus said to the Tempter: Man lives by "every word that proceedeth out of the mouth of God."

100, 106-107). See also John W. Klotz, *"The Philosophy of Science in Relation to Concepts of Creation Vs. the Evolution Theory," *Creation Research Society Quarterly,* III (July, 1966), 3-12.

17. Cf. Alfred M. Rehwinkel, *The Flood* (St. Louis: Concordia Publishing House, 1951); John C. Whitcomb and Henry M. Morris, *"The Genesis Flood* (Philadelphia: Presbyterian and Reformed Publishing Company, 1961); and the recent book by geographer Donald W. Patten, *The Biblical Flood and the Ice Epoch* (Seattle: Pacific Meridian, 1966).

3. The Historicity of Jonah

Previous sections of this essay have set the stage for the present discussion: Readers will be able easily and accurately to predict the opposing views of Positions A and B in regard to Jonah! Position A, consistent with its attitude toward Genesis, regards the historicity of Jonah as very questionable, but, in any case, as a matter of little importance; after all, the "didactic narrative" clearly conveys the basic message of Law and Gospel: God's judgment on those (such as Jonah) who flee from His word and His saving grace to those (such as the Ninevites) who repent and acknowledge Him.[18]

Position B again opts for the facticity of the biblical narrative, and considers the question of Jonah's historicity to be of great importance. As to evidential considerations, advocates of Position B cite such telling points as these:

> Any assessment of the historical character of the book of Jonah must take into consideration the following facts. First, Jonah himself was without doubt an historical figure, a prophet of Jehovah in Israel (II Kings 14:25). Secondly, the book is in the form of straightforward historical narrative, and there is no positive indication in the book that it is to be interpreted in any other way. Thirdly, if the book is parable or allegory, it is unique and without analogy among the books of the Old Testament. Fourthly, neither Jews nor Christians have ever, until recently, regarded Jonah as anything else but a record of actual fact, whatever interpretations they have placed on its message. Finally, our Lord Jesus Christ clearly believed that the repentance of the men of Nineveh was a real occurrence, and it is most natural to take His allusion to Jonah's 'three days and three nights in the whale's belly' (Mat. 12:40, 41) in the same way. In addition it may be urged that the whole force of Jehovah's self-vindication to Jonah demands an actual mission to a heathen city with an actual repentance and 'sparing' of it. It is not easy to believe that the challenge, 'Should not I spare Nineveh?' was presented to the people of Israel through the inspired writer as a purely hypothetical consideration.[19]

Position B sees the Jonah issue as not just a question of the truth of a "whale story"; this story is part of the totality of Holy Writ and one's attitude toward it (in regard to its miraculous content, for example) will have a bearing on one's evaluation of other portions of the Bible. In particular, the view one takes of Jonah will condition one's attitude toward the teachings of Christ Himself:

> Some of the "minor" problems confronting the church are not so minor as they appear at first glance. Many people are concerned about matters like the authorship of the Pentateuch, Isaiah, and Psalm 110 or the historicity of Jonah, not because of the intrinsic importance of these

---

18. Position A on Jonah has been given detailed expression by Alfred von Rohr Sauer in a mimeographed essay on the subject. This essay has received a careful tape-recorded critique by the Old Testament specialist Gleason L. Archer, Jr. (cf. note 10 above).

19. D. W. B. Robinson, in *The New Bible Commentary*, ed. F. Davidson (Grand Rapids, Michigan: Eerdmans, 1953), p. 714.

questions but because they feel that some current answers to these questions are contrary to what they understand Christ and the New Testament to be saying. They are thus concerned for the *sola Scriptura* principle: Do these "new" interpretations suggest that the Bible is unreliable? If the Bible is unreliable in these points, may I trust it when it tells me about my Savior? These people are also concerned about the *solus Christus* principle: Do these "new" interpretations imply that Christ was wrong? And if Christ was wrong, then He was not omniscient; and if He was not omniscient, then He was not God; and if He wasn't God, how could He be my Savior? If I cannot trust Christ's words on such matters, can I trust them on *any* matter?[20]

4. The Person and Work of Christ

Current theological discussion in our Church is by no means restricted to Old Testament problems. Our Lord's parallel between Jonah's experience and His own forthcoming death and resurrection (Matt. 12:39-40) shows how intimately connected the two Testaments are. We have already seen that corresponding to the documentary approach to Genesis is a form-critical treatment of New Testament texts. Thus it will not come as a surprise that Positions A and B take different approaches even on so central a New Testament issue as the interpretation of Christ's person and work.

The following represents the general orientation of Position A:

> Jesus' unique Sonship is not manifest in terms of perfect knowledge, unique powers, or other trappings of pagan "divinity." He is a man locked in a particular history and culture. He derives his images, parables, similes from his cultural and geographical setting. He is capable of *ad hominem* argumentation. He lives, speaks and thinks as a first-century Palestinian Jew. But his obedience to the Father is unbroken.[21]

Just as Position A uses the Near Eastern environment to establish the "symbolical" meaning of Old Testament persons and events, so here Jesus Himself is seen as "a man locked in a particular history and culture." The Old Testament was regarded primarily as a species of Near Eastern literature, and the criteria of the latter were applied to the former; here Jesus is viewed principally as "a first-century Palestinian Jew" and the characteristics of the latter become the standard for the former. Palestinian Jews do not have perfect knowledge or unique powers, so one ought not to attribute these to Jesus; indeed, miracle-working and omniscient judgments are characteristic of "pagan divinity," not

---

20. Ralph A. Bohlmann, °"Principles of Biblical Interpretation in the Lutheran Confessions," in *Aspects of Biblical Hermeneutics* ("Concordia Theological Monthly. Occasional Papers," No. 1; St. Louis, 1966), p. 46, n. 51.

21. Walter R. Bouman, "Jesus As the Christ" (mimeographed essay presented as a closed seminar paper at the Concordia Teachers College, River Forest, Illinois, on November 15, 1965). The author has given me general permission to quote his essay. In "An Open Letter to the Proviso Teachers Conference" (June 29, 1966) Professor Bouman attempted to clarify the meaning of his statement; his explanations have not, in my judgment, softened the force of the original assertion (cf. below, the appendix to the present volume ["A Critic Criticized"]).

of the Jewish Messiah. Jesus' "unique Sonship" is seen in His unbroken obedience to God, i.e., in His perfect accord with the Law and His perfect proclamation, in word and deed, of the Gospel.

Position B is even less willing to allow a Law-Gospel reductionism of Jesus than it was to permit a symbolical interpretation of Old Testament content. For Position B, every one of the miracles attributed to Christ in the New Testament really happened, and Jesus' unique powers of thought and action as recorded by the Evangelists were anything but pagan attributes. Position B emphasizes the manifest Deity of Christ in Scripture, and refuses to subject God Incarnate to limitations imposed by the cultural environment.[22] Advocates of Position B are quick to point out, in fact, that a basically humanistic, environmentally-conditioned Jesus is the natural outcome of an approach to the whole of Scripture which de-emphasizes its uniqueness and attempts to understand it by analogy with the non-revelatory, the finite, and the sinful.[23]

If it is objected that Position B does not take proper cognizance of the self-limitation of God to the human sphere — the limitation (*kenosis*) spoken of in Philippians 2:6-8 — Position B replies that Philippians 2 is badly misconstrued when it is used to justify an anthropocentric picture of Christ:

> Jesus Himself gives us an indication of what the explanation is when He says: "I have power to lay My life down, and I have power to take it again" (John 10:18). Hereby Jesus actually says: "I have the power to refrain from using My power — and to die. I also have the power to use My power — and to live." He does *not* say: "I relinquish My power; I cease to have the power." The same thing applies to His omniscience: The Son knows the Father (Matt. 11:27), and in the person of the Son "are hidden all the treasures of wisdom and knowledge" (Col. 2:3). Still He knows not the day nor the hour of His return to judgment (Mark 13:32). According to His eternal deity He knows everything — according to His human nature He does not know everything. He has *not* said of Himself: "I relinquish My omniscience; I cease to be omniscient." But it is the case that in His divine and human existence He does not speak anything of Himself but only what the Father directs Him to speak (John 12:49) and what He hears from the Father (John 8:26). Consequently when the Father does not initiate the human nature of the Son in regard to the time of His return, then this knowledge lies dormant in the eternal deity of the Son during the time of His earthly life. . . .

---

22. See John Warwick Montgomery, °*History & Christianity* (HIS Magazine Reprints, 4605 Sherwood, Downers Grove, Illinois), and °*The Shape of the Past* (Ann Arbor, Michigan: Edwards Brothers, 1963), especially pp. 138-45, 181-82.
23. A further ramification of Position A, which I cannot discuss here for want of space, is its universalistic focus; at a recent Institute on the Church in Mission held at Concordia Seminary, St. Louis, Professor John H. Elliott described the Church's task not as that of bringing Christ to people, since God's redeeming and judging presence is already among men everywhere today, but rather as that of proclaiming the presence of Christ in the social milieu of our time (cf. *The Lutheran Witness Reporter*, September 4, 1966, pp. 1-2).

In other words: He laid aside His *function* as ruler and judge during His life on earth — but none of His divine *attributes* or *consciousness*.[24]

Position B insists on retaining the full stress of Scripture itself on Christ's divine self-consciousness and miraculous attributes, especially in a day when the gravitational pull toward humanistic theologies is becoming continually stronger.[25]

5. Immortality and Resurrection

A special problem which has divided Positions A and B in our Church is the nature of man's state after death. Position A contends that the idea of a disembodied soul existing after the dissolution of the body is essentially a pagan Greek concept, and that the Christian Church unfortunately incorporated the notion into its teaching early in its history and allowed it to obscure the truly Hebrew-Christian position, viz., the resurrection of the total person at the Last Day.

> We cannot properly speak of death as a separation of body and soul. Nor can we speak of the "soul" going anywhere. A relationship cannot be separated from me. A relationship cannot go anywhere. . . .
>
> Heaven and Hell are not "places" in the perspective from which we must now view reality. They are descriptive of our relationship with God. Hell is the final verdict of God's wrath upon my unfaith and rebellion.[26]

Especially in light of the modern scientific rejection of a soul-body dualism (the separability of personality and body), Position A calls on the Church to revise its understanding of life after death.[27]

Adherents of Position B agree that Scripture lays powerful stress on the resurrection of the body at the end of the age (I Cor. 15), but they insist no less strongly that immortality is a clear biblical teaching ("Jesus said unto him [one of the crucified thieves], Verily I say unto thee, Today shalt thou

---

24. Olav Valen-Sendstad, °*The Word That Can Never Die,* trans. Madson and Strand (St. Louis: Concordia Publishing House, 1966), pp. 43, 47 (Valen-Sendstad's italics). This clear and penetrating book is highly recommended to laymen who wish to examine current theological views of Christ and of Scripture in the light of the Bible's own teachings; chaps. 2 and 3 are especially pertinent in this regard.

25. Cf. John Warwick Montgomery, °*The 'Is God Dead?' Controversy* (Grand Rapids, Michigan: Zondervan Publishing House, 1966). The Rutz Foundation lecture on which this book is based will appear shortly in a Random House anthology on the death-of-God movement.

26. Walter R. Bouman, "The Last Things" (mimeographed essay presented as a closed seminar paper at the Concordia Teachers College, River Forest, Illinois, on December 6, 1965). General permission to quote the essay has been given to me by the author.

27. The universalistic tendency referred to in note 23 has a bearing on Position A's view of eternal life: belief in immortality requires an immediate separation of the saved and the damned after death and a continuation of conscious existence for both; but if cessation of personal existence precedes the final resurrection, and Christ alone gives life, then perhaps the resurrection will be solely a resurrection to life in the Father's presence.

be with me in paradise" — Luke 23:43; "We are confident, and willing rather to be absent from the body, and to be present with the Lord" — II Cor. 5:8; etc.). Position B grants that the biblical view of immortality differs greatly from the classical Greek idea (the notion that man's immortality is a sign of his inherent worthiness and god-likeness), but one does not properly make the distinction between pagan and biblical teaching by rejecting a valid aspect of the biblical message simply because it has something in common with non-Christian ideas. Position B refuses to make an invidious comparison by setting immortality and resurrection against each other. The truly biblical view of immortality (that all men face God's judgment after death — Heb. 9:27 — and immediately enter heaven or hell — Luke 16:19-31) is to be joined with the equally scriptural view of the general resurrection at the end of time. We may not be able to understand how precisely these two doctrines co-ordinate with each other, but if they are both taught in Scripture, they must both be accepted and preached.[28] Moreover, Position B notes, recent work in the field of parapsychology does much to remove the objection of scientistic behaviorism that human personality cannot function apart from a living body.[29]

6. The Moral Law in the Christian Life

The Reformers, both Lutheran and Calvinist, distinguished three uses or functions of the moral Law: the "political" (as a restraint for the wicked — to keep sinners from destroying themselves), the "theological" (as a "school-master to bring us to Christ" — Gal. 3:24), and the "didactic" (as a guide for the Christian believer). Position A argues, on the basis of another Reformation principle ("the Law always accuses"), that the Third or Didactic Use of the Law is really indistinguishable from the other two uses, and should not be taught as a separate function.[30] The claim is made that to urge a distinct and positive use of the Law for Christians is to reduce the Christian life to a static, biblicistic legalism; in actuality, the Holy Spirit and *Agape*-love (self-giving love) provide the only positive guidance the Christian needs to live a God-honoring life. The Christian, after all, is still a sinner, so the Law continues to drive him to Christ, and Christ's loving Spirit then dynamically directs his living.

Position B, however, insists on holding to a distinct Third Use of the Law for believers — and appeals to the last of the Lutheran confessional writings, *The Formula of Concord,* which devotes an entire article (VI) to setting it forth. For adherents of Position B, Lutherans have only two legitimate choices in the matter: either they must accept the confessional teaching on the Third

---

28. Cf. *The Abiding Word,* ed. Theodore Laetsch, Vol. I (St. Louis: Concordia Publishing House, 1953), chap. 26 ("The Doctrine of the Last Things"), pp. 544-60, and chap. 27 ("Eternal Life"), pp. 561-82.
29. Cf. Gardner Murphy, *Challenge of Psychical Research: A Primer of Parapsychology* ("World Perspectives"; New York: Harper, 1961); and F. W. H. Myers, *Human Personality and Its Survival of Bodily Death,* ed. Susy Smith (New Hyde Park, New York: University Books, 1961).
30. Advocates of Position A generally rely for their view on Werner Elert's *The Christian Ethos,* trans. Carl J. Schindler (Philadelphia: Muhlenberg Press, 1957), pp. 294-303.

Use of the Law, or they must find another Church commitment which does not require subscription to this article of faith. But aside from its plea for confessional integrity, Position B maintains that the issue of the Law's Third Use is of paramount significance for the Church's entire ethical stance. True, the Law does "always accuse," for neither Christian nor non-Christian ever fulfills God's Law perfectly in this life. But the Christian has been made a "new creature" in Christ (II Cor. 5:17), and to hold that his relationship to God's Law has undergone no change is to deny any real sanctification.[31] The believer does what no unbeliever can: he *loves* God's Law (Ps. 119; 1; 19) and desires to learn more and more of God's will for his life through reading Holy Scripture. To de-emphasize the Third Use of the Law in favor of *Agape*-love and the Spirit's inner guidance is to drive the Christian within himself instead of to the resources of God's scriptural revelation (and the scriptural Word, after all, is the only touchstone of the Spirit: apart from Scripture one has no sure way of testing the inner promptings that can as well be the voice of self as the voice of God!).[32] Ours is a day of "new morality" and "situation ethics," and the tendency is everywhere present to substitute vague existential and personal morality for the unchanging standards of God's scriptural Law.[33] Position B is convinced that the Third Use of the Law — the "law of Christ" (Gal. 6:2) — must be retained if our Church is to lead both its children and its adults to holy living and to the true joy that comes only when our lives are brought into accord with Divine precept and example.

7. The Inspiration of Scripture

Every one of the six theological issues we have been discussing has driven us one way or another to the doctrine of Holy Scripture. It could not be otherwise, for, as the Reformers consistently declared, Scripture is the "formal principle" of all theology, and one's attitude toward it conditions one's stance on all substantive questions of belief. Thus we not unnaturally discover a fundamental cleavage in viewpoint between Positions A and B on the nature of biblical inspiration.

Position A uses the term "inspiration" in several ways, and it is important to spell these out so that ambiguity will be avoided. Here are the most

---

31. See my article, "The Law's Third Use: Sanctification," *Christianity Today*, VII (April 26, 1963), 722-24 (reprinted in the present volume as Essay V).
32. For a classic Lutheran treatment of the place of the Law in the Christian life, see Adolf Köberle, °*The Quest for Holiness*, trans. John C. Mattes (Minneapolis: Augsburg Publishing House, 1938). Cf. also Ernest F. Kevan, °*Keep His Commandments* (London: Tyndale Press, 1964).
33. The better-known advocates of the "new morality" are Bishop John A. T. *Robinson* (*Christian Morals Today* [London: SCM Press, 1964]), Joseph Fletcher (*Situation Ethics* [Philadelphia: Westminster Press, 1966]), and Bishop James Pike. I have analyzed and criticized the latter's views in °*The Sunday School Times*, CVIII, No. 18 (April 30, 1966), 311-12, 317; and No. 19 (May 7, 1966), 327-38, 343. Excellent general critiques of the "new morality" are: Arnold Lunn and Garth Lean, °*The New Morality* (London: Blandford Press, 1964) and *The Cult of Softness* (London: Blandford Press, 1965); and A. G. Bamford, *et al.*, *Second Thoughts on the New Morality* (Bristol, England: Evangelical Christian Literature, 1965).

common: "Holy Scripture is inspired, not in conveying inerrant propositions about God and the world, but in acting as a vehicle for true Christian experience"; "Holy Scripture is inspired, not in its scientific or historical statements, but in the theological truths it conveys"; "Holy Scripture is inspired, not as a conveyer of infallible information, but because and insofar as it testifies to the person of our Lord and Savior Jesus Christ"; "Holy Scripture is inspired in an inerrant way — so that it always fulfils God's purpose of proclaiming Law and Gospel — not in the static sense of always conforming to objective scientific or historical fact."[34] Here is a typical composite statement of Position A:

> Inspiration in this view refers to the entire activity of the Spirit by which he dwells in the Church and attends the proclamation of the Word. In the older theory, inspiration is too static and finally too anemic. It seems to assume that the Spirit can convince of the truth only through a book without errors. The Spirit has a much more powerful means than this at his disposal, namely the "two-edged sword of the Word" through which he creates faith. The question, therefore, of whether or not there may be human errors of one sort or another in scripture is of no particular importance. Just as the pastor on Sunday morning may make errors of one sort or another in preaching and still preach the Word so also with scripture. . . .
>
> Often the question is asked of this method, "If you admit that there are errors in the little things how do you know that they didn't make errors in the big things as well, i.e., once you start admitting errors, where do you stop?" To this the only answer is . . . the faith born out of the law-gospel experience.[35]

It will be observed that Position A is especially concerned to distinguish the inspiration of Scripture from belief in its factual inerrancy. In recent years attempts have been made to show that biblical passages traditionally held to affirm the inerrancy of the Word do not in fact make such claims;[36] and advice has been given to fellow Lutherans to "refrain from using the term 'inerrancy'" since "where the stress is on a religious purpose, his [the biblical writer's] concern with the precise and literal accuracy of concomitant historical or scientific detail may recede into the background," and also since we should apply to Scripture the principle of "the economy of miracles" (i.e., the actual occurrence of the miraculous ought to be held to a minimum there).[37] Others have listed what they consider to be unarguable cases of factual error in Scripture — cases that supposedly demonstrate that the assertion "the Bible is inerrant, 'that is, contains no error,' simply cannot be

---

34. I discuss in considerable detail (with examples) these several definitions of biblical inspiration in my article, "Inspiration and Inerrancy: A New Departure," *Evangelical Theological Society Bulletin*, VIII (Spring, 1965), 45-75 (reprinted in the present volume as Essay I).

35. Gerhard Forde, "Law and Gospel As the Methodological Principle of Theology," in *Theological Perspectives: A Discussion of Contemporary Issues in Lutheran Theology* (Decorah, Iowa: Luther College Press [1962]), p. 65.

36. E.g., Richard Jungkuntz, "An Approach to the Exegesis of John 10:34-36," *Concordia Theological Monthly*, XXXV (October, 1964), 556-65.

37. Arthur Carl Piepkorn, "What Does 'Inerrancy' Mean?" *Concordia Theological Monthly*, XXXVI (September, 1965), 577-93.

supported by the biblical evidence itself.[38] That this is not an isolated judgment can be seen from the following answer to a query on the subject:

> According to the *Oxford English Dictionary* the word "error" may have, among others, the following meanings: (a) a departure from moral rectitude; (b) something incorrectly done . . . through inadvertance, (c) the difference between an approximate result and the true determination.
>
> No one here [on the faculty of Concordia Seminary, St. Louis] holds that the Bible contains error in the sense of (a). While we caution against every use of the word "error" in the context of speaking about the Sacred Scriptures without very careful explanation of the sense in which it is used, we must allow that Matt. 1:8, for example, would come under definition (b) . . . . Many of the biblical numbers would fall under definition (c).[39]

Position B, in contrast, holds unqualifiedly that biblical inspiration implicates inerrancy, and that Holy Scripture, as the God-breathed product of the Divine Spirit of Truth (II Tim. 3:16) is free from factual error and contradiction in whatever it teaches or touches.[40]

> What is really the case with the so-called mistakes in the material reported in Scripture? It is remarkable that the nature of these so-called mistakes generally varies to correspond to the hearts and eyes that are contemplating them. In the course of the years I have made repeated attempts to probe theological claims that this or that is a "mistake," or in contradiction with something else in Scripture. In doing so, I have invariably experienced the following: When, in trying to understand the "contradictions" of which the theologians spoke, I applied what I choose to call a synthetic-integrative method in a *both-and* assumption, i.e., that both parts are correct, I discovered that surprisingly simple connections arose consistently to establish harmony. However, when I proceeded along the lines of what I choose to call an atomistic or analytic-disjunctive method, sharpening the differences to an *either-or* edge, i.e., until contradictions appeared, then matters consistently became highly complicated and incomprehensible. The synthetic-integrative method removes most of the difficulties from the Scriptures. I won't go so far as to say that all difficulties are removed from Scripture. But the difficulties that remain become more deeply entrenched when viewed with a skepticism which is analogous to viewing the words and activities of Jesus with skepticism.[41]

---

38. Robert Scharlemann, Letter to the Editor, *The Lutheran Scholar*, April, 1963. In my "Inspiration and Inerrancy" article (see above, note 34) I have treated the alleged biblical errors and contradictions he cites.
39. Letter of 27 May 1963 from President Alfred O. Fuerbringer to the Effingham-Altamont Circuits, Central Illinois District of the Lutheran Church-Missouri Synod. Dr. Fuerbringer replies to the question: "Do all members of the St. Louis faculty believe that the Bible is without errors of fact?"
40. Cf. Robert Preus, *"Notes on the Inerrancy of Scripture," *Evangelical Theological Society Bulletin*, VIII (Autumn, 1965), 127-38; and the same author's paper, *"The Doctrine of Revelation in Contemporary Theology," *Evangelical Theological Society Bulletin*, IX (Summer, 1966), 111-23.
41. Valen-Sendstad, *The Word That Can Never Die* (Cited above in note 24), pp. 50-51.

Advocates of Position B readily grant that "the Bible is not a textbook of science or history," but they note that all knowledge — theological, historical, and scientific — forms one whole, and that if one can only separate the provinces of truth arbitrarily outside of Scripture, how much less can one do in a historical revelation which unites earth and heaven at every point and comes to focus on the Incarnation: God entering history and becoming part of it! Thus Position B is unwilling to regard problems such as Matthew 1:8 as "errors" in any sense; here is how one learned advocate of this position handled the difficulty:

> Now, it must be said, in the first place, that Matthew cannot have been ignorant of the names of the kings whom he does not mention, because every page of his Gospel evinces a thorough acquaintance with the Old Testament. In the second place, we must say that it would be absurd to suppose that Matthew tried to deceive his readers. His book was intended for people who knew the Old Testament, and a juggling, on his part, of the facts with which we are concerned would immediately have been detected. The names of the kings in question were well known, and Matthew cannot have made this omission in the hope that it would remain unnoticed. But what could have induced him to draw up a list of this kind? A simple explanation is that he used current genealogical tables, in which, probably for reasons of symmetry, certain names had been dropped. He wished to present proof that Jesus was the Messiah, who, according to prophecy, was to be a descendant both of Abraham and of David. To do this, he appeals to the genealogical tables of the Jews themselves and shows that their own official documents prove Joseph, the legal father of Jesus, to have been a son of Abraham and a son of David. If viewed thus, we shall no longer find the omission of these names inexplicable or embarrassing.[42]

Position B is convinced that all alleged errors or supposed contradictions can be treated in comparable God-honoring ways, so as not to impugn the veracity of the Scripture or of its Divine Author. In this connection, the stand of Luther himself is recalled, who maintained that "the Scriptures have never erred" (W.A., XV, 1481) and that "it is impossible that Scripture should contradict itself; it only appears so to senseless and obstinate hypocrites" (W.A., IX, 356); and the united testimony of the classical Lutheran dogmaticians is marshalled as well:

> The canonical Holy Scriptures in the original text are the infallible truth and free from every error, or, in other words, in the canonical Holy Scriptures there is found no lie, no falsity, no error, whether in the things or in the words; but all things, and each single one, that are handed down in them are the most true, whether they pertain to doctrine or morals or history, chronology, topography, or nomenclature; no ignorance, no thoughtlessness or forgetfulness, no lapse of memory, can or

42. William F. Arndt, *Does the Bible Contradict Itself?* (5th ed.; St. Louis: Concordia Publishing House, 1955), pp. 56-57. Cf. also Arndt's *Bible Difficulties: An Examination of Passages of the Bible Alleged To Be Irreconcilable with Its Inspiration* (St. Louis: Concordia Publishing House, 1951).

dare be ascribed to the amanuenses of the Holy Ghost in their penning of the sacred writings.[43]

Position B holds that this is an accurate description of the Bible's own attitude toward itself. When one observes the teaching and example of Christ and of His chosen Apostles on the subject of scriptural authority, one is overwhelmingly impressed by the attitude of *total trust* involved; nowhere, and in no particular, and on no subject is Scripture subjected to criticism. Passages are quoted authoritatively from the most obscure corners of the Old Testament; individual words are forced to bear the weight of heavy doctrinal teaching; passages from diverse periods and from the pens of many authors are quoted together and sometimes conflated, obviously implying their consistency and common Divine authorship; no attempt is made to distinguish "theological" or "moral" truth from veracity in historical or secular matters; and (as previously noted) the reader is told that man lives "by every word that proceedeth out of the mouth of God" (Matt. 4:4, quoted Deut. 8:3).

For Position B, then, a scripturally grounded doctrine of inspired authority implicates (in the strictest sense) an inerrant, non-contradictory Bible, and qualitatively distinguishes Scripture from all extra-biblical materials, such that none of them can be used to judge or criticize Holy Writ. If it is objected that a standard of consistency is here being imported into the doctrine of inspiration, Position B replies that man is incapable of comprehending anything where the law of contradiction is disregarded, so a "revelation" involving contradiction would reveal nothing at all. Moreover, from a contradiction anything follows, so that the presence of any contradictions in God's word would require the immediate testing of all its alleged truths — an impossible task in the very matters most vital to salvation. Thus the earlier-quoted analogy between the Scripture and a sermon breaks down ("just as the pastor may make errors of one sort or another in preaching and still preach the Word so also with Scripture"): the only way one knows that a sermon *does* reveal God's truth is by comparison of its teachings with Scripture; but there is no Bible-to-the-second-power by which to test the veracity of the *Bible's* salvatory teachings. And (to quote the warning Jesus gave to Nicodemus when He preached the Gospel to him): "If I have told you earthly things, and ye believe not, how shall ye believe, if I tell you of heavenly things?" (John 3:12).

Position B fully agrees with Position A that the Bible points to Christ, declares Law and Gospel, and is a means of grace whereby the Holy Spirit brings men into the living presence of the Savior; but it refuses to set the "earthly things" of Scripture over against these "heavenly things." Indeed, Position B is convinced, with classical Protestant theology, that "assent to" and "trust in" the biblical Christ cannot be sustained apart from the factual soundness of God's written revelation, which, after all, is our only objective source of knowledge concerning Christ and His plan of salvation for us.[44] Position B,

---

43. J. A. Quenstedt (1617-1685), *Systema*, I, 112; quoted in the comprehensive discussion of biblical authority in Franz Pieper's °*Christian Dogmatics* (4 vols.; St. Louis: Concordia Publishing House, 1950-1957), I, 223.

44. It is characteristic of Position A to object strenuously to the grounding of "assent" and "trust" in biblical "knowledge"; see Bouman's "The Teaching of Religion: A Theological Analysis" (cited in note 3 above), p. 54.

then, must not be regarded as static, formal, or intellectualistic because of its concern for the verbal and propositional truth of the Bible; this concern stems directly from an overarching conviction that the biblical message of forgiveness and personal acceptance of the saving Christ will suffer in direct proportion to the weakening of scriptural foundations.[45]

CONFLICT IN BIBLICAL INTERPRETATION: THE ISSUES IN PERSPECTIVE

In treating each of the seven major theological issues in dispute, Positions A and B have displayed quite different "hermeneutic" — or interpretive — understandings of Holy Writ. So basic is the problem of sound biblical interpretation to all current theological discussion that we shall now focus attention on it in an effort to sharpen the issues with which we have been dealing. As previously, we shall begin with Position A.

When approaching the Genesis accounts of Creation, Fall, and Flood, the Book of Jonah, Jesus' references to "Moses' words," etc. — all of which in themselves give the impression of being straight factual material — Position A feels impelled to interpret them non-factually where extra-biblical considerations (Near Eastern mythologies, contemporary scientific theories, modern documentary approaches, etc.) dictate or encourage the symbolical handling of the biblical data. If extra-biblical data come into conflict with biblical material, Position A is willing to regard the Scripture as erroneous in its factual assertions. One of the most basic interpretive principles of Position A is, therefore, that one can arrive at sufficient certainty in extra-biblical matters to allow for (and often to necessitate) the interpreting of Scripture along lines which would not be evident from Scripture itself and which on occasion reveal that Scripture contains erroneous information. Expressed otherwise, Position A holds the non-biblical facts and interpretations can be more certain and clear than biblical assertions. In contemporary theological terms, the "circularity principle" of the so-called "New Hermeneutic" is frequently appealed to: the view that Scripture can never be understood objectively or on its own terms, but must enter into a "dialectic relation" with its ancient and modern interpreters, so the biblical understanding always arises from a joint contribution both of the biblical and of the extra-biblical.[46]

A second fundamental interpretive principle with which Position A operates is that just as the presence of errors can be discovered in Scripture, so can the existence of unresolvable internal contradictions in matters of fact. Such contradictions are not regarded as incompatible with the divine inspira-

---

45. Two superlative, recent, and non-technical presentations of the historic Christian view of biblical inspiration (Position B) are: J. I. Packer, °God Speaks to Man: Revelation and the Bible (Philadelphia: Westminster Press, 1965); and John H. Gerstner, °A Bible Inerrancy Primer (Grand Rapids, Michigan: Baker Book House, 1965). Cf. also Kenneth Kantzer, °Christ and Scripture (HIS Magazine Reprints, 4605 Sherwood, Downers Grove, Illinois).

46. I have discussed the "New Hermeneutic" and its current Lutheran expressions in considerable detail in my essay, "Lutheran Hermeneutics and Hermeneutics Today," in Aspects of Biblical Hermeneutics (cited above in note 20), pp. 78-108 (reprinted in the present volume as Essay II).

tion of Holy Writ; quite the contrary: as we saw from our examination of the approach of Position A to Genesis 1 and 2, factual contradictions in Bible narratives are held to convey a higher truth (for example, that God did not intend us to discover from Scripture the point enmeshed in the contradiction, but instead wished us to focus on a more general aspect of biblical teaching).

Thirdly, Position A employs in its interpretation of Scripture the earlier noted principle of "the economy of miracles." In practice, this means that where a non-factual or symbolical interpretation of a biblical passage will reduce the miraculous element without altering the theological or moral lesson of the passage, it is legitimate and desirable. We have encountered concrete examples of the economy-of-miracles principle in the "didactic" interpretation of the Book of Jonah; in the post-dating of the last half of Isaiah and of Synoptic material so that their prophecies could be understood as descriptions of already fulfilled events; and in the hesitancy to attribute to Jesus perfect knowledge and unique powers, on the ground that they are "trappings of pagan 'divinity'."

A fourth characteristic of Position A's interpretive method is its emphasis on the general rather than the specific. Having opted for *de facto* contradictions in Scripture, Position A not infrequently finds itself in the awkward role of dealing with what it sees as irreconcilable doctrinal conflicts in the Bible (e.g., immortality of the soul and resurrection of the body). In such situations, Position A takes the more general teaching (in this case, resurrection) and drops the other, attributing it to foreign ("non-Hebraic," etc.) influences. This stress on the general to the exclusion of the specific is particularly evident in Position A's employment of general theological themes (the most common in our circles is "Law and Gospel"). We are told that instead of being concerned with questions of concrete historical facticity, we should simply seek to discover the Law-Gospel lesson the text would teach us. Indeed, advocates of Position A tell us, scriptural inspiration as such has reference to general theological truths of the Law-Gospel variety, and we should not mistakenly assume that inspiration guarantees the scientific or historical accuracy of biblical particulars. The Bible must be viewed in broad theological terms, and must be seen not as a revelation of propositionally sound data but as a pointer to spiritual experience. Truth itself, we frequently hear from adherents of Position A, is not conformity to fact but "existential," "I-Thou" encounter between God and man; and the Bible must be interpreted accordingly.

Position B regards the foregoing interpretive philosophy as nothing less than ruinous. It sees there two of the most destructive tendencies in the entire history of theology: rationalism and subjectivism. Position A is rationalistic because it imposes its own intellectual view of the world upon Scripture; it is subjectivistic because it imports its own subjective orientation into the Bible. Rationalistically, Position A holds that the knowledge it obtains outside of Scripture has preferential status as compared with Scripture's own claims, and that the "economy-of-miracles" principle, employed operationally in ordinary life, can be imposed on God's own miraculous revelation of Himself in the Bible. Subjectivistically, Position A sets personal experience above the God-given law of contradiction, thereby permitting the Bible to pass into

101

logical nonsensicality except for the "higher" truths one subjectively draws from it; and Position A reduces the whole counsel of God in Scripture to the general principles (Law-Gospel, etc.) that are subjectively acceptable to it and that accord with its arbitrary depreciation of "factual truth" as compared with "personal-existential truth."

Position B is especially troubled by the lesson of history: the sad panorama of instances in the history of the Church Militant where reason and subjective experience have gained sway over Scripture and have corrupted it to the point where its message of salvation has gone unheard. Position B insists that Scripture maintain lordship over reason and subjective experience, not the reverse; that the God of Scripture create us in His image, not that we arrogate the privilege of re-doing His revelation in the cultural image of past or present.

Position B finds support for its stand in the historic refusal of Lutheranism to allow anything, rational or experiential, to judge Holy Writ. At Worms, when his very life hung in the balance, Luther testified: "My conscience has been taken captive by the Word of God," and he never willingly allowed any human opinion or personal conviction to judge God's Book. "Scripture alone," he flatly stated, "is the true overload and master of all writings and doctrines on earth" (*W.A.*, VII, 308 ff.); and the Lutheran Confessions make this position binding on all pastors and teachers of the Church:

> Dr. Luther himself . . . has expressly drawn this distinction, viz. That God's Word alone is and should remain the only standard and rule, to which the writings of no man should be regarded equal, but to it everything should be subordinated.[47]

The greatest systematic theologian of the Lutheran Church-Missouri Synod echoed the same position, over against views identical with many of those we have been discussing:

> Exegesis [the interpretation of Scripture] loses its theological character if the exegete does not adhere throughout to the "*Scriptura Scripturam interpretatur*" [Scripture is the interpreter of Scripture] and "*Scriptura sua luce radiat*" [Scripture gleams by its own radiance]. No extra-biblical material, philological or historical, may determine the exegesis. That holds true particularly with regard to historical circumstances. Interpreting the words of Scripture according to a "historical background" not furnished by Scripture itself but, wholly or in part, by contemporary secular writers, is false exegesis.[48]

The theologians of classical Lutheranism have seen that to mold Scripture by an extra-biblical environment, past or present, is to suffocate its unique, revelatory character — a procedure as reprehensible as that of molding Christ the living Word by standards derived from the behavioral study of men in general. Lutherans have always objected in the strongest terms to the

---

47. *Formula of Concord* (Solid Declaration), Summary Formulation.[9]
48. Pieper, *°Christian Dogmatics* (cited above in note 43), I, 101. Walter R. Bouman quoted this passage from Pieper and subjected it to criticism in his essay in defense of evolution presented at the Valparaiso University debate on October 21-22, 1965 (see above, note 12).

Calvinist aphorism, "the finite is incapable of the infinite," by which the Calvinist argues that he knows what a finite human body is and that human bodies can't be everywhere at once, so Christ's body is not really present in the Sacrament. But does not Position A operate in precisely this way on Scripture? The finite book cannot be inerrant and free from contradictions; we know what religious literature is capable of, so there is no sense in attributing fanciful characteristics to the Bible. Tragically, observes Position B, the application of Position A's interpretive principles could well tear the heart out of Lutheranism's historic approach to the living, the sacramental, and the written Word.

What, then, are Position B's principles of biblical interpretation? Having illustrated them in the previous section of this paper, we shall do no more than summarize them here:[49]

1. A passage of Holy Writ must be taken as veracious in its natural sense (*sensus literalis*) unless the context of the passage itself dictates otherwise, or unless an article of faith established elsewhere in Scripture requires a broader understanding of the text.

2. The prime article of faith applicable to the hermeneutic task is the attitude of Christ and His Apostles toward the Scriptures: their utter trust in Scripture — in all it teaches or touches — must govern the exegete's practice, thus eliminating in principle any interpretation which sees the biblical texts as erroneous or contradictory in fulfilling their natural intent.

3. Harmonization of scriptural difficulties should be pursued within reasonable limits, and when harmonization would pass beyond such bounds, the exegete must leave the problem open rather than, by assuming surd error, impugn the absolute truthfulness of the God who inspires all Holy Scripture for our learning.

4. Extra-biblical linguistic and cultural considerations must be employed ministerially, never magisterially, in the interpretation of a text; and any use of extra-biblical material to arrive at an interpretation inconsistent with the veracity of the scriptural passage is to be regarded as magisterial and therefore illegitimate. Extra-biblical data can and should put questions to a text, but only Scripture itself can in the last analysis legitimately answer questions about itself.

5. Not all literary forms are consistent with scriptural revelation; the exegete must not appeal to literary forms (such as Near Eastern mythology) which cast doubt on the truthfulness or the morality of the Divine Author of Scripture.

6. The exegete should employ all scholarly research tools that do not involve rationalistic or subjectivistic commitments. Such methodologies are identifiable by their presuppositions, which either (like Bultmann's demythologizing) do violence to articles of faith, or (like certain documentary theories) oppose the perspicuity of the received biblical texts and the facticity of the events recorded in them, or (like the "circularity principle" of the so-called "New Hermeneutic") give to the sinful cultural milieu, past and present, a

---

49. For the applicability of these principles to current theological discussion in Synod, see the Appendix to this essay.

constitutive role in the formulation of biblical teaching. These and other unscriptural techniques are to be scrupulously avoided in carrying out the interpretive task.[50]

The comparison of Positions A and B on the vital matter of scriptural interpretation has opened a vista from which we can perhaps better understand the theological difficulties our Church faces at the present time. Position B stands revealed as the historic Lutheran view, endeavoring to emphasize the "whole counsel of God" as conveyed in a totally reliable, divinely authored Scripture; Position A, on the other hand, by its de-emphasis on the miraculous and its insistence that Christ is just like other men and the Bible just like other human books, displays theological characteristics more typical of positions (such as Rationalism, Pietism, and Modernism) which orthodox Lutheranism has consistently opposed. Why, it may well be asked, has Position A risen to trouble Zion at this time?

The answer is in many ways sociological. The Lutheran Church-Missouri Synod is an immigrant Church, and the standard pattern among immigrant groups is to remain walled off from the new society by language and by tradition for a time, and then for a younger generation to react violently to its past and to seek to identify completely — generally to over-identify — with the new environment. During its first century of existence, Missouri isolated herself in many ways from American religious life. To a certain extent this was fortunate, since American theology was passing through successive stages of heresy: subjectivistic revivalism, the economic religiosity of big business and the self-made man, and the Modernism of the Fosdick era. In other respects, Missouri's isolation was anything but desirable. (Do we not all have true stories in our bag such as the one told me by one of Springfield Seminary students? His grandfather had nearly been excommunicated for religious "Unionism" because he played checkers in the Y.M.C.A.!)

When the theologs of the present generation woke up to their Church's in-grown condition, they reacted violently to it. They set their faces resolutely against their past — and the more of a past they had, the more violent, generally, was the reaction. (Have you noticed that the advocates of Position A are very commonly offspring of long-established, "distinguished" clerical families in Synod — with a strong tradition of strict, in-Synod education?) Both the good and the bad suffer in a sociological reaction; Synod has become more "relevant" in American life, but this has happened at a time theologically when to embrace ecumenical Lutheranism (to say nothing of mainline non-Lutheran theologies) is to court disaster: the disaster of dialectic Neo-Orthodoxy, subjectivistic Existentialism, and now the humanistic, universalistic "secular Christianity" typified by the death-of-God movement. Like the Germany of Missouri's forbears, which attained the power and influence of a national state late in life, in the dangerous era when armaments made global

---

50. This hermeneutic summary (and some other material in the present essay) has been derived from my soon-to-be-published paper, "The Approach of New Shape Roman Catholicism to Scriptural Inerrancy: A Case Study," which was given as an invitational presentation at the international Seminar on the Authority of Scripture (Harold John Ockenga, Chairman), held at Gordon College, Wenham, Massachusetts, June 20-29, 1966.

destruction possible, the Missouri Synod is coming out of her shell at a time when theology is entering a new humanistic phase, in many ways more destructive of historic Christianity than the old Liberalism.[51]

How tragic if, at this key juncture in our Synodical history, we allow ourselves, in the legitimate quest for maximum cultural and theological relevance, to discard the very treasure of God's Word which He has permitted us to retain while so many churches have pursued the mirage of other gospels! Our greatest need today is for more maturity among our theologians: the maturity to see real sociological blindspots in our past, yes; but the even greater maturity not to discard the scriptural remedy for our ailments in the course of treating them. Can we not learn from history and the mistakes of others? Can we not benefit from the insights of the great theologians of the past, who have reminded the Church that its greatest treasure is the Word, and that to lose it is to lose everything? Can we not, in short, see the fundamentally spiritual nature of our problem, and seek by God's grace to "arrive at real maturity — that measure of development which is meant by 'the fullness of Christ' "?

> We are not meant to remain as children at the mercy of every chance wind of teaching and the jockeying of men who are expert in the crafty presentation of lies. But we are meant to hold firmly to the truth in love, and to grow up in every way into Christ, the head. For it is from the head that the whole body, as a harmonious structure knit together by the joints with which it is provided, grows by the proper functioning of individual parts to its full maturity in love.[52]

APPENDIX: AN ILLUSTRATION OF CURRENT CONFLICT OVER PROPER PRINCIPLES OF BIBLICAL INTERPRETATION

I. *Action of the Board of Control of Concordia Seminary, St. Louis, on Resolution 2-37 of the Detroit Convention of the Lutheran Church-Missouri Synod*

The resolution reads:

> "WHEREAS, Dr. Norman Habel on request originally prepared an essay, 'The Form and Meaning of the Fall Narrative,' and presented it to a joint conference of the faculties of the Springfield and St. Louis Seminaries with the Council of Presidents for the purpose of study and discussion; and
> "WHEREAS, Dr. Habel on invitation by the Iowa District West presented this same essay at a special conference of the District; and
> "WHEREAS, The Iowa District West has indicated certain concerns in reaction to this essay; therefore be it
> "RESOLVED, That in recognition of the concerns expressed by Iowa District West the Synod advise the District —

---

51. See E. L. Mascall, *The Secularisation of Christianity* (London: Darton, Longman & Todd, 1965); Carl F. H. Henry, *°Frontiers in Modern Theology* (Chicago: Moody Press, 1966); and my *°The 'Is God Dead?' Controversy* (cited above in note 25).
52. Eph. 4:13-16 (Phillips' paraphrase).

"1. to present all concerns involving heremeneutical method to the Commission on Theology and Church Relations; and

"2. to direct any request pertaining to the classroom teaching of this material to the appropriate Board of Control, as specified in the synodical *Handbook*; and be it further

"RESOLVED, That the Synod advise the Board of Control of Concordia Seminary, St. Louis, Mo., to decide whether the interpretive method employed in this essay should be used at the seminary before the Commission on Theology and Church Relations has completed its study on hermeneutics

"ACTION: This resolution was adopted."

Preamble:

Resolution 2-37 does not ask the Board of Control to pass judgment on the *content* of the essay, nor on the classroom use of this content. It rather advises the Iowa District West "to direct any request pertaining to the classroom teaching of this material to the appropriate Board of Control, as specified in the synodical *Handbook*." To date no such request has been received. Furthermore, Resolution 2-37 does not ask the Board of Control for a decision as to whether all principles of interpretation employed in the Habel essay have received proper emphasis or consistent application in the essay. In accordance with section 1 of the first "Resolved" of the Detroit convention resolution "All concerns involving hermeneutical method" are to be considered as being in the study assignment given to the Commission of Theology and Church Relations and should be communicated to this commission. In the light of these considerations, we present the following resolution:

WHEREAS, Resolution 2-37 calls upon the Board of Control of Concordia Seminary, St. Louis, Missouri, "to decide whether the *interpretative method* employed in this essay should be used at the seminary before the Commission on Theology and Church Relations has completed its study on hermeneutics;" and

WHEREAS, Dr. Habel's interpretive method in this essay is based on the following principles (compare pages 1-2 of Habel's printed essay):

1. The approach of the Lutheran exegete is governed by his faith in Jesus Christ.

2. The Lutheran exegete must relate all of Scripture to its center, Jesus Christ, that is, the message of justification by grace *propter Christum* through faith.

3. The Lutheran exegete must follow the rule that Scripture interprets Scripture.

4. The Lutheran exegete follows the norm that the Old Testament must be interpreted in the light of the New Testament.

5. The Lutheran exegete must assume an attitude of subservience to the Scriptures as the inspired word of the living God which is designed to lead men to salvation. He will always seek to determine the message which *God* intends to communicate in any given passage.

6. By seeking to ascertain the intended sense of a given passage the

Lutheran exegete is applying the principle *sensus literalis unus est.*

7. When attempting to determine the intended sense of a given text of Scripture, the Lutheran exegete must employ all the tools at his disposal to discover the character or nature of the text with which he is dealing.

8. The Lutheran exegete must pay special attention to the *usus loquendi* of the Biblical writer, that is, he must try to ascertain what the terms, concepts, imagery, forms, etc., of a given text meant in the culture and specific historical situation of the audience to which the passage was originally addressed; and

WHEREAS the Board of Control acknowledges that these principles of biblical interpretation are thoroughly Lutheran and have been employed by exegetes of the Lutheran church in all periods of her history; therefore

BE IT RESOLVED, that the Board of Control affirms that the interpretive method employed at Concordia Seminary must continue to follow these principles; and be it further

RESOLVED, that since the significant differences between this exposition of Genesis 3 and earlier exegesis current in our synod has produced considerable negative reaction and since members of the Board of Control do not find themselves in full agreement with all of the applications of these principles and the conclusions reached in the essay and therefore do not find the paper completely acceptable, the Board asks Dr. Habel, in collaboration with his colleagues, to make a careful reexamination of his application of the hermeneutical principles in order to insure that in all of his exegetical work he produces sound biblical interpretation, and be it further

RESOLVED, that questions with regard to Dr. Habel's application of these principles in his essay be referred to Dr. Habel himself and then, if they need to be pursued further, to the seminary president and Board of Control.

28. February, 1966.

II. *Reply by the Iowa District West, Lutheran Church-Missouri Synod, to the Action of the Board of Control of Concordia Seminary, St. Louis, on Resolution 2-37 of the Detroit Convention*

The Board of Control, having listed eight principles of biblical interpretation deriving from Professor Norman Habel's essay, "The Form and Meaning of the Fall Narrative," affirms that these principles "are thoroughly Lutheran and have been employed by exegetes of the Lutheran church in all periods of her history" and therefore resolves that "the interpretive method employed at Concordia Seminary must continue to follow these principles."

We herewith register objection to this judgment, on the ground that ambiguity in the statement of Professor Habel's principles and imprecision as to the mutual relations among the principles yield the grave possibility that they may be employed to justify an utterly un-Lutheran conception of biblical inspiration and hermeneutics; and we therefore respectfully request the Board of Control to revise its judgment and tighten the hermeneutic controls at the St. Louis Seminary before other essays similar to Professor Habel's result from the employment of his principles.

Specifically, principles 3, 5, 7, and 8 manifest an exceedingly perilous ambiguity. Principle 5, while affirming that the Lutheran exegete "will always seek to determine the message which *God* intends to communicate in any given passage," does not indicate how the divine intent is to be determined. As Luther made clear, the intent of any biblical passage must be established, first and foremost, on the basis of the literal meaning of the passage itself: "Anyone who ventures to interpret words in the Scriptures any other way than what they say, is under obligation to prove this contention out of the text of the very same passage or by an article of faith" (*Works,* American ed., XXXVII, 32). Non-literal interpretation of a given passage must therefore not be construed as God's intent unless the passage itself or the exigencies of basic Christian doctrine demands this. True, as principle 3 asserts, "the Lutheran exegete must follow the rule that Scripture interprets Scripture," but this does not mean that in interpreting a passage which in itself conveys a literal meaning, the exegete can give it non-literal force by the citation of other passages of Holy Writ. Such a faulty exegesis was employed by Professor Habel in using Ezekiel 28 to argue for a non-literal interpretation of Genesis 3, and the hermeneutic principles accepted by the Board of Control leave the door open to such baneful exegesis. This is precisely the hermeneutic orientation employed by the Calvinists, Zwinglians, and Enthusiasts of the Reformation period to argue (on the basis of such passages as John 6) that Luther and the Lutheran Confessions were hopelessly literalistic in their interpretation of the Verba.

Principle 7 affirms that the Lutheran exegete "must employ all the tools at his disposal to discover the character or nature of the text with which he is dealing." Unfortunately, this statement does not distinguish between legitimate and illegitimate tools in biblical interpretation. It affords the exegete the opportunity to use any "tools at his disposal," presumably including such methodologies as higher or literary criticism that subjectively allows the realignment and re-interpretation of biblical material according to hypothesized "documents" or "forms" assumed to underlie the text established by lower criticism. The ambiguity of principle 7 lies in its failure to reject exegetical tools that permit the interpreter to assume a magisterial rather than ministerial stance in relation to the scriptural text. In a word, principle 7 should exclude all use of hermeneutic methods in which rationalistic presuppositions (such as "the economy of miracles," or the "circularity principle" of the post-Bultmannian New Hermeneutic) play a role.

Because of the vagueness of principle 7, the door is opened to principle 8, which encourages the employment of an exegetical method of the most unhealthy kind. According to principle 8, the *usus loquendi* of a biblical writer is to be ascertained by determining "what the terms, concepts, imagery, forms, etc., of a given text meant in the culture and specific historical situation of the audience to which the passage was originally addressed." Owing to lack of any indication as to the relation between this principle and principle 3

("Scripture interprets Scripture") and owing also to the above-noted ambiguity of principle 5, principle 8 actually gives ground for the fundamental error of Professor Habel's essay: the determination of biblical meaning on the basis of the Near Eastern Cultural situation, rather than on the basis of the clear and literal meaning of the biblical text taken on its own ground. Professor Habel, through an "analysis of the Fall narrative in the light of the culture of ancient Israel and her neighbors," endeavored to show that "it is legitimate to consider this narrative a literary form which may be described as a 'symbolic religious history,' but that we should not confuse the truth that the writer is stating with this particular mode of saying it, a mode which is especially appropriate for the world in which he lived, and a mode which has at least partial analogies in the epic literature of his day." Here Scripture is reduced to a reflection of the Near Eastern environment, and special revelation is absorbed into a non-revelatory, sinful human idealogical situation. Of course, extra-biblical linguistic and cultural considerations are to be used in scriptural study, but, as Luther stressed, they can never legitimately be employed to arrive at an interpretation of a biblical passage which is not fully consistent with the literal force of the text taken by itself. If Scripture is God's unique and special revelation, then it is self-interpreting; and principle 8 is remiss in not limiting cultural and situational considerations to a ministerial function in relation to the perspicuous scriptural text.

Rudolf Bultmann could readily accept principles 7 and 8 as justifying his exegetical relegation of the saving events of our Lord's ministry to "the language of mythology" on the ground that "the origin of the various themes can easily be traced in the contemporary mythology of Jewish Apocalyptic and in the redemption myths of Gnosticism" (*Kerygma and Myth*, ed. Bartsch, tr. Fuller, p. 61). Here the cultural audience determines what is "form" as distinct from "true content" — thereby totally destroying the gospel. Professor Habel is employing strictly analogous methodology in his non-literal exegesis of Genesis 3, and principle 8 makes such methodology permissible in principle.

We therefore respectfully submit that Professor Habel and his colleagues be required to operate with hermeneutic principles that are in fact unambiguously Lutheran, viz. [here follow principles 1, 4, and 6 substantially as given in the text of the present essay at note 49].

25. May, 1966.

IV.

CURRENT THEOLOGICAL TRENDS IN THE LUTHERAN CHURCH - MISSOURI SYNOD

Or: A Brief Plea for the Introduction of
Minimal Logic into our Doctrinal Discussions
before We Scuttle the Ship

Only an inebriated mole would claim that the Missouri Synod is not in theological ferment. Even the highest administrators of the Synod (who, though they are not prone to liquor, tend to see things perpetually quiet in Zion) quite readily agree that the Church is facing tempestuous waters. Six years have passed since President A. O. Fuerbringer of Concordia Seminary, St. Louis, earmarked the theological situation as the Church's "newest frontier," stating that "our published theology is heavily weighted with systematic theology and dogmatics," that "we have simply concluded that we have the answers or sufficient basis for the answers" and warning that "we cannot continue to coast or muddle our way through."[1]

It is the contention of this essayist that "muddle" constitutes *le mot juste* — the exact descriptive term — for the current theological scene in the Missouri Synod. The nature of this muddle derives, I am convinced, from the impassioned desire of a number of theologians to achieve a new and "relevant" Lutheran theology through chucking the theological orientation Missouri has displayed in its first century of existence. Here one observes, with mixed agony and incredulity, another instance of blithe discarding of baby and bathwater — a phenomenon so frequent in church history that it could serve as a Leitmotiv for an entire treatment of the church's past.

Now it is characteristic of baby-and-bathwater dumpings (whether secular or religious) that they reflect both sin and irrationality. Not wishing to involve myself in the sticky realm of identifying sinful motivations (the passion to "hear some new thing," to be feted theologically outside of Synod, to achieve ecumenical relations at all cost, etc.), I shall devote myself here strictly to pointing out some of the representative logical blunders characteristic of the present efforts to re-do Missouri's theology. Irrationality revealed does not, of course, necessitate correction of abuses (change of heart, not just change of mind, is always required for that), but perhaps some service can be rendered by showing that a powerful corrective to theological balderdash lies simply in keeping one's wits.

---

1. *The Lutheran Witness*, October 4, 1960, p. 522.

The General Tone of Theological Revision

To obtain a picture of the over-all revisionary scene, we shall briefly discuss representative essays by two Missouri Synod advocates of change: Walter R. Bouman, an assistant professor at Concordia Teachers College, River Forest, Illinois, and Richard J. Gotsch, pastor of Grace Lutheran Church, Northbrook, Illinois. Choice of these writers has been determined solely by their explicit advocacy of new theological avenues, not because they offer the most profound statement of the new views; indeed, Missouri Synod proponents of new theology are in almost every case but pale reflections of neo-orthodox, existentialist, or other European theological giants. But we must make do with what we have.

In the 1965 Yearbook of the Lutheran Education Association, Bouman picks up Missouri Synoder F. Dean Lueking's distinction between "scholastic confessionalism" and "evangelical confessionalism,"[2] and argues:

> Scholasticism reached its first peak in the 13th century. . . . Elert's acute analysis of Luther's *evangelical* point of departure led him to locate the decisive shift in basic approach which characterized the actual rise of *Lutheran* scholasticism in the 17th century. The 19th century witnessed a revival of Lutheran scholasticism. . . . It did not learn from history; and it again missed Luther's *evangelical* point of departure in both its formal (doctrine of Holy Scripture) and material (doctrine of the Atonement) principles. The neo-scholasticism of the 19th century became the dominant theological approach of the Missouri Synod. The *Book of Concord,* the Reformation and the Scriptures themselves were read in the light of neo-scholasticism. Franz Pieper became its great theological spokesman.[3]

Bouman claims that Luther's "Law-Gospel" distinction stands in radical opposition to this "scholasticism," and that the Missouri Synod's educational materials are banefully tainted by scholastic influences. He concludes:

> Scholasticism ruins a church. It can do this because it has a moralistic view of sin, an intellectualistic understanding of faith, and a legalistic ethic devoid of evangelical impulse. . . . Scholasticism — in both its medieval and Lutheran form — has accommodated itself to the sinner in man, to the legalist in man, the god that man would be. The educational materials prepared and authorized by the Missouri Synod give evidence that a reformation is under way. They also give much evidence that a reformation is needed.[4]

Now observe carefully the nature of this argument. (We leave aside all consideration of the technical scholarly errors in it, e.g., Bouman's depreciation of the 17th century Lutheran dogmaticians on the basis of tertiary sources such as liberal Calvinist A. C. McGiffert's *Protestant Thought before Kant,* and his

---

2. Set forth in Lueking's *Mission in the Making* (St. Louis: Concordia Publishing House, 1964).
3. Bouman, "The Teaching of Religion: A Theological Analysis," in John S. Damm (ed.), *The Teaching of Religion: Twenty-second Yearbook* (River Forest, Illinois: Lutheran Education Association, 1965), p. 33 (Bouman's italics).
4. *Ibid.,* p. 60.

total disregard of such decisive counter-treatments as Robert Preus' *The Inspiration of Scripture: A Study of the Theology of the Seventeenth-Century Lutheran Dogmaticians.*) Bouman begins by semantically loading the issue: he employs the term "scholastic" to designate what he dislikes in Missouri, and the term "evangelical" to cover the new position he advocates. Since no Protestant can think of "scholasticism" in a neutral way, and since all of us place the "evangel" close to our hearts, we tend naturally and uncritically to look with favor on Bouman's case.

But consider the case. He would have us accept the amazing view that (1) classical 17th century Lutheran theology, which above all endeavored faithfully to systematize the revealed truth of a Scripture it considered inerrant, and to perform its theologizing in accord with strict (*quia*) subscription to the Lutheran confessions and especially to Luther's own theological insights, ought properly to be paralleled with 13th century medieval scholasticism (Aquinas, *et al.*), whom Luther vehemently opposed; and (2) the Missouri Synod, whose great theologian Walther was responsible for a classic work on *The Proper Distinction between Law and Gospel*, established itself in this same scholastic morass, intellectualized faith, moralized sin, legalized ethics, misunderstood Law and Gospel, and "accomodated itself to the sinner in man, to the legalist in man, the god that man would be." For Bouman, the theology of Missouri, as expressed in Pieper's *Christian Dogmatics* and as reflected in its educational instruction, is essentially a scholasticism that betrays the Reformation and ruins the church. Quite a charge! And not one — we hope — to be accepted without incontrovertible evidence, since even at law a defendant is innocent until proven guilty, and since most of us have the overwhelming experiential conviction that we *did* hear the "evangel" of God's grace in Christ and not moralistic scholasticism in Missouri. But let us move on.

Bouman expresses his dissatisfaction with Missouri's theological orientation by way of educational materials; for Richard J. Gotsch, a new theological stance is dictated by ecumenical considerations. In a short article in the December, 1965, issue of the *American Lutheran,* Gotsch correctly notes that Missouri's approach ecumenically has been determined by her "principle of unity through doctrinal agreement," that this principle is based upon the presupposition that "in the Scriptures we have a single theological system," and that "a very concrete example of this point of view can be seen in our synodical catechism."[5] But Gotsch disagrees with this fundamental assumption that Scripture presents a single theology: "It is precisely this assumption which needs to be re-examined in the light of the Scriptures themselves. . . . The central point I wish to make is that within the New Testament itself the church is confronted with a rich variety of theological systems and viewpoints. It is certainly significant that the Holy Spirit used more than one human author. . . . A careful examination of the Gospel tradition reveals that even within a single work, such as the Gospel of Luke, a variety of theological viewpoints can be found."[6] Gotsch then ties the alleged theological diversity

---

5. Gotsch, "New Testament Theology and Church Unity," *American Lutheran,* XLVIII (December, 1965), 13-14.
6. *Ibid.*

of the New Testament documents to the primitive church: "Not only are we confronted with a variety of theologies in the New Testament, but beneath these theologies we encounter a number of Christian communities whose doctrinal viewpoints were certainly not uniform." Now comes the ecumenical consequence for Missouri today:

> Rather than saying that we have the reservoir of pure truths, we ought to think of our theological system as a witness. Since the Holy Spirit inspired more than one apostle and at least four evangelists to proclaim the good news, ought we not reconsider the assumption that the Holy Spirit has deposited all truth with one synod of the Christian family? We should also look upon our theology as a conditioned theology. It is subject to the limitations which we have as human beings in history.[7]

Here the logically unwary reader is led down the garden path by such a rhetorical question as, "Ought we not reconsider the assumption that the Holy Spirit has deposited all truth with one synod?" The answer is patently Yes (and even the most rock-ribbed 19th century Missourian never denied it!), but this does not happen to be the question on which the original argument depends, namely, "Does the New Testament (or Scripture as a whole, for that matter) convey a single theology capable of unified expression, on which church bodies must agree for God-honoring ecumenical union?" The historic churches of Christendom, whether Catholic, Lutheran, or Reformed, have always maintained, contra Gotsch, that God reveals a single and coherent truth, subject to confident theological proclamation. The fact that God chose more than one biblical writer to record His revelation no more proves a diversity of theological viewpoints than the twelve-man jury system proves that no court can ever reach a unanimous verdict! Obviously Gotsch regards the theology of the Bible as stemming primarily from its human writers (who are many), rather than from its Divine Author (who is one). Here again, we shall not emphasize the factual unsoundness of the argument (biblical scholarship in recent years has powerfully stressed the unity both of Old and of New Testament theology); we wish only to expose logical blunders which, if unrecognized, can divert us from Missouri's powerful historic stand in behalf of God's univocal revelation of truth. Clear thinking should make us pause as long before chucking Synod's Catechism à la Gotsch as we paused before dumping Pieper à la Bouman.[9]

A central thrust in the move to update Missouri's theology is the assertion that the formal, propositional systematics of 17th century orthodoxy, of Pieper's *Dogmatics*, and of such teaching tools as the Synodical Catechism "intellectualize" the faith, demanding a basis in fact or knowledge to precede both

---

7. *Ibid.*, pp. 14-15.
8. Cf. Edmond Jacob, *Theologie de l'Ancien Testament* (Neuchatel et Paris: Delachaux & Niestle, 1955); Ethelbert Stauffer, *New Testament Theology*, trans. John Marsh (New York: Macmillan, 1956); and especially Rudolf Schnackenburg, *La Theologie du Nouveau Testament: Etat de la question*, ("Studia Neotestamentica Subsidia," I; Bruges: Desclée de Brouwer, 1961).
9. Having entered Missouri in no small part because of the lucid presentation of Scriptural truth in the Synodical catechism, I must be pardoned for obtuseness in not seeing its unevangelical character!

the salvatory relation to Christ and ecumenical church relations. Particularly offensive to advocates of reform is the classical understanding of faith as "knowledge" (*notitia*), "assent" (*assensus*), and "trust" (*fiducia*), since, it is argued, the grounding of faith in knowledge exhibits unfaith, and permits the substitution of an inerrant Scripture or doctrinal propositions about faith for the Gospel of living faith itself. Thus Bouman, in an article appearing in the same issue of the *American Lutheran* as Gotsch's essay, condemns Lutheran orthodoxy because in its theology Scripture was "identified with God's Word. . . . Holy Scripture replaced the Gospel as the object of faith. Indeed, the doctrine of Holy Scripture became the guarantee for the veracity of the Gospel."[10] In his previously cited LEA Yearbook essay, Bouman blasts the following example of what he considers the "scholastic approach" and the "intellectualization of faith" in Missouri educational materials: "What is faith? First we have to '*know* what God says about Himself in the Bible.' Then we have to '*believe* that what God says about Himself is true.' And finally we must 'rely on Him with firm confidence.' Here faith has become what Regin Prenter has called a 'middleclass virtue' to be filed away with our insurance policies, bonds, and bank books."[11]

Again we are faced with a very odd kind of reasoning. Softened by a reference to "middleclass virtue" (does *anyone* want to be middleclass?) and a safety-deposit-box analogy (surely we don't want our faith to be like *that*!), we prepare to opt for faith simply as a "relationship" in the Gospel — which will bypass the cold, "intellectualistic" propositions of Scripture and remove those doctrinal barriers that have impeded church union. But wait! Suppose one asks (and it is certainly a legitimate question when so many different religious and denominational views clamor for our attention): "Shall I experience the faith relationship with Christ as Christian Science understands the Gospel? or as Unitarianism understands it? or as the Lutheran understands it?" Perhaps the question will strike even deeper: "Why a relationship with Christ and not with another?" Possibly the relationship ought to be with "Being uncreate"[12] and its cosmic egg?

> Upon a rock, yet uncreate,
> Amid a chaos inchoate,
> An uncreated being sate;
> Beneath him, rock,
> Above him, cloud.
> And the cloud was rock,
> And the rock was cloud.
> The rock then growing soft and warm,
> The cloud began to take a form,
> A form chaotic, vast and vague,
> Which issued in the cosmic egg.

10. Bouman, "What is Lutheran in Theology," *American Lutheran*, XLVIII (December, 1965), 12.
11. Bouman, "The Teaching of Religion: A Theological Analysis," *op. cit.*, p. 54 (Bouman's italics).
12. In all probability, a blood relative of Tillich's "Being itself" and of existential theologian John Macquarrie's "beingful Being."

Then the Being uncreate
On the egg did incubate,
And thus became the incubator;
And of the egg did allegate,
And thus became the alligator;
And the incubator was potentate,
But the alligator was potentator.

A bizarre relationship, you say. But no less "potentator" than any number of religious claims to true spiritual "relationships" that mislead people every day. The Lutheran fathers saw what ought to be transparently clear to us, living in a religiously pluralistic age: "assent" and "trust" are not of value in themselves; they are meaningful and significant only when they rest in the proper object. One must assent to and trust in *Christ* if one is to be saved, and all other religious "assents" and "trusts" are, in the last analysis, demonic. And by "Christ" we mean the Christ of *Scripture*, not a "Christ" created in mystic experience. If "knowledge" (i.e., the facticity of God's scriptural revelation of the historic Christ) does not ground faith, the result is a chimerical self-salvation. This is why Luther replied to the enthusiast Müntzer's depreciation of the Bible in favor of inner experience ("Bible, Babel, bubble!") that apart from God's written revelation he would not listen to Müntzer even if "he had swallowed the Holy Ghost, feathers and all."[13]

Stress upon the objective truth of God's scriptural Word and upon the Christ there revealed is not "intellectualism." Quite the contrary: it is the only means by which our assent and trust are preserved from becoming slaves of some clever intellectualistic world-view that would rob us of eternal life. No one of us is strong enough to withstand the subtle reworking of our faith into selfish channels; only as long as our assent and trust are grounded in an objective and inerrant Word outside of ourselves will faith remain saving faith. Apart from the scriptural Word, the true Gospel cannot be separated from the multitude of other gospels which are not gospels at all (Gal. 1:6-9).

Some Specific Isues in Theological Revision

The general tone of theological "advance" in our circles does not give us great confidence (whether viewed as *fiducia* or not!) when we approach the individual points of argument characteristic of the new positions. Space forbids us from analyzing more than a few representative contentions on the part of those who press for a more "relevant" perspective, but, unless I am mistaken, your native good sense will be sufficiently appalled by the types of reasoning I shall adduce that there will be little picketing for more examples.

Our last section brought us to the question of biblical authority. Let us therefore focus our attention here upon the key issues of the Bible's inspiration and interpretation. Missouri's great dogmaticians, exegetes, and teachers (Pieper, Walther, Mueller, Engelder, Arndt, *et al.*) consistently maintained that the Bible is inerrant and perspicuously self-interpreting: as God's Word it stands above all human criticism and speaks a clear and unambiguous message

13. *WA*, XVII, Pt. 1, 361-62.

to those who will approach it on its own ground. In taking this position, our theologians were simply echoing Luther and the Confessions: Luther asserted that the Scriptures "never yet have erred" and flatly declared, "Scripture alone is the true overlord and master of all writings and doctrines on earth";[14] the Confessions quote Luther directly on the point, making his attitude to biblical authority normative and obligatory for Lutheran Christians: "God's Word alone is and should remain the only standard and norm of all doctrine, and no human being's writings dare be put on a par with it, but everything must be subjected to it."[15]

Since the rise of modern humanistic rationalism in the 18th century, however, the Bible has been less and less treated as a unique revelation from God. Rather, it has come to be viewed from within the framework of cultural humanism: as the reflection of the human religious ideas of a Semitic people and therefore subject, like everything else, to rational criticism from other human perspectives. This trend has by no means been limited to moderns outside the Christian churches; indeed, it is a truism to say that at the present time the Missouri Synod is one of very few Protestant bodies holding officially to an inerrant Scripture.

To many theologians outside of Missouri, therefore, the Synod's position appears hopelessly anachronistic; and for some of those within the fold it has become difficult to believe that "everyone is out of step but Johnny" (or better, Johann). Thus endeavors have been made of late to re-think Missouri's attitude toward Scripture. Characteristic of such rethinking is Richard Jungkuntz's attempt, in an essay appearing in the October, 1964, issue of the *Concordia Theological Monthly*, to argue that Jesus' assertion in John 10:34-36, "Scripture cannot be broken" (the verse, not so incidentally, which Engelder used as the title of his massive book defending biblical inerrancy) does not mean "if Scripture says something, that something is a fact" but is a Law-Gospel preachment, equivalent to "Scripture cannot be kept from fulfillment."[16] (Aside from the *prima facie* oddity of this exegesis, it is perhaps worth noting that even Jungkuntz finds "both the modern and traditional interpretations" united against his own.)

A more recent issue of the *Concordia Theological Monthly* contains Arthur Carl Piepkorn's article, "What Does 'Inerrancy' Mean?"[17] in which the author advises his readers "to refrain from using the term 'inerrancy'" on such grounds as (1) the absence of the original autographs of the biblical books (a venerable old clinker of an argument, presented by opponents of biblical inspiration generations ago and decisively answered by many orthodox theologians);[18] (2) the principle of "the economy of miracles" (pardon us for asking, but is

---

14. *WA*, VII, 316-17.
15. FC SD, Summary Formulation, 9.
16. Jungkuntz, "An Approach to the Exegesis of John 10:34-36," *Concordia Theological Monthly*, XXXV (October, 1964), 556-65.
17. Piepkorn, "What Does 'Inerrancy' Mean?" *Concordia Theological Monthly*, XXXVI (September, 1965), 577-93.
18. For example, Carl F. H. Henry, *The Protestant Dilemma: An Analysis of the Current Impasse in Theology* (Grand Rapids, Michigan: Eerdmans, 1949), pp. 43-121 (especially pp. 72-85).

the principle of keeping the miraculous to a minimum *really* appropriate when evaluating a book that purports to reveal God's special actions in the world for man's salvation?); and (3) the contention that "where the stress is on a religious purpose, his [the human biblical author's] concern with the precise and literal accuracy of concomitant historical or scientific detail may recede into the background" (and *how* do we distinguish the "historical" and the "scientific" from the "religious" in a revelation that thoroughly unites the earthly and the heavenly, as the Incarnation shows? And what about our Lord's query in John 3:12: "If I have told you earthly things and ye believe not, how shall ye believe if I tell you of heavenly things?")

Even more to the left are Missourians such as Robert Scharlemann who flatly claim the existence of errors and contradictions in the biblical text. Elsewhere[19] I have discussed the three examples Scharlemann provides as particularly overwhelming evidence that the assertion "the Bible is inerrant, that is, contains no error," simply cannot be supported by the biblical evidence itself.[20] These illustrations are the different word-order of the superscriptions on the cross in Matthew and Luke, Matthew's apparent ascription to Jeremiah of a quotation found in Zechariah, and the 15th Nisan date of the crucifixion in the Synoptics vs. the 14th Nisan date in John. The first "contradition" appears plausible only if we conveniently forget that the superscription appeared in three languages, obviously with different word-order in each; the second was nicely handled by St. Augustine in the 5th century and by numerous other orthodox theologians since (one simple solution: "Jeremiah" was a covering rubric for the several prophetic books bound with it in Jewish times); and the 14th-15th Nisan problem has been set in an entirely new light recently by the Dead Sea Scroll discovery that *two* calendars were in use in Palestine when Jesus was crucified, thus permitting the conclusion that John and the Synoptics employed different (but equally legitimate) calendar systems.[21] Perhaps, like the great saints of the past, we would do well to stand fully under the authority of the Word, seek to resolve its difficulties as best we can, and trust that the future will take care of the minor problems that remain; history has had a remarkable way of vindicating Scripture while shooting down its confident critics.

The inerrancy question leads naturally into the interpretive question: Must we understand the Bible as representing factual truth? For Luther and for the historic Lutheran church, the Bible had to be interpreted literally and factually unless the text itself dictated otherwise. "All 'figures'," writes Luther against Erasmus, "should rather be avoided, as being the quickest poison, when Scripture itself does not absolutely require them."[22] Thus the Missouri Synod has refused to allegorize or parabolize the Genesis account of Creation, Fall, and Flood, the narrative of Jonah and the Leviathan, etc.

---

19. Montgomery, "Inspiration and Inerrancy: A New Departure," *Evangelical Theological Society Bulletin*, VIII (Spring, 1965), 45-75 (reprinted in the present volume as Essay I).
20. Robert Scharlemann, Letter to the Editor, *The Lutheran Scholar*, April, 1963.
21. Cf. my article, "The Fourth Gospel Yesterday and Today," *Concordia Theological Monthly*, XXXIV (April, 1963), 206, 213.
22. *WA*, XVIII, 701.

Recently, however, attempts have been made to argue for non-literal, mythico-poetic, *midrash* interpretations of such ostensively literal passages as those just mentioned. The contention is that alongside of the traditional literal view, one should be permitted to teach a "symphonic" interpretation of the Creation story and a "didactic" view of Jonah.[23] A particularly telling example of the new hermeneutical approach is Norman C. Habel's essay, "The Form and Meaning of the Fall Narrative,"[24] in which the author through an "analysis of the Fall narrative in the light of the culture of ancient Israel and her neighbors," contends that "it is legitimate to consider this narrative a literary form which may be described as a "symbolical religious history,' but that we should not confuse the truth that the writer is stating with this particular mode of saying it, a mode which is especially appropriate for the world in which he lived, and a mode which has at least partial analogies in the epic literature of his day."

The impressive marshalling of philological detail in the essays of such exegetes as Habel, Sauer, and Gehrke leaves the reader momentarily stunned and almost ready to yield the right of private interpretation to an exegetical priesthood. But then it dawns that the basic question is not one of philology but of the *use* of philology. Suppose (which is hardly the case) that every ostensively literal, factual event and statement in Scripture could be paralleled with cultural myths of the ancient Near East; would that prove that the Bible was *likewise* presenting myths?[25] As the logicians say: If two clocks strike the hour at the same time, do we conclude that one causes the other to strike? Obviously not;[26] the "Near Eastern culture" argument gratuitously *assumes* a causal relationship between Scripture and its cultural milieu such that the Scripture can be explained by its enviroment. But that is exactly what the Christian position on special revelation has always denied; Christians have always held that the Bible is unique, for it is *God's* Word, and therefore uniquely self-interpreting. To make it a chameleonic reflection of the Near Eastern environment is to absorb special revelation into a non-revelatory, sinful human ideological situation, thereby destroying special revelation. Of course, extra-biblical linguistic and cultural considerations are to be used in scriptural study; but (as our Lutheran fathers stressed) they must always be used *ministerially* (as a servant), never *magisterially* (as overlord) in relation to the biblical text.

Consider other impossible difficulties in which this "cultural relevance"

23. These positions are advocated in two mimeographed papers by Alfred von Rohr Sauer. Cf. also Ralph D. Gehrke, "Genesis Three in the Light of Key Hermeneutical Considerations," *Concordia Theological Monthly*, XXXVI (September 1965), 534-60.

24. Presented to Missouri's Conference of College Presidents and Seminary Faculties on December 2, 1963 (and subsequently to several District meetings of the Missouri Synod), and copyrighted by the author in April, 1965.

25. In point of fact, recent biblical scholarship has stressed the *contrast* between the scriptural world-view and that of the ancient world; see G. Ernest Wright, *The Old Testament Against Its Environment*, and Floyd V. Filson, *The New Testament Against Its Environment*.

26. This is the venerable *"post hoc, propter hoc"* fallacy known to every student of elementary logic (but to relatively few professional theologians strange to say).

approach to Scripture places us: It requires us to separate the "form" of biblical address from its "content." This, however, is like peeling an onion — and the result is (or should be) theological weeping, for only subjective criteria tell us whether we are to stress as content or de-emphasize as form a given aspect of the biblical narrative. In the case of Genesis 1-3, for example, why not hold that the very concept of God is one of the forms that primitive Near Eastern man used to interpret his world — and that the *true* content is the desire (à la Eliade and Jung) to bring about a "conjunction of opposites" in human experience? Moreover, where in Scripture do we draw the line in applying the "cultural relevance" approach? No criteria (other than subjective likes and dislikes) exist here either, and since *all* biblical events occurred in an environment, why aren't they *all* to be considered reflections of it? Why not interpret Jesus' claims that he came to "give his life a ransom for many" as a "form" explainable in terms of the 1st century world, where, in the rite of Taurobolium, the religious initiate descended into a ditch and was bathed in the blood of a sacred bull slain above him? In such a way, by the mere logical application of the proposed new approach to biblical hermeneutics, one can totally destroy the scriptural revelation and its saving message. Granted that *we* may not go this far, but, once the approach is accepted as legitimate, what will prevent others from consistently carrying it out?

A further refinement of the new interpretive orientation is "Law-Gospel exegesis." Bouman begins with the claim: "The distinctive characteristic of Lutheran theology, and therefore of Lutheranism itself, is the antithesis between Law and Gospel. This antithesis is not just one of many Lutheran 'doctrines.' It is rather the central and decisive perspective for everything Lutheran."[27] From here he moves to biblical interpretation, arguing that the true Lutheran is not concerned about matters of factual inerrancy in Scripture, but about Law-Gospel. "If God deals with us in Law and Gospel, then we will look for *that* and be struck by *that* in Genesis, Joshua, and the Ascension story. And we will recognize that whatever the cosmology — our own or that of the Bible — God calls our idolatrous use of His world into question with the Law and creates everything — even sinners — anew out of nothing through the Gospel."[28] Following this line, Thomas W. Strieter, an instructor at Concordia Teachers College, River Forest, informs us how revolutionary it was that Reformation Lutherans had thoroughgoing Copernicans among them, "because Copernicanism differed with the cosmology in the Book of Judges. But this did not concern the Lutherans because it was *not a threat to the Gospel*."[29]

Now what exactly is going on here? First, the Law-Gospel distinction is asserted to be the center of Lutheran theology. This may or may not be the case (there is excellent reason to hold that the center is the Incarnation, as distinct from Calvinism's stress on God's transcendent sovereignty and Roman

27. Bouman, "What is Lutheran in Theology," *op. cit.*, p. 11.
28. Bouman, "The Teaching of Religion: A Theological Analysis," *op. cit.*, p. 43 (Bouman's italics).
29. "Strieter's Letter Suggests Educational Changes," *Advance*, XIII (May, 1966), 7 (Strieter's italics).

Catholicism's emphasis on magisterial, ecclessiastical authority).[30] But even if Law-Gospel is allowed to represent the center of Lutheran theology, one can hardly tolerate a jump to the totally unwarranted conclusion that it is the *whole* of Lutheran theology and biblical interpretation. The argument proceeds to depreciate all that is *not* Law-Gospel in Scripture, and allows for a cavalier attitude toward the cosmological and historical claims of the Bible. This is sheer, unmitigated reductionism: the restriction of the whole counsel of God to Law-Gospel. The result is a special kind of existential reductionism, no different in principle from Bultmann's. As Bultmann reduces the historical resurrection of Christ to an existential, "heart resurrection ("self-understanding," "authentic existence"), so the Law-Gospel exegete reduces God's *ex nihilo* creation of the world described in Genesis to a "calling of our idolatrous use of the world into question with the Law" and a recreating of sinners "out of nothing through the Gospel." As a matter of fact, Reformation Copernicans such as Kepler were not blithely unconcerned about harmonizing Joshua and the new cosmology; they worked hard, long, and faithfully on the problem,[31] for they knew full well that if God's Word represented faulty human opinion at this point, then it could be called into question on any other point — including Law-Gospel and the very plan of salvation itself!

But aside from such concrete factual howlers in the Law-Gospel argument, it should be evident that this entire line of reasoning illogically assumes that biblical statements can be translated willy-nilly into Law-Gospel statements and their obvious literal meanings ignored or regarded as non-revelatory. Such a treatment of Scripture makes one think of Greenwich Village cartoonist Jules Feiffer's analysis of the Huntley-Brinkley show:

> It is time for a serious critical evaluation of this season's TV news programs. Number one — the Huntley, Brinkley show. It is not the news that is important in this program. Rather, it is the complex relationship of the two heroes. The viewer is compelled to ask, Do they like each other today? Would David prefer to work in New York? Would Chet prefer Washington? When Chet seems depressed by events we worry, not because of the event, but because of its effect on Chet.[32]

Thus do Bouman, Streiter, *et al.* attempt to argue that "it is not the factual, historical news that is important in the biblical program. Rather, it is the

30. Cf. my essay, "Evangelical Unity in the Light of Contemporary Orthodox Eastern-Roman Catholic-Protestant Ecumenicity," *The Springfielder*, XXX (Autumn, 1965), 8-30.
31. See especially Kepler's introduction to his *Astronomia nova* of 1609 (in the Frisch edition of Kepler's *Opera omnia*, III, 153 ff.). Since this was one of the areas of my doctoral work at Strasbourg, I feel a bit sensitive about sloppy, misleading generalizations based upon secondary sources. Cf. Montgomery, "Cross, Constellation, and Crucible: Lutheran Astrology and Alchemy in the Age of the Reformation," *Transactions of the Royal Society of Canada*, 4th ser., I (1963), 251-70 (also published in the British periodical *Ambix, the Journal of the Society for the Study of Alchemy and Early Chemistry*, XI [June, 1963], 65-86, and shortly to appear in French in *Revue d'Histoire et de Philosophie Religieuses*).
32. Jules Feiffer, *Hold Me!* (New York: New American Library Signet Books, 1964), p. [72].

complex Law-Gospel relationship"! And the pseudo-sophisticated argument is as unrealistic in the one case as in the other.

Ironically, moreover, Law-Gospel exegesis does exactly what the new theologians claim they are counteracting: it substitutes an abstract, cold, formalistic principle for the living dynamic of God's salvatory actions and words. Instead of experiencing the creative and redemptive life pulsating through a totally revelatory Word, one floats into the realm of idealistic abstraction. Law-Gospel comes to function as an independent philosophical principle (like those of 19th century German idealism) by which Scripture is judged; and the Bible takes on the role of a book of illustrations for the principle. Not so the Reformers' view of Law-Gospel; for them, it derived *from* Scripture, and, like all other theological truths, it could be affirmed only on the ground of the total reliability of God's Word.[33]

A further clarification is required before leaving the question of biblical authority. Several of the theologians advocating the new approach to Holy Writ contend that the truth (or even the "infallibility") of Scripture is not impugned if the Bible contains errors or contradictions. "After all," it is said, "cannot God reveal through error and contradiction? You conservatives don't trust the Holy Spirit to work even through a fallible text!" But again the argument confuses the issue. Certainly God can and does "work" through fallible and even sinfully perverse agents (e.g., Nebuchadnezzar — or us!); the "whole world," as the spiritual puts it, "is in His hands." But to "reveal" through error or contradiction is in itself a contradiction in terms. From a contradiction, as any student of elementary logic knows, *anything* can follow; thus a "revelation" containing contradictions can "reveal" anything and everything, and so reveals nothing. And a "revelation" through error reveals an erroneous God, who, presumably, cannot be trusted. Moreover, as I have pointed out at length elsewhere,[34] if God's revelation contains errors or contradictions, then some criterion is absolutely essential for locating what *is* untrustworthy there, so as to free the true and non-contradictory material from deserved criticism; but such a criterion would, by the nature of the case, have to come from outside Scripture, and this would mean a revelation-of-the-second-power to interpret the Bible. That such a revelation in tradition, church authority, or any other source does not exist, the Reformers maintained with all their strength; they saw the argument for what it was: an infinite regress that denies the ability of God to reveal Himself veraciously in Holy Writ.

If space permitted, we could show how the theological revisionists, starting from the biblical orientation already described, are endeavoring to shift substantive Lutheran doctrines in a more "relevant" (i.e., Law-Gospel and anthropocentric) direction. The fact that the Law-Gospel dichotomy has be-

---

33. For further discussion of these hermeneutic issues, see the papers by Ralph A. Bohlmann and by the present essayist in *Aspects of Biblical Hermeneutics* ("Concordia Theological Monthly. Occasional Papers," No. 1; St. Louis, 1966). My paper has been reprinted in the present volume as Essay II.

34. Montgomery, "The Theologian's Craft: A Discussion of Theory Formation and Theory Testing in Theology," *Concordia Theological Monthly,* XXXVII (February, 1966), 67-98 (especially pp. 80-85).

come an aprioristic presupposition standing above and in judgment upon both Scripture and the Confessions is apparent from the current attempt to eliminate a distinct Third Use of the Law[35] — a teaching so important to the authors of the Formula of Concord that they devoted an entire section (VI.) of their Confession to it.[36] The revisionists' anthropocentric thrust (we have already met it in the effort to reinterpret Scripture from the standpoint of its human authors and its "cultural situation") is appallingly evident in the retranslation of the biblical Christ. Thus Bouman writes in his Concordia, River Forest, seminar paper, "Jesus As the Christ":[37]

> Jesus' unique Sonship is not manifest in terms of perfect knowledge, unique powers, or other trappings of pagan "divinity." He is a man locked in a particular history and culture. He derives his images, parables, similes from his cultural and geographical setting. He is capable of *ad hominem* argumentation. He lives, speaks and thinks as a first-century Palestinian Jew. But his obedience to the Father is unbroken.

Any resemblance (as the cinematographic title has it) between this Jesus and the New Testament Jesus is purely coincidental! In the New Testament, Jesus' ministry is one of supernatural knowledge and unique powers — of miracle in word and deed; it is a ministry of One who, far from being locked in His culture, "came down from heaven," trailing heaven's glory in everything He did. He did *not* employ the fallacious *ad hominem* form of argument; in the face of his divine cogency, men "could not answer him a word." He perceived men's thoughts and knew what was in their hearts; no man spoke as He spoke; and when brought face to face with His life and death, those not blinded by their own self-centeredness cried, "Surely this was the Son of God."

Three Concluding Axioms

This is the day of the enigmatic Zen Koan, and it would be a delight to close with several pithy enigmas, such as, "Once theology has been made fully

35. See Robert J. Hoyer, "On Law and Gospel," *The Cresset*, XXIX (February, 1966), 8-9; and Bouman, "The Teaching of Religion: A Theological Analysis," *op. cit.*, p. 42, n. 22. (Incidentally, Helmut Thielicke, in his *Theological Ethics*, Vol. I [Philadelphia: Fortress Press, 1966], pp. 133 ff., especially p. 134, n. 7, eloquently argues for the presence of the Third Use of the Law in Luther's own teachings; thus one tends to look with a jaundiced eye on Bouman's misleading assertion: "Luther never uses the term." My appreciation to Dr. George W. Forell, who first brought this reference to Thielicke to my attention.)

36. Cf. my article, "The Law's Third Use: Sanctification," *Christianity Today*, VII (April 26, 1963), 722-24 (reprinted in the present volume as Essay V).

37. Presented in mimeographed form on November 15, 1965, with the caveat, "not to be quoted without permission." (I have received oral permission from Professor Bouman to quote the essay.) The title of the paper deserves careful note: not "Jesus Christ," but "Jesus *As* the Christ" (the contemporary theological wedge is driven between "the historical Jesus" and "the Christ of faith," in the manner of Tillich). In opposition to such thinking, see Carl F. H. Henry's symposium volume, *Jesus of Nazareth: Saviour and Lord* (Grand Rapids, Michigan: Eerdmans, 1966), containing my essay, "Toward a Christian Philosophy of History" (pp. 225-40).

'relevant' to sinful culture, old and new, what theology remains?" But our substantive description of the new theological emphases in the Missouri Synod has provided us with all the vagaries we can endure for the moment, so let us conclude with three crystal-clear axioms. (1) The truly relevant theology has always been the theology that is to the greatest degree faithful to God's revelation — that in no sense stands in criticism of it, but which becomes a channel for the Word to reach out in judgment and grace to a lost world. (2) Those who continually talk about "relevance in the human situation" are invariably the least relevant, for "he who would seek life shall lose it, but he who loses his life for My sake, the same shall find it." (3) As in politics, so in the church, people get the government they deserve. "The secret of freedom is courage," said Pericles in his Oration on the Athenian Dead, and he was precisely correct. If you want to preserve the freedom of the church to proclaim an unadulterated Word and a scriptural Gospel, then you must have the courage to say to your church leaders: I shall not tolerate the corruption of eternal truth in my church, for my Lord means too much to me for that, and the needs of the unbelieving world are too great to permit the attenuating of Christian witness. As Walther well put it in his sermon, "The Sheep Judge Their Shepherds": "Oh, my dear friends, if you at one time had realized that the office of judge belonged to you, you would not have entered upon so many and such dangerous bypaths."

V.

THE LAW'S THIRD USE: SANCTIFICATION

In 1528 — only a decade after the posting of the Ninety-five Theses — Erasmus asserted that "the Lutherans seek two things only — wealth and wives (*censum et uxorem*)" and that to them the Gospel meant "the right to live as they please" (letter of March 20, 1528, to W. Pirkheimer, a fellow humanist). From that day to this Protestants have been suspected of antinomianism, and their Gospel of "salvation by grace through faith, apart from the works of the Law" has again and again been understood as a spiritual insurance policy which removes the fear of hell and allows a man to "live as he pleases."

Sanctification Twice Desanctified

The claim that Protestantism is essentially antinomian seemed to have an especially strong basis in fact in the nineteenth century. Industrialization and urbanization brought about social evils which were overlooked and rationalized by many professing Protestants. Inevitably a reaction occurred, and in the social-gospel movement of the late nineteenth and early twentieth centuries one encounters a textbook illustration of what Hegel called the antithesis. In its fear that Protestantism had become ethically indifferent, the social-gospel movement of Washington Gladden and Walter Rauschenbusch identified the Christian message with social ethics. From an apparent justification without sanctification, the pendulum swung to a "sanctification" which swallowed up justification. In their eagerness to bring in the kingdom of God through social action and the amelioration of the ills of the industrial proletariat, the social gospelers generally lost track of the central insight of the Reformation: that the love of *Christ* must constrain the Christian, and that we can experience and manifest this love only if we have personally come into a saving relationship with the Christ who "first loved us" (I John 4:19) and gave himself on the cross for us (I Peter 2:24).

World War I burst the optimistic bubble of the social gospel; no longer did there seem to be much assurance that human beings had the capacity to establish a sanctified society on earth. But the reductionist biblical criticism with which the social-gospel movement had allied itself did not die as easily. So loud had been the voices of modernism against a perspicuous, fully reliable Scripture that in the most influential Protestant circles it was believed that a return to a propositional biblical ethic could never take place. The result was (and is, for the movement is by no means dead) an existential ethic.

The Protestant existentialists do not of course go to the length of the atheist Jean-Paul Sartre, who says in *Existentialism and Human Emotions,*

"There are no omens in the world." But when Sartre follows this assertion with the qualification that even if there were omens (as the Christian believes), "I myself choose the meaning they have," he comes very close to the approach of the contemporary Protestant existentialist. The latter, unable to rely (he thinks) on a biblical revelation which is objectively and eternally definitive in matters ethical, must himself "choose the meaning" of Scripture for his unique existential situation. In practice he agrees with Simone de Beauvoir when she says that man "has no need of any outside guarantee to be sure of his goals" (*The Ethics of Ambiguity*). Right or wrong is never determined absolutely in advance; the Bible is not a source of ethical absolutes — it is rather the record of how believers of former times made ethical decisions in the crises of their experience. What distinguishes the Christian ethic from the non-Christian, in this view? Only the motivation of love. The Christian has experienced God's love, and so is in a position to bring that love to bear upon the unique existential decisions he faces. This existential approach, at root highly individualistic, has in recent years been given a "group discussion" orientation by such writers as A. T. Rasmussen, who, in his *Christian Social Ethics* (1956), asserts that existential decision should take place in "the higher community of God," where "Christian discussion" serves as "the channel through which the Holy Spirit moves in the dialectic or give-and-take of genuine spiritual intercourse to provide ethical guidance."

The contemporary existential ethic in Protestantism is a second instance of desanctifying sanctification, for it inevitably devolves into ethical relativism. Sartre, when asked advice by a young man who, during World War II, was torn between a desire to join the Free French Forces and a feeling that he should stay in France to take care of his mother, could only say, "You're free, choose, that is, invent." Likewise, the Protestant existentialist can never appeal to absolute law; he can only say, "You're free, choose to love." But what does this mean in concrete terms? Theoretically it can mean "anything goes" — an antinomianism indeed — for each existential decision is unique and without precedent. Thus the housemother in *Tea and Sympathy* who committed adultery out of self-giving (*agape?*) love in order to prove to a student that he was not incapable of heterosexual relationships, cannot be condemned for her decision. As for Rasmussen's ethic of social existentialism, one can see that it merely compounds the problem on the group level. George Forell has well characterized this approach as "inspiration by bladder control," for the person who stays longest in the group discussion is frequently the one whose "responsible participation" determines the "contextual and concrete" ethic of the moment. The absence of an eternal ethical standard either in individualistic or in social existentialism totally incapacitates it for promoting Christian holiness.

Answer of Classical Protestantism

In the Protestantism of the Reformation, antinomianism is excluded on the basis of a clear-cut doctrine of the Law and a carefully worked-out relation between the Law and the Gospel. The Reformers assert, first of all, that no man is saved on the basis of Law. As the *Apology of the Augsburg*

Confession puts it: *Lex semper accusat* ("The Law always indicts"). Whenever a man puts himself before the standard of the Law — whether God's eternally revealed Law in the Bible or the standard of Law written on his own heart — he finds that he is condemned. Only the atoning sacrifice of Christ, who perfectly fulfilled the demands of the Law, can save; thus, in the words of the Apostle, "by grace are ye saved through faith; and that not of yourselves: it is the gift of God: not of works, lest any man should boast" (Eph. 2:8, 9).

But God's Law, as set forth in Scripture, remains valid. Indeed, the Law has three functions (*usus*): the political (as a restraint for the wicked), the theological (as "a *paidagogos* to bring us to Christ" — Gal. 3:24), and the didactic (as a guide for the regenerate, or, in Bonhoeffer's words, "as God's merciful help in the performance of the works which are commanded"). Few Protestants today dispute the first and second uses of the Law; but what about the third or didactic use? Do Christians, filled with the love of Christ and empowered by His Holy Spirit, need the Law to teach them? Are not the Christian existentialists right that love is enough? Indeed, is it not correct that Luther himself taught only the first two uses of the Law and not the *tertius usus legis?*

Whether or not the formulation of a didactic use of the Law first appeared in Melanchthon (Helmut Thielicke [*Theologische Ethik*] and others have eloquently argued for its existence in Luther's own teaching; cf. Edmund Schlink, *Theology of the Lutheran Confessions*), there is no doubt that it became an established doctrine both in Reformation Lutheranism and in Reformation Calvinism. One finds it clearly set out in the Lutheran *Formula of Concord* (Art. VI) and in Calvin's *Institutes* (II, vii, 12 ff.). It is true that for Luther the pedagogic use of the Law was primary, while for Calvin this third or didactic use was the principal one; yet both the Lutheran and the Reformed traditions maintain the threefold conceptualization.

An Essential Doctrine

The Third Use is an essential Christian doctrine for two reasons. First, because love — even the love of Christ — though it serves as the most powerful impetus to ethical action, does not inform the Christian as to the proper *content* of that action. Nowhere has this been put as well as by the beloved writer of such hymns "I Heard the Voice of Jesus Say" and "I Lay My Sins on Jesus"; in his book, *God's Way of Holiness*, Horatius Bonar wrote:

> But will they tell us what is to regulate service, if not law? *Love,* they say. This is a pure fallacy. Love is not a *rule,* but a *motive.* Love does not tell me *what* to do; it tells me *how* to do it. Love constrains me to do the will of the beloved one; but to know what the will is, I must go elsewhere. The law of our God is the *will* of the beloved one, and were that expression of his will withdrawn, love would be utterly in the dark; it would not know what to do. It might say, I love my Master, and I love his service, and I want to do his bidding, but I must know *the rules of his house,* that I may know *how* to serve him. Love without law to guide its impulses would be the parent of will-worship and confusion, as surely as terror and self-righteousness, unless upon the supposition of an inward miraculous illumination, as an equivalent for law.

Love goes to the law to learn the divine *will,* and love delights in the law, as the exponent of that will; and he who says that a believing man has nothing more to do with law, save to shun it as an old enemy, might as well say that he has nothing to do with the will of God. For the divine law and the divine will are substantially one, the former the outward manifestation of the latter. And it is *the will* of our Father which is in heaven" that we are to do (Matt. 7:21); so proving by loving obedience what is that "good and acceptable, and perfect *will of God*" (Rom. 12:2). Yes, it is he that doeth "the *will* of God that abideth forever" (I John 2:17); it is to "the *will of God*" that we are to live (I Peter 4:2); "made perfect in every good work *to do his will*" (Heb. 13:21); and "fruitfulness in every good work," springs from being "filled with the knowledge of *his will*" (Col. 1:9, 10).

Secondly, the doctrine of the Third Use is an essential preservative for the entire doctrine of sanctification. The Third Use claims that as a result of justification, it is a nomological fact that "if any man be in Christ he is a new creature: old things are passed away; behold, all things are become new" (II Cor. 5:17). A man in Christ has received a new spirit — the Spirit of the living God — and therefore his relation to the Law is changed. True, in this life he will always remain a sinner (I John 1:8), and therefore the Law will always accuse him, but now he sees the biblical Law in another light — as the manifestation of God's loving will. Now he can say with the psalmist: "I delight in Thy Law" and "O how I love Thy Law!" (Ps. 119; cf. Ps. 1 and 19). Only by taking the Third Use of the Law — the "law of Christ" (Gal. 6:2) — seriously do we take regeneration seriously; and only when we come to love God's revealed Law has sanctification become a reality in our lives. Ludwig Ihmels made a sound confession of faith when he wrote in *Die Religionswissenschaft der Gegenwart in Selbstdarstellungen:* "I am convinced as was Luther that the Gospel can only be understood where the Law has done its work in men. And I am equally convinced that just the humble Christian, however much he desires to live in enlarging measure in the spirit, would never wish to do without the holy discipline of the *tertius usus legis.*" The answer to antinomianism, social-gospel legalism, and existential relativism lies not only in the proper *distinction* between Law and Gospel, as C. F. W. Walther so effectively stressed, but also in the proper *harmony* of Law and Gospel, as set forth in the classic doctrine of the Third Use of the Law.

VI.

MISSOURI COMPROMISE & AFTERMATH

Missouri Compromise

1.

"How are things in Glocca Morra?" asks Sharon in *Finian's Rainbow*. The answer is "Grandish" for an Irish lass whose utopia is the green of Erin. Evangelicals will be saddened to learn that in the Lutheran Church-Missouri Synod, once a utopian model of conservative theology (as represented by such luminaries as Walther and Pieper) and of missionary zeal (one thinks especially of Walter Maier), things are now far from grandish.

They are, in fact, compromisish; and so serious is the problem on doctrinal, ecumenical, and administrative levels that unless the forthcoming Convention of the Church at Denver in July reverses the trend, Missouri will certainly go the way of all flesh: into irreversible theological confusion and unionistic indifferentism.

Is it really possible that doctrinal disunity now characterizes the Lutheran Church-Missouri Synod, a church body whose hallmark has been rigorous adherence to Reformation confessions as true expressions of the teaching of the inerrant Scriptures? Here is the depressing answer of the greatest living orthodox Lutheran dogmatician, Hermann Sasse, formerly of Erlangen and now a professor of theology in Australia: "It is exactly twenty years that I set out from Germany for St. Louis to discover with deep disappointment that your church was divided. Through all these years I have shared the grave concern of the conservatives in your church. My prayer is that Denver will mean a turning point. There will be a new presidency. If this is to be only a repetition of the politics of uncertainty and compromise, it would mean the fall of the last great confessional Church" (communication of May 13, 1968).

In the 1940s, a cloud no larger than a man's hand arose in Missouri in the so-called "Chicago Statement of the 44," a manifesto of clergy dissatisfied with the synod's strict position on church fellowship. The "Statementarians" had some good points to make, but their real concerns went far beyond the fellowship issue; they desired a Missouri Synod in which more emphasis would be placed on ecumenical involvement. The synod administration did not air the problem or deal with it decisively. It was swept under the rug by persuading all concerned to "withdraw" (but not retract) the Chicago Statement (pastoral letter of President Behnken, January 18, 1947). The consequence was the established presence of an informal but articulate "liberal" faction in Missouri, devoted to modernization.

In the intervening years, those of liberalizing mind-set have vastly increased their influence, particularly in the administrative and publications echelons of the excessively centralized denomination, and in its two major educational institutions: Concordia Seminary, St. Louis, and Concordia Teachers College, River Forest, Illinois.

So fractured is doctrinal unity in Missouri that a group of Eastern District liberals has actually formulated a resolution to make Missouri a full member of the NCC, LWF, and WCC on the ground that "it is utter audacity to assume this unified orthodoxy (or Theological agreement) is even a remote possibility within our own Synod."

The Missouri Synod has been particularly noteworthy both for its uncompromising stand on biblical inerrancy (in line with the Lutheran Formula of Concord), which expressly states, following Luther, that "God's Word alone is and should remain the only standard and rule, to which the writings of n man should be regarded equal, but to it everything should be subordinated"), and for its insistence on the verbal proclamation of the propositional, biblical Gospel through a Christian school system and by all available communications media. Now, however, both message and its clear proclamation are under question.

The doctrine of scriptural inerrancy is outrightly denied by some Missouri Synod clergymen (e.g., Robert Scharlemann), and no disciplinary action is taken. Professors such as Walter Bouman at River Forest and Robert H. Smith at St. Louis distinguish the "scholastic" inerrancy view of traditional Missouri theology from their own allegedly "evangelical" view of the Bible. Writes Smith in October, 1968, *Lutheran Forum*: "In the scholastic view the Bible alone is inspired and inerrant, and it is therefore the sole authority in all matters of doctrine, history, science, and what have you. In the confessional or evangelical view every Christian is inspired when he believes in and bears witness to Jesus as Lord."

The effect of this downgrading of the Bible has been a corresponding lack of confidence in presenting its propositional message. Thus Dr. John Elliott, in a series of lectures at Missouri's annual Mission Institute in 1966, offered a non-verbal approach to evangelism that seriously confused the Gospel with social action. At the close of the institute, one of the most respected communications specialists in the Synod, Dr. Herman Gockel (author of *What Jesus Means to Me*), wrote to Professor Elliott: "The position which you have taken in this respect is untenable." And Elliott himself, after a meeting on the subject with the undersigned and others, wrote quite frankly of the "manifestation of two quite different, if not irreconcilable, approaches toward the understanding and interpretation of both the Sacred Scriptures and the Lutheran Symbols."

Prior to the 1967 Convention of the Missouri Synod in New York, the Free Evangelical Lutheran Church of Finland sent a fraternal warning to her sister church in America. One of the closing paragraphs of that monitum well expresses the path Missouri must take if her present doctrinal situation is to be remedied:

"The witness of the Lutheran Church-Missouri Synod during the past decades, resulting especially from internal unity, has echoed throughout the world. Now, that unity has disappeared and it is openly stated that a portion of the Synod is conservative, a portion, super-conservative, and a portion, liberal. Nevertheless, the Confessions prescribe agreement in doctrine as a necessary qualification for the preservation of the unity of the church. We believe that the prevailing situation can be corrected only with the help of efficient, objective, doctrinal discipline, which God has commanded and for which He has provided the weapons (I Pet. 4:11; Gal. 1:8; 5:9; II Cor. 6:14; Tit. 3:10, 11 etc.). If the great majority (some believe as much as 90 per cent) of the Synod is still obedient to God's Word, it should not be impossible to restore doctrinal unity. If all those faithful to God's Word join the fight against liberalism and ecumenism and choose as their weapon the doctrinal discipline prescribed by God's Word, the precious heritage of the Reformation will be saved and Christ's name will be glorified among us."

2.

So stands the internal, doctrinal aspect of the current crisis of belief in the Lutheran Church-Missouri Synod. Now something needs to be said about the external consequences of this mid-twentieth-century Missouri Compromise: the very real possibility that the July convention of the synod in Denver will declare "pulpit and altar fellowship" with The American Lutheran Church.

"And what could possibly be the matter with *that?*" interjects the ecumenically minded reader. "Doesn't the ALC have a similar ethnic background, the same Lutheran confessions, and a tradition of powerful orthodox theology, as represented by the exegetical labor of Lenski and the dogmatic and historical scholarship of Reu? Haven't joint commissioners of the ALC and the Missouri Synod arrived at common agreements as to fellowship? Didn't the ALC in its Omaha convention on October 18 declare the pulpit and altar fellowship with Missouri? And hasn't the official resolution of Missouri's 1967 New York convention stated that 'the task is not to create or fashion a basis for unity. This Scriptural and confessional basis exists. From this basis the Synod now seeks to move forward with whatever steps are necessary for a full realization of altar and pulpit fellowship'?"

Now it is certainly the case that the ALC has expressed its desire for full fellowship with Missouri. But such an agreement must be bilateral, and Missouri's final decision in the matter will not be made until its Denver convention. Some feel there are significant reasons why this proposed agreement should not be carried out.

The ALC of today is not the ALC of Lenski or Reu. Can one imagine, for example, Lenski's participation in the opening communion service of the ALC's Omaha convention, where the reredos posed the questions, "Whom Shall I Send? Who Will Go for Us?," accompanied by pictures of four men: Gandhi, who explicitly refused the name of Christian; Schweitzer, who, consistent with his lifelong denial of Jesus' deity, joined the International Unitarian Association shortly before his death; Martin Luther King, whose Boston University theology was little more than social-gospel humanism; and, inevitably, Martin Luther, who would have felt as uncomfortable there as Lenski, if not more so,

Or take Reu, author of the classic *Luther and the Scriptures*, which so painstakingly demonstrates from the sources Luther's conviction that "the Scriptures have never erred" (WA, 15, 1481) and "it is impossible that Scripture should contradict itself; it only appears so to senseless and obstinate hypocrites" (WA, 9, 356)—can one visualize him working happily side by side with religion professor Paul Jersild of the ALC's Luther College, who writes: "We who teach at Luther College cannot subscribe to scriptural inerrancy" (*Luther*, Spring, 1967)?

The high doctrinal assertions of the ALC-Missouri Synod joint commissioners do not represent what is actually being taught in ALC religion departments and seminaries. My own roommate at Cornell University chose the ALC's Luther Seminary for his pastoral training so that he would not be subjected to the demise of doctrine at the schools of his own denomination, and then lost his belief in the inerrant authority of the Bible there—principally because of instruction received from Warren Quanbeck. Quanbeck's activities in ecumenical Lutheranism have resulted in such productions as the weak and muddy "Study Document on Justification" prepared for the 1963 LWF Assembly in Helsinki. Quanbeck holds a thoroughly neo-orthodox view of the Bible, and incorporates into his thinking on the subject the un-Lutheran idea that the finite is incapable of the infinite: "Since human language is always relative, being conditioned by its historical development and usage, there can be no absolute expression of the truth even in the language of theology" (*Theology in the Life of the Church*, ed. Robert Bertram [1963], p. 25).

"But," one may ask, "have you not said there are instances of doctrinal deterioration in the Missouri Synod? Doesn't this indicate that both bodies are more or less in the same boat and have no reason to remain apart?"

To this, two things need to be said. First, systematic efforts are being made, especially on the lay and congregational level, to do something about Missouri's theological difficulties; but in the ALC little or nothing is being done to preserve doctrinal integrity. The theological deviants in the ALC are "untouchables"—they can write or preach without any fear of being forced to toe the confessional mark. As Klaas Runia correctly noted in a series of articles for *Christianity Today* some years ago, the presence of heresy does not make a denomination heretical, but refusal to do anything about it does. Should Missouri join the ALC when, unlike Missouri, the ALC appears to have lost its concern for the disciplined purity of church teaching?

131

Secondly, there has been greater deterioration on the parish level in the ALC than in the Missouri Synod. In Missouri, theological weakness is still largely confined to particular schools and publications; the grass roots is still (for the present at least!) very solid.

This is clear from two surveys. Jeffrey Hadden's study of the beliefs of U.S. Protestant ministers (summarized in *Christianity Today*, October 13, 1967) revealed that whereas 95 per cent of Missouri clergy believe that the Virgin Birth was a physical miracle, only 81 per cent of ALC pastors hold this belief. As to the inerrancy of the Bible, 76 per cent of Missouri pastors hold to it, but only 23 per cent—less than a fourth!— of the ALC clergy regard Scripture as entirely trustworthy (and if only ALC pastors under thirty-five years of age are considered, the affirmations of scriptural inerrancy drop to 6 per cent). The 1965 Glock-Stark survey of lay Protestant convictions showed that whereas 86 per cent of Missouri laymen maintain an unqualified belief in original sin, only 49 per cent of ALC laymen—less than half—do so. On the deity of Christ, only 74 per cent of ALC laymen affirmed it, while 93 per cent of lay Missourians said they believed in it. Missouri laymen were 70 per cent willing to express "certainty" as to religious belief; only 48 per cent of ALCers could do so.

Would not pulpit and altar fellowship with the ALC (a member of the LWF and the WCC, which Missouri has consistently regarded as unionistic) greatly accelerate the synod's doctrinal decline? Might not such a step put it beyond the hope of recovery? Is not this issue a watershed? These are the questions that will be answered one way or the other at Denver.

President Kreiss of the Missouri-affiliated Free Lutheran Church of France and Belgium surely speaks for many when he says: "For my part, 1969 and the outcome of elections in Denver and of certain issues like intercommunion with ALC and LWF membership will be absolutely decisive. If there is no right-about switch then, I'll step out."

3.

At the conclusion of his volume on *American Protestantism* (1961), noted church historian Winthrop S. Hudson observed that Lutheran denominations have experienced rapid growth rates since World War II, "with the Lutheran Church-Missouri Synod making the greatest gains," and saw in this phenomenon a bright hope for U.S. Protestantism, since Lutheranism has been "less subject to the theological erosion" experienced by other American churches. But, as we have seen, the last few years have considerably dampened such hopes. "Theological erosion" has taken place, and its results are concretely visible.

The synod's gigantic 1967 "Ebenezer" fund drive was a sorry failure, and no small reason for this was the dissatisfaction of lay Missourians with the leaders of their church who have done little to stop the advance of theological deviations and who appointed as head of the fund drive the president of the Concordia (River Forest) Teachers College, a consistent defender of his institution's latitudinarian religion department. While enrollments in accredited theological schools in the United States have increased significantly this academic year, the Missouri Synod seminaries have experienced a marked decline (see *Christianity Today*, *News*, Dec. 6, 1968). Why is Missouri's trumpet no longer sounding a clear note, and what can be done to remedy the situation?

The reason for Missouri's current theological crisis is to a large extent sociological. Here one observes the "ghetto" phenomenon so characteristic of immigrant groups. During the first century of its existence, the Missouri Synod remained largely walled off from theological erosion because of its commitment to the orthodox doctrinal position (and even language) of its Saxon founders, who had left Germany expressly to avoid politically enforced ecumenical union. World Wars I and II, however, required germanically-suspect Missourians to justify themselves as true Americans, and the common tendency to go from one extreme (ingrownness) to the other (cultural absorption) has been manifest in Missouri's theology in recent decades. Sad to say, some Synod leaders have not been sufficiently aware of this problem to offer the mature leadership required for steering the church's ship between Scylla and Charybdis.

In a very real sense, the core problem in the Missouri Synod exists at the administrative level, and if improvement is to take place anywhere it must begin in the church's highest offices. At first such a judgment may seem inconsistent with the polity of the denomination, since on paper Missouri is one of the most decentralized churches imaginable—fully congregational in organization, But in practice, as conservative Springfield Seminary President J. A. O. Preus has shrewdly observed, the Germanic spirit of authoritarian centralism has counterbalanced the synod's theoretical congregationalism; the grass roots tends to be uncritical of what emanates from the professors and the presidents at the denomination's "Vatican," St. Louis. During the first century of the Synod's existence, parish pastors and laymen followed an orthodox line of march set in St. Louis; now, though the tune being piped is significantly different, the churchwide posture of servility is much the same.

Some feel that the central administration of the synod now typifies what C. S. Lewis called "that hideous strength": bureaucratic religiosity. Parkinson's law often seems more in evidence than either the law of Moses or the New Testament law of love. Some key administrators are now using their positions and their publications in an effort to turn the overwhelmingly orthodox but docile grass roots toward an ecumenical theology.

Here are a few recent examples:

• The editorial direction of the *Lutheran Witness* and the *Lutheran Witness Reporter* is now in the hands of the liberal faction. This leaves only the *Lutheran Layman* (lately returned to a sound theology) as an orthodox general communications medium in the church. The *Reporter* even went so far, on November 17, 1968, as to produce a special supplement ostensibly neutral on the ALC fellowship issue but actually pushing the ecumenical proposal by unfortunate half-truths and innuendos.

• The book editor of the Concordia Publishing House readily publishes ecumenical literature but manages to obfuscate decision on orthodox submissions, obtains negative sales judgments on them, and (if they do occasionally get published) provides substandard promotion for them.

• The *Concordia Theological Monthly*, while maintaining a facade of objectivity, changes material in orthodox articles without the permission of the authors (a Missouri missionary scholar suffered this treatment recently) or endeavors to pressure orthodox authors into accepting changes by introducing them in galley proof. When three years ago the Council of District Presidents (the "bishops" of the church) voted to have some orthodox essays published in the *CTM*, they were conveniently issued in a "special number" of the journal; this had the effect of limiting their circulation (general subscribers never received them) and keeping them out of the journal index.

• The Lutheran Academy for Scholarship, begun to promote higher-level academic contributions within the church, now serves largely as a promotional device for new theological ideas. Lutheran liberals such as Warren Quanbeck, Joseph Sittler, and Krister Stendahl are invited to address its sessions; if conservatives receive invitations (which is very rare), they function as "reactors" and their contributions are not included in the published reports.

• The synod's president is now surrounded by administrative personnel who try to influence him continually in a broad-church direction. At first it appeared to be a classic case of the weak king with bad advisers. Now, however, king himself appears to have been pushed to disastrous policies. In his address to the Council of District Presidents on September 11, 1968, he endeavored to whitewash ALC theology. Then he blundered by identifying his will in the matter with "the will of this Synod" and said that "officials who cannot in good conscience carry out what Synod has asked, be prepared to relinquish their office."

Professor Wilhelm Oesch of the synodically-related Lutherische Theologische Hochschule in Germany has said of the Missouri compromise: "Missouri is not the great exception at the end of all church history so that it can demand of God to 'have it both ways.' " Exactly, *May* not some people have to relinquish their offices? But who?

As the synod meets at Denver in July [1969], the decision will have to be made. Many hope and pray that the Church of the "Lutheran Hour" will experience a theological emancipation that will release it from its new posture of compromise and insure continued commitment to its historic legacy.

Missouri Turns a Corner

The crucial 1969 Denver convention of the Lutheran Church-Missouri Synod has come and gone, leaving mystified observers shaking their heads in bewilderment here and abroad. Hardly had the convention begun when Dr. J. A. O. Preus, the conservative president of synod's Springfield seminary, replaced (almost on the first ballot) the mediating-to-liberal incumbent synodical president Oliver Harms. A few days later, the same convention voted its approval of pulpit-and-altar fellowship with the American Lutheran Church—a move consistently opposed by Preus and other synod conservatives because of the ALC's latitudinarianism on the doctrine of biblical inerrancy, its fellowship with the liberal Lutheran Church in America, and its membership in the unionistic Lutheran World Federation and World Council of Churches.

Having witnessed at close range the kaleidoscopic shifts in the French political climate, I was perhaps better prepared for these apparently inexplicable results than would otherwise have been the case. In France one learns that inconsistency in surface behavior can often be explained consistently if one strikes deeper.

The election of Dr. Preus cannot be attributed—as sour-grapes liberal inside and outside the synod are claiming—to "underground," "anti-harmonistic," "reactionary" forces that endeavored to gain control of the synod for their "nefarious right-wing purposes." Certainly efforts were made to convince delegates to vote a particular way. But this activity was carried on by both sides, as it inevitably is in any democracy. The election itself was entirely aboveboard, and the delegates were free to make their own decisions, which they did.

The post-convention complaints of the losing side merely illustrate an immature liberal syndrome: the attribution of conservative success to "hidden right-wing forces" (c. Stringfellow and Towne's *The Bishop Pike Affair*, which argued in all seriousness that attempts in the Episcopal Church to discipline the bishop for his doctrinal deviations were the product of reactionary elements endeavoring to undermine our democratic society!). Both the far left and the far right continually find bogeymen under their beds (whether "underground anti-democratic forces" or "the international Communist conspiracy"). Preus was elected simply because the Missouri Synod had had enough of leadership that was characterized by an enormous credibility gap and that, step by step, was leading Missouri to compromise its historic doctrinal heritage.

But why, then, the positive vote on the ALC fellowship issue? Unlike the presidential vote (which the incumbent administration could not very well influence before the convention without betraying its fear that its time was running out), the ALC proposal had been advocated in all official church publications for months. And at the convention itself, the pressure actually increased in intensity: delegates found it extremely difficult to resist the repetitious refrain that to oppose the fellowship resolution would be to oppose Christ's own prayer for unity in the church. After Preus's election, some liberals actually went so far as to tell undecided conservatives: "Now that God has given us a firmly conservative leadership again, we have nothing to fear in entering into fellowship with a less conservative body"!

Considering the quantity, intensity, and emotional overtones of the pro-ALC propaganda, it is quite remarkable that the delegates passed the fellowship motion only by a narrow margin. That says something about the theological acumen of Missouri's grass roots; in most large denominations such a vote would have been 98 per cent for fellowship, and the other 2 per cent would have been burned in effigy on the one inviolable heresy charge in the twentieth century church: anti-ecumenicity.

As a whole, Denver was indeed a conservative, not a liberal, victory. Had the seemingly paradoxical vote been reversed—against ALC fellowship but for the continuation of the Harms regime—the cause of confessional Lutheranism would have been lost in the Missouri Synod. For the liberal propaganda emanating from St. Louis would have continued unabated, and, in the absence of a comparable official avenue for presentation of the other side, the ALC fellowship proposal would have inevitably passed at a future convention anyway. Moreover, the steady shift in the direction of a liberal ministerium would have persisted, for nothing would have been done to correct the present latitudinarian atmosphere at such synodical schools as Concordia Seminary, St. Louis, and Concordia Teachers College, River Forest.

As things stand now, there is every hope of a new day in the Missouri Synod. Because of the Germanically authoritarian aura of prestige surrounding the synod's presidential office, Preus is in an ideal position to reverse the trends of the last two decades. But this will come about only if two measures are rigorously carried out—uninhibited by fear or the confusion of Law and Gospel that is continually pressed on Missouri's conservatives in the name of brotherly sentimentality.

First, the President must courageously rid the synod, and particularly its teaching offices, of those persons who by their public teachings have advocated views of Scripture disharmonious with the Church's express belief that the Bible is God's inerrant Word ("everything should be subordinated" to Scripture—*Formula of Concord*, S.D, Summary, para. 9). Martin Scharlemann of the Concordia, St. Louis, faculty has recently stated that in a meeting with liberally oriented district presidents, Preus "specifically promised that no heads will roll." Certainly no vendetta must occur, but unless the heads of a number of liberals are rolled out of Missouri into churches where their owners can maintain their un-Lutheran views with integrity, Missouri will continue to deteriorate. Scriptural defection is a cancer that has destroyed too many denominations for anyone to think naively that it can be treated by a remedy less acute than surgery.

Secondly (and this may irritate the extreme right as much as measure number one infuriates the liberals), the educational system of the synod must be revamped from bottom to top. No longer can the Church be satisfied with lock-step, Germanic indoctrination, whether orthodox or heterodox, or with a slavish adherence to bureaucracy. Missouri's people, from parochial school to seminary, need to learn to *think*—to discover the "reason for the faith that is within them," so that in contact wih the complex ideologies and heresies of our day they will display an active, informed, relevant, socially sensitive, truly biblical faith. Only by such thoroughgoing reeducation will Missouri come into the kind of ecumenical alignments it really needs—with other Bible-believing churches who share Luther's evangelical conviction that "there's none other God" than Christ Jesus and that "he holds the field for ever."

The Last Days of the Late,
Great Synod of Missouri?

"One day it was there, the next it was gone," writes Curt Gentry in his apocalyptic novel, *The Last Days of the Late, Great State of California*, describing the effect of a cataclysmic earthquake on "the superlative state" —the state with "all the accoutrements of the 'good life.'" A fictional production, to be sure; and yet the recent earthquake damage in California and the continuing menace of the San Andreas fault have given it a prophetic quality. Uncomfortable parallels exist with that bastion of the doctrinal "good life," that "superlative synod" of biblical orthodoxy, the Lutheran Church-Missouri Synod. The theological seismologist has no difficulty at all observing the deep tremors of this church body, and one need only extrapolate from present conditions to predict an ecclesiastical earthquake of the direst proportions.

Our foregoing discussions have sufficiently analyzed the formation and present character of the Missouri Synod's peculiar San Andreas fault. The intensive strains that may well result in the total fracturing of this church at its July, 1971, Milwaukee Convention are caused by (1) an over-reaction to the ghetto-like ingrownness of the synod's early days, such that many in the church are seeking undisciplined theological "relevance" whatever the doctrinal cost; (2) the authoritarian, Germanic tendencies of the synod, which place loyalty to the organization and to its officialdom above virtually all other values, including—on occasion—even loyalty to Scripture and the confessions; (3) the untouchable role of professors at the seminaries, teachers' colleges, and other educational institutions of the synod, by which in recent years a non-evangelical theology that espouses non-inerrancy has been able to make considerable inroads into the synod's parishes; and (4) the synod's latest ecumenical involvements, not with consistently confessional, evangelical bodies, but with the American Lutheran Church (only 23 per cent of whose clergy hold to the entire trustworthiness of the Bible) and the Lutheran Council in the U.S.A. (embracing the ALC and the even less orthodox Lutheran Church in America).

The consequences of this deterioration of the grass-roots level are now appearing. Wrote a Missouri pastor recently in a private communication: "Here briefly is my present theological stance: Christianity is essentially theistic humanism. The Gospel is always good news to a bad situation—therefore the Gospel is always conditioned by the situation. The Church from Paul onward has usually misrepresented Christianity as a Compendium if Creeds and doctrines which must be intellectually accepted rather than a positive force for social and psychological renewal. Genesis 1-11 is poetic myth. I fully agree with O.T. reconstruction, JEPD, Redaction history, etc. Scripture *contains* the Word of God, but is not coterminous with it. I believe in the afterlife, but have serious doubts about the existence of hell. . . . I find the people are not as well versed in doctrine and Bible to dispute the discoveries of modern scholarship. I've also discovered that people appreciate a 'breath of fresh air.' Basically, my theology is an admixture of Job—Jesus—and Kahlil Gibran."

With "fresh air" like this blowing about the synod, it was not unnatural that concerned laity and pastors elected conservative theologian J.A.O. Preus to the presidency of the church body at its Denver Convention in 1969. The hope was that Dr. Preus would exercise the firm hand necessary to effect a general doctrinal clean-up. This presidential choice left nothing to be desired in either orthodoxy or scholarship (while president, Preus, a Ph.D. in classics, has published a massive translation of seventeenth-century dogmatician Chemnitz's *De duabus naturis*—a work that probably no other church president in the world today could read, to say nothing of translating!); but the last two years have shown no significant change in the synod's condition.

Why? The answer, much as one hates to give it, is the addiction of the president to the besetting sin of twentieth century administration: politicking. Instead of acting on pure principle—on the clear teaching of Scripture and the confessions—Dr. Preus has allowed himself to be pushed to and fro by real or imagined pressure groups. At the very convention at which he was elected, he had every opportunity to oppose the ALC fellowship resolution. Not only did he neglect to do so, but he has subsequently permitted its implementation on levels where presidential action could certainly have deterred this unfortunate involvement.

When theological liberals in the synod issued their "Call to Openness and Trust" in January of 1970, expressly affirming that differences of opinion should be tolerated in the Missouri Synod on "the question of factual error in the Bible" and "the definition of the presence of Christ in the Lord's Supper," President Preus should have immediately disciplined those responsible for violation of their ordination vows. When the American Lutheran Church in 1970 officially approved the ordination of women, contrary to Missouri's doctrinal stand, Dr. Preus had the right and obligation to suspend fellowship with that body on the ground of de jure and de facto doctrinal disagreement. Nothing has, however, been done on either count; and the highly publicized theological investigation of the central trouble-spot, Concordia Seminary in St. Louis, seems to suffer from hopeless political roadblocks. Moreover, why did not the president initiate such an investigation the morning after taking office, and not a year and a half later?

Hermann Sasse, doubtless the greatest living Lutheran dogmatician, has recently (25 January, 1971) written from Australia condemning present Lutheran doctrinal indifferentism in America. He points to Missouri's forthcoming Milwaukee Convention and warns that unless a stand is taken there "Missouri will be swallowed by the great union of American Protestants

138

which is coming"; and he reminds his readers of Tertullian's observation that Christ has called himself *Veritas* (the Truth), not *Consuetodo* (the Customary).

Even now, many pastors and congregations of the Missouri Synod (including the undersigned) are declaring themselves *in statu confessionis*—in a state of protest against the toleration of error and false doctrine in the church body. Milwaukee appears to by a point of no return. If the president of the synod does not act unequivocally, an earthquake is inevitable, and the consequence will be either the formation of a new pan-Lutheran body of authentic confessional commitment or the movement of vast numbers of Missouri people to such consistently Lutheran and evangelically relevant bodies as the Evangelical Lutheran Synod. In order not to preside over the demise of the Missouri Synod, President Preus must move beyond translating Chemnitz to reincarnating him. He has our prayers.

VII.

THE UNBRIDGEABLE CHASM:
Gospelism or the Scriptural Gospel?

C. S. Lewis says somewhere that good and evil never remain inactive: good "sharpens to a point" and so does evil. On September 1, 1972, President Preus fulfilled the mandate of the 1971 Milwaukee Convention by issuing his *Report* on the doctrinal situation of the St. Louis Seminary; he regretfully concluded on the basis of "abundant" evidence that Seminary professors were holding "views contrary to the established doctrinal position of the Synod" and that the Seminary president, John Tietjen, had failed "to exercise the supervision of the doctrine of the faculty" (pp. 146-47). He called upon the Seminary's Board of Control to insist that the faculty cease to depart from the Synod's doctrinal position through the use of "any method of interpretation which casts doubt on the divine authority of the Scriptures and thus also on the Gospel itself, questions the historicity or factuality of events described in Scripture as actually having taken place, calls into question the reality of any Biblical miracle," or "casts a shadow on the factualness of the Gospel accounts of the ministry of Christ" (*ibid.*).

On September 8, 1972, Dr. Tietjen published his reply, *Fact Finding or Fault Finding?* in which he claimed that his faculty had in no way departed from orthodoxy, and, using the slogan, "Garbage in, garbage out," rejected wholesale the Preus *Report* as "completely unreliable": the "Report is anything but a reliable presentation of what faculty members believe, teach, and confess" (p. 4). Now, in response to the request on September 21 by the Synod's Council of Presidents, the faculty itself has issued a clarification of its position. This document, entitled *Affirmations of Faith and Discussions of Issues*, was approved by the Concordia faculty on November 21 in an effort to assure the church "that we do indeed teach in accord with the doctrinal position of the Lutheran Church-Missouri Synod."

Every member of the Synod—and all those Christians in other communions who have been following this conflict which may be one of the most important for the future of confessing orthodoxy in the church at large—should thank the Concordia faculty for its consistency and candor. On the basis of the *Affirmations and Discussions*, no possible doubt remains that (1) the Preus' *Report* accurately records the views of the Seminary faculty; (2) these views are utterly incompatible with the biblical orthodoxy expressed in the historic Lutheran Confessions to which the Missouri

Synod is officially committed; and (3) the repeated assurance of orthodoxy on the part of Dr. Tietjen and his faculty is based upon an entirely wrong-headed conviction that it *is* Lutheran to operate with a personalistic, fideistic view of Christian truth, to baptize historical-critical method (source analysis, form history, redaction history) for the interpretation of Scripture, and to reduce the whole counsel of God in the Bible to a vague Gospelism.

The document, as its title indicates, consists of two parts: "affirmations" and "discussions." The Preamble informs the reader that the faculty subscribes to the Affirmations section "without reservation." This is not especially helpful, however, since the brief Affirmations portion of the document is a rather lyrical and stylistically inferior expansion of the three articles of the Creed, and carefully avoids any reference to the controverted points at issue. The disputed questions are the subject of the second part of the document, the Discussions. Here the warning is given: "We are not suggesting that each member of the Faculty binds himself to the precise wording"; however, "we also agree that these Discussions present positions responsibly taken on the basis of our Scriptural and Confessional commitment"; indeed, "we, as a Faculty, agree that the principles employed in the following Discussions are Gospel-oriented and therefore Lutheran." It is exceedingly important to note that although the faculty is willing to allow for viewpoints other than those set forth in its Discussions, it insists that its own viewpoints as contained therein *are genuinely Lutheran and fully compatible with Synodical teaching.* This, needless to say, is precisely what must be determined. Let us examine the Discussions in terms of their major emphases: Creation and Fall (Discussions 1 and 2), miracles (Discussion 3), and the historicity, inerrancy, and proper interpretation of the Bible (Discussions 4-9).

The faculty's treatment of the biblical accounts of Creation and Fall introduces us at once to the method that operates throughout their paper. The purpose of the scriptural narratives is to elicit faith, not to provide any guaranteed knowledge of how God made the world or man. "The biblical accounts of God creating the world call for a response of praise and wonder, not biological or geological investigation." "The message remains the same whether we consider the text of Genesis 2-3 a literal historical account or some other kind of literature." Just as the questions of creation, cosmology, and evolution "have engaged the minds of scientists, the imagination of poets, and the faith of worshipers for centuries," so "similarly biblical men of faith, operating with the same limitations of human language in a given culture, were moved by the Spirit to portray the creative work of God in diverse ways." Note well the position here espoused: the biblical writers suffer from exactly the same human limitations as non-inspired writers as to the facticity of what they convey; *the Bible thus has no facutal advantage over extra-biblical material.* The Holy Spirit's work is to see that the message imparts faith, not to guarantee historicity or facticity.

141

Is it possible to maintain that such a conception is Christian, much less Lutheran? The faculty commits the Platonic error of holding that "the finite is not capable of the infinite": that God's Spirit cannot inspire the human authors of Scripture to speak veracious, factual truth in spite of the "limitations of human language." The faculty drives a wedge between personal faith and factual truth, between the Gospel message and historical accuracy, thereby contradicting the very incarnational heart of Christianity. And the faculty turns credible, historical revelation into personalistic fideism—indistinguishable from the vaguest and least supportable Gnostic theosophy.

Having established their pattern of operation in dealing with Creation and Fall, the faculty's approach to miracles follows easily (Discussion 3). Christians are misled when "they demand an absolute acceptance of each detail of the miracle, precisely as it is reported, as a test of their own faith and the faith of others." After all, a miracle such as the feeding of the five thousand "was important only as a means of leading them to know and trust in Jesus Christ."

Here we observe that the facticity of New Testament miracles is of no more consequence to the faculty than the historicity of the Creation and Fall narratives. Faith in Christ is separated from the miraculous events of His life and allowed to float free, without any necessary factual grounding. When the faculty tells us that "any discussion of God's miracles or wonders in the Scriptures" is dependent upon His reconciliation of "the world to Himself for us," the biblical pattern is turned upside down and destroyed. In Scripture, the miracle objectively comes first, and faith and reconciliation follow from and are dependent on it (cf. the miraculous healing of the paralytic in Mark 2, on the basis of which Jesus shows His power to forgive sins and reconcile). Why the scriptural pattern of miracle-then-faith and not faith-then-miracle? To keep the Gospel *estra nos*—objectively over against us—so that we do not make its miraculous power dependent on our subjective faith experience. The faculty's viewpoint, however, pulls the gravitational center away from God to man, vitiating Luther's theocentric "Copernican revolution in theology" by bringing the church back like a dog to the vomit of anthropocentrism.

By far the largest segment of the Discussions pertains to the general question of the authority of the Bible, especially in regard to the disputed areas of historicity, inerrancy, and proper interpretive method. Here, as might be expected, the faculty generalizes the position already exhibited in its analysis of Creation, Fall, and miracles. As to the historicity of biblical material, the faculty reiterates that it is "a misunderstanding of the nature of the Gospel" to "insist on a public acceptance of the historicity of every detail of the life of Jesus as recorded by the evangelists, as if that were a test of our faith"; "our faith," the faculty tells us, "rests in the promise of a faithful God, not in the accuracy of ancient historians" (Discussion 5). Thus the evangelists—and the other

142

human authors of the Bible—are placed on the same level as "ancient historians" in general, with no better claim to precision or accuracy than they. The irony of this attempt to make Christian belief rest on "the promise of a faithful God" and not on a reliable scriptural revelation is, obviously, that *apart from the Bible we do not know what God's promises are.* If the details of Christ's life and the other facts in Holy Writ need not be accurate or worthy of public acceptance in the church, what value have the promises conveyed by these same facts? What makes the evangelists and other biblical writers suddenly more accurate than secular historians at the point of the promises of God they record?

But it is already clear that the faculty is not interested in dealing with questions of facticity, even where the "promises" are concerned. Faith, not intellect, accepts the promises. Indeed, the faculty totally embraces the fideistic error of contemporary theology, by which matters of belief are separated from questions of scriptural accuracy, and—as an inevitable consequence—one can claim commitment to Christianity *even while subjecting all biblical statements to non-factual interpretation.* It thus follows inexorably that the faculty should claim that "in and of itself so-called 'historical-critical' methodology is neutral," that "all the techniques associated with 'historical-critical' methodology, such as source analysis, form history, and redaction history, are legitimated," and that one can use such methodology "on the basis of Christian presuppositions" (Discussion 9).

The faculty's "Christian presuppositions" are in reality its *non-Christian* conviction that the factual accuracy of the Bible is unnecessary—for source-, form-, and redaction-critics all necessarily presuppose that the text is not the product of veracious reporting, that it contains errors and contradictions due to oral transmission, and that the events recorded represent an admixture of what happened and what the writers introduced because of their personal or communal situation-in-life. Consider, for example, the following summary of the method by a philosopher who has no axe to grind as to the Christian or non-Christian nature of higher-critical operations, but who simply wishes to analyze the necessary assumption of the methodology:

> The source critic wonders if the author relied on, or even reproduced, some earlier documents which have not survived independently. The idea of literary dependence or borrowing is a frame within which *contradictions, non sequiturs* and unevenness of style in the Gospels are seen as traces of their construction out of earlier documents or 'sources', which might even be reconstituted word for word from these remains.
>
> Those earlier documents, or the gospels themselves, must have depended on information which came to their writers by word of mouth. *Unless those informants were contemporaries of Jesus,* one or more stages of oral transmission must have intervened. Form-critics set themselves to assess the likely effects of this on the tradition. Here the idea that, *in repeating a story, people emphasize and interpret*

what they are interested in, serves as a frame within which the detailed point and manner, the 'form' of the Gospel paragraphs appears as a trace of their origin or of their development.*

Note how the practitioner of historical criticism must, by the very nature of the method, operate with texts displaying "contradictions" and "non sequiturs" (illogical arguments in which the conclusions do not follow from the premises—as a result of clumsy editorializing), and must assume non-primary source reporting which conveys later interpretation and traditional development of the original message. It is inconceivable that a Christian could legitimately treat the biblical materials in this manner when they claim to be recording exact, primary, factual truth. What is one to do with Luke's express claim that his narrative derived from "those who from the beginning were eyewitnesses" (Luke 1:1-4), or Peter's flat assertion that "we did not follow cleverly devised myths when we made known to you the power and coming of our Lord Jesus Christ, but we were eyewitnesses of His majesty" (II Peter 1:16)? The Bible's own concern with its historicity and factual veracity stands poles apart from the faculty's denigration of truth questions, substitution of personalistic fideism for scriptural reliability, and wholehearted acceptance of critical methods that are incompatible with the Bible's own claims to perfect trustworthiness.

Finally, the Concordia document endeavors to eliminate the Bible as a basis for faith in the interests of "the Gospel." To "begin with the assumption that the doctrine of scriptural infallibility guarantees the validity of our theology" "would not be Lutheran. We, as Lutherans, start with the Gospel of Jesus Christ." "We are saved by grace through faith in Christ alone, not through faith in Christ *and* something else, even if that something else be the Bible itself" (Discussion 4). Here we have the very heart of the faculty's thrust and the overarching issue before the Synod: can a church legitimately operate on the basis of the material principle (the Gospel) without unqualified acceptance of the factual truthfulness of the Bible (the formal principle)? President Preus says no; Dr. Tietjen and his faculty say yes.

We could readily cite page upon page of references to Luther and the Confessions to show that Lutheranism at its very core has always insisted on the formal principle, and that the issue has never been whether faith in the Bible saves alongside faith in Christ. The *Formula of Concord*, Epitome, 7, is certainly not setting up a parallel means of salvation when it unqualifiedly asserts: "The distinction between the Holy Scripture of the Old and New Testaments and all other writings is maintained, and Holy Scripture remains the only judge, rule, and norm according to which as the only touchstone all teachings should and must be understood and judged as good or evil, right or wrong." Here nothing less than the absolute

---

* Humphrey Palmer, *The Logic of Gospel Criticism: An Account of the Methods and Arguments Used by Textual, Documentary, Source, and Form Critics of the New Testament* (London: Macmillan, 1968), pp. 47-48. (Italics ours.)

inerrancy of Scripture is demanded, for no human writing or datum extrinsic to Scripture can stand in judgment on it to show that it is mistaken; Scripture judges all—nothing judges Scripture.

Rather than such a view being a threat to the Gospel, it is the sole preservative of it. Consider: if, as the faculty holds, true Lutherans start with "the Gospel of Jesus Christ" and not with the infallibility of Scripture, how do they discover what that Gospel is and who Jesus Christ is? The only proper source of such understanding *is* Scripture, and it is either an infallible or a faillible Scripture. If fallible, then *so is the Gospel of Jesus Christ* contained therein. There is no escape from this conclusion. A fallible Bible, whether in actuality or potentially, places the very Gospel of our Lord Jesus Christ in precisely the same jeopardy.

When the faculty asks the church to hold to an infallible Gospel not guaranteed by an inerrant Scripture, it asks the church to remove the Gospel from Scripture and elevate it to the status of an eternal principle without historical guarantes. This is Gnosticism, not Christianity. More specifically, the operation can be termed *Gospelism*: the creation of a total religion out of a minimalistic statement of the Gospel, whose certainty is assured by inner faith only, not by biblical documents (the latter being always subject to negative evaluation through historical criticism).

Christian faith and the .Bible itself are redefined through this Gospelism: anything in Scripture that does not directly teach it is unimportant at best and may be erroneous at worst; in any case, no question of biblical fact can ever touch it, since it stands sublimely above all historical questions in the realm of pure fideism. The "whole counsel of God" (Acts 20:27) and the "whole armor of God" (Ephesians 6:11) are reduced to minimal soteriology, and even this is put at the mercy of the faith-experience of the faculty, whose subjection of Scripture to their anthropocentric criticism should leave the church with little confidence in the stability of their Gospel pronouncements.

To return to a point made at the outset of this analysis: the Concordia faculty should receive the thanks of the church for so explicitly setting forth its views and for assuring us that in its best judgment "these Discussions present positions responsibly taken on the basis of our Scriptural and Confessional commitment." No leaway now exists for reconciling the views of the faculty and the Synod President. The church assembled must decide between two incompatible views of Lutheran commitment. It must decide whether the Bible is to retain its position as the formal principle of all doctrine and the standard by which all else is judged—or whether it shall be relegated to the position of a fallible witness to a fideistic Gospelism. Since the genuine Gospel of Christ is derived only from Scripture, the issue really lies between that Gospel and the faculty's Gospelism. Accept the latter, and the united voice of church history assures you that the Gospel itself will soon disappear in the same fideistic, critical quicksand that has swallowed biblical authority. Many other church bodies and modern theologians have taken this route, and the Lutheran World Federation churches and the majority of American Lutheran Church theologians are among them. The question is: Will the Missouri Synod wake up in time? Will it insist that its officials engage in cancer surgery before the entire body dies? When the Son of man comes, will he find faith on the earth?

* * * * *

A bibliographic addendum to this essay is warranted by the citations "for further study" after each Discussion unit in the Concordia faculty's statement. These references to journal articles and pamphlets by faculty members and their friends are most illuminating, for they demonstrate my contention in the preceding essays of this book, first published in 1967, that many influential Missouri Synod theologians have consistently held to the positions espoused in the recent faculty declaration for many years and that their publications have long advocated a theology of Gospel reductionism and a noninerrancy view of Holy Scripture. Readers who would like to verify this contention and obtain more detailed treatment of particular views than the present essay allows are referred to the following pages in the present volume, where articles and authors recommended by the Concordia faculty statement are specifically mentioned:

Faculty recommendation	"Crisis" reference
Wegner, "Creation and Salvation,"	
CTM (September, 1966)	I, 87
Habel, Form and Meaning of the Fall	
Narrative	I, 87, 105-109, 118
Gehrke, "Genesis Three,"	
CTM (September, 1965)	I, 118
Piepkorn, "What Does 'Inerrancy' Mean?"	
CTM (September, 1965)	I, 96, 116
Jungkuntz, "John 10:34-36,"	
CTM (October, 1964)	I, 96, 116
Harrisville (on hermeneutics)	I, 16, 56

Two other brief notes on the faculty's bibliographic citations: (1) the references to publications by Hermann Sasse and Robert Preus (Discussion 8) are entirely misleading, since these theologians, both contributors to Volume II of the present work, categorically oppose the faculty views set forth in the statement; and (2) the citation of an article by John Elliott and the dependence of Discussion 7 on his views should remind us of Elliott's 1966 Mission Institute lectures which offered a non-verbal approach to evangelism which confused the Gospel with social action and led Dr. Herman Gockel to write to Elliott: "The position which you have taken in this respect is untenable." After a day of close theological discussion with Elliott myself, I could only second Dr. Gockel's judgment.

Elliott saw the issue clearly himself when he subsequently wrote of the manifestations of two quite different, if not irreconcilable, approaches toward the understanding and interpretation of both the Sacred Scriptures and the Lutheran Symbols.''

APPENDIX

A CRITIC CRITICIZED

As indicated in the Acknowledgements, Essay IV ("Current Theological Trends in the Lutheran Church-Missouri Synod") was originally prepared for and presented by invitation at the Proviso Lutheran Teachers Conference, Hinsdale, Illinois, on May 6, 1966. Three weeks later (June 29, 1966), Walter R. Bouman, whose identification of the Missouri Synod's historic theological position with "scholasticism" was scored in the essay, sent a mimeographed "Open Letter" to all members of the Proviso Teachers Conference. This document, which exceeded Essay IV in length, endeavored to justify its author's theological stance and at the same time to raise doubts as to the scholarly soundness of Essay IV. Subsequently, Professor Bouman requested *Lutheran News* to publish his "Open Letter," and a portion of his critique received dissemination in that periodical.

One of the major thrusts of Professor Bouman's "Open Letter" was the claim that his negative evaluation of Lutheran orthodoxy, based on secondary and tertiary sources such as Werner Elert's writings, warranted acceptance by the fact that recognized specialists in the area — particularly Dr. Robert Preus, author of the classic work, *The Inspiration of Scripture: A Study of the Theology of the Seventeenth Century Lutheran Dogmaticians* (2d ed.; Edinburgh: Oliver and Boyd, 1957) — are in substantial agreement with his judgments. In view of the sharp dichotomy between the theology of Professor Bouman and that advocated in the present work, it is of more than routine interest to obtain additional light on the question as to where scholarly and theological soundness really lies. I have therefore requested Dr. Robert Preus (Department of Systematic Theology, Concordia Seminary, St. Louis) to evaluate Professor Bouman's "Open Letter." Here follow the relevant portions of Dr. Preus' communication, written to me on September 6, 1966, with a copy sent on the same date to Professor Bouman:

"I think Prof. Bouman must have felt rather uncomfortable using my book to bolster his opinion that the emphases of Lutheran orthodoxy 'had and are still having . . . fateful and even disastrous consequences.' Could I have really suggested such a thing? I wanted to make the old Lutheran theologians look good; Bouman has me make them look bad. I hope he does not use his other secondary and tertiary sources the same way. But why cite all the secondary sources (you learn much more about Pelikan and Elert when reading their books about seventeenth century Lutheranism than you do about seventeenth century Lutheranism)? Why not go to Chemnitz, Chytraeus, Gerhard, yes, even Calov (and especially him, since he has been so maligned by the historians), and see what they have to say about Christ, faith, Law and Gospel, and Scripture? This is what Walther did, after he had first gone to Luther and the Confessions; and he learned to appreciate these great champions of orthodoxy and by his own confession he became a better theologian for it. . . .

"It would appear from . . . Bouman's works (e.g. his speech on Creation at Valparaiso of some time back [see above, Essay III, notes 12 and 48]) that he holds a highly questionable view relative to the inerrancy of Scripture. It is as though the Law-Gospel motif somehow makes inerrancy unimportant. If this is the position of Prof. Bouman — and I know it is the position of certain ALC men — I fail to see any sense in it at all. The Lutheran Law-Gospel motif does not vitiate the infallibility and inerrancy of Scripture, any more than the *sola gratia* and *sola fide* vitiate the *sola Scriptura*. . . .

"I recall that somewhere in my book I point out that it is the old Lutheran doctrine of the inspiration and inerrancy of Scripture which has marked Lutheran orthodoxy more than anything else and made it unacceptable to modern theologians. I think this is the case with Elert (cf. his chapter "Unzulänglichkeit der Inspirationslehre" in his *Der Christliche Glaube*, 3d ed., pp. 169 ff., where he cruelly attacks the old Lutheran doctrine of inspiration after having caricatured it completely), Schlink and even the earlier Sasse (I too respect the name of Sasse, *really so*; but why don't our Lutheran scholars today who love to quote him cite his latest contributions on inspiration and inerrancy, e.g. in the *Reformed Theological Review*, Vol. XIX, No. 2 [July, 1960], pp. 33 ff?). I hope Prof. Bouman has not followed this line and followed his European mentors at their weakest point. I think Walther and Pieper and even our exegete Stoeckhardt may have loved the dogmaticians all the more because of their adherence to the Biblical doctrine of the inspiration and truthfulness of Scripture; and were these fathers of our Synod less evangelical than an Elert or a Schlink? . . .

"I wish our young theologians would call a moratorium on blasting the fathers of our Synod. Until they do this they will be suspected and severely criticized; and rightly so, I believe. It is the writings of men like Walther and Stoeckhardt which have given many of us in the Missouri Synod a deeper appreciation of the Gospel and led us deeper into the Confessions and the Scriptures. We therefore take it personally when such great teachers and examples are attacked."

INDEX OF NAMES

DATE DUE

Demco, Inc. 38-293